D0122504

Germany, Poland and Europe

Published in our
centenary year
~ **2004** ~
MANCHESTER
UNIVERSITY
PRESS

ISSUES IN GERMAN POLITICS
Edited by
Professor Charlie Jeffery, Institute for German Studies
Dr Charles Lees, University of Sheffield

Issues in German Politics is a major series on contemporary Germany. Focusing on the post-unity era, it presents concise, scholarly analyses of the forces driving change in domestic politics and foreign policy. Key themes will be the continuing legacies of German unification and controversies surrounding Germany's role and power in Europe. The series includes contributions from political science, international relations and political economy.

Already published:

Annesley: *Postindustrial Germany: Services, technological transformation and knowledge in unified Germany*

Bulmer, Jeffery and Paterson: *Germany's European diplomacy: Shaping the regional milieu*

Green: *The politics of exclusion: Institutions and immigration policy in contemporary Germany*

Gunlicks: *The* Länder *and German federalism*

Harding and Paterson (eds): *The future of the German economy: An end to the miracle?*

Harnisch and Maull: *Germany as a Civilian Power? The foreign policy of the Berlin Republic*

Hyde-Price: *Germany and European order: Enlarging NATO and the EU*

Lees: *The Red–Green coalition in Germany: Politics, personalities and power*

Longhurst: *Germany and the use of force: The evolution of German security policy, 1990–2003*

Rittberger (ed.): *German foreign policy since unification: Theories and case studies*

Sperling (ed.): *Germany at fifty-five: Berlin ist nicht Bonn?*

Germany, Poland and Europe

Conflict, co-operation
and Europeanisation

Marcin Zaborowski

Manchester University Press
Manchester and New York

Distributed exclusively in the USA by Palgrave

Published by Manchester University Press
Oxford Road, Manchester M13 9NR, UK
and Room 400, 175 Fifth Avenue, New York, NY 10010, USA
www.manchesteruniversitypress.co.uk

Distributed exclusively in the USA by
Palgrave, 175 Fifth Avenue, New York,
NY 10010, USA

Distributed exclusively in Canada by
UBC Press, University of British Columbia, 2029 West Mall,
Vancouver, BC, Canada V6T 1Z2

British Library Cataloguing-in-Publication Data
A catalogue record for this book is available from the British Library

Library of Congress Cataloging-in-Publication Data applied for

ISBN 0 7190 6816 9 *hardback*

EAN 978 0 7190 6816 4

First published 2004

13 12 11 10 09 08 07 06 05 04   10 9 8 7 6 5 4 3 2 1

Typeset
by Carnegie Publishing Ltd
Printed in Great Britain
by Biddles Ltd, King's Lynn

For my parents,
Andrzej Zaborowski and Zofia Zaborowska

Contents

Figures

Acknowledgements

This book had many helpers; my family, my friends, the people who became friends as well as the many individuals whom I met since embarking on the writing of my PhD in 1996 in Birmingham. As much as I feel that I should, I cannot name everyone to whom my work remains indebted. The list would be too long and probably unreadable. Instead, I will thank those few individuals without whom this book would never been finished, or even begun.

I would like to begin with my wife Kerry Longhurst. Ever since meeting Kerry she has been not only a source of inspiration in my private life, helping me through many difficult moments while in Birmingham, but she also provided guidance in my academic career by introducing me to the world of International Relations, helping me in the process of learning how to write an academic paper and finally by correcting my imperfect English.

This book is based on my PhD, which was supervised by Adrian Hyde-Price. I am extremely grateful to Adrian not least for his readiness to discuss the often bizarre ideas I proposed to him in the early days of my doctoral studies. Adrian introduced me to alternative approaches in International Relations theory and German foreign policy. I have been always keen to follow Adrian's advice, including his dancing lessons at the 'Cul-de-sac' disco in Warsaw.

I would like to thank Professor Willie Paterson and Professor Charlie Jeffery, whose skilful 'wrangling' with many administrative obstacles made my enrolment at the University of Birmingham possible. I still do not know how they did it but I remain extremely grateful to both of them. Both Charlie and Willie have also inspired my thinking about Germany's and Poland's European policy and the chapters on EU enlargements are greatly influenced by their work.

I also would like to thank Dr Judy Batt, who was the first person I spoke to about my PhD idea. I would have never begun this work without her words of encouragement. Judy has also been a source of great help throughout the entire period of my work in Birmingham, including her most useful comments on the final draft. I am also indebted to Dr Vladimir Handl, whom I consulted regularly on my PhD during his time in Birmingham and whose useful remarks greatly improved my work. Vladimir also facilitated many of my contacts both in Germany and in the Czech Republic.

I would like to thank my colleagues: Arthur Hoffman, who became my very good friend, and Stuart Graham, who offered his support in my uncomfortable relationship with the world of computers. Finally, I am grateful to Henning Tewes, Vanda Knowles and Heather Grabbe who contributed to my thesis through numerous discussions, comments on my publications and through being such great company.

Introduction

Germanic-Polish relations have been some of the most troublesome in Europe ever since the eighteenth century when the kings of Prussia, Frederick I and then his son Frederick II, pursued aggressive policies towards the Polish–Lithuanian commonwealth, which eventually led to the partition and demise of this state by 1795. Subsequently, western Poland remained under Prussian and then German occupation until 1918, after which date the Polish state was briefly resurrected only to be threatened by the Weimar Republic and then Nazi Germany, which consequently led to the outbreak of Second World War. This historical conflict heavily influenced the national movements in both countries, with implications felt arguably to this day. Emerging in the mid-nineteenth century, German nationalism espoused an expansionist view of Germany's position towards the East. This idea clearly conflicted with Polish nationalism, which came to perceive Poland's western neighbours as inherently aggressive and undermining Polish aspirations at state-building. The two nationalisms were therefore born and developed in opposition to each other, a situation which did not change until the end of the Cold War.

Polish–German antagonism has always been of more than just bilateral or even regional significance and, as European history demonstrates, it has proved to be of consequence for the whole of Europe. It is clear, for example, that the conflict has had profound geopolitical implications. At the time when Frederick II co-engineered the partition of the Polish–Lithuanian commonwealth in the late eighteenth century, it was the largest state in Europe. The commonwealth's subsequent demise fundamentally changed the geopolitical landscape of Central and Eastern Europe, leading to the emergence of imperial Prussia and transforming Russia into a major European power. Later, the Second World

War began with the German invasion of Poland and ended with the Polish annexation of a quarter of German territory and expulsion of millions of Germans from these areas. In subsequent years, one of the 'hottest' conflicts of the Cold War period was the border dispute between communist Poland and capitalist West Germany, which only solidified the hostilities and animosities between these nations.

But the conflict also had far-reaching cultural ramifications. The partition of the Polish–Lithuanian commonwealth marked a clear violation of the principles of Treaty of Westphalia of 1648, hence bringing an end to the vision of international relations in Europe as being orderly and peaceful. In addition, the incorporation of western Poland into Prussia meant that the eastern part of this country remained ethnically Slavic and, despite the subsequent policy of forceful 'Germanisation', remained unassimilated into Prussian and then German society. This development had a profound impact on the formation of German identity that came to be based on ethnicity, and hence exclusive and hostile towards minorities.[1] The implications of this cultural trait were to affect German and European history throughout the twentieth century, and made it one of the key factors leading to two world wars.

With the end of the Cold War, Poland and Germany had a real chance to build a completely new relationship for the first time since 1795. The end of bipolarity meant that the structure of the international environment became conducive to a major transformation in bilateral relations. Both Germany and Poland are now ruled by compatible, democratic governments and the two states operate in a highly institutionalised context of European integration and Transatlanticism.

This book looks at the developments in the relationship during the second half of the twentieth century, when the relationship underwent a dramatic transformation. While, as argued above, the two nations had been in conflict since the late eighteenth century, their relations were at an all-time-low at the end of Second World War. The subsequent Cold War prevented a genuine reconciliation between these societies and until the 1970s Poland remained engaged in a severe diplomatic conflict with West Germany over the Oder-Neisse border and the status of East Germany. Following West Germany's *Ostpolitik* some elements of co-operation began to emerge in Bonn-Warsaw relations from the 1970s onwards; however, it was not until the end of the Cold War that a genuine rapprochement could take place between these states. During the 1990s the relationship improved spectacularly, with the two states finding a congruence of interests and perspectives – in particular, over the question of the Eastern enlargement of the European Union (EU). The history of the relationship during the latter part of the twentieth century can therefore be divided into three respective phases, referred to here as *conflict, co-operation* and '*Europeanisation*', all of which are addressed in this book.

In many respects this relationship remains strikingly comparable with Franco-(West) German relations, which went through a similar historical evolution. In fact, as often admitted by both Polish and German politicians, Franco-West German rapprochement was seen as a model for Warsaw and Bonn when they embarked on the transformation of their relations after 1989. Consequently, Franco-(West) German relations are frequently referred to in this book. Although, as will become apparent later, these cases are not always comparable, there is no doubt that Franco-(West) German relations are particularly useful to look at when studying issues of 'Europeanisation'.

'Europeanisation' is not interpreted here as an EU-focused process but rather a broader normative and cultural phenomenon with ramifications for international relations and, in this case, bilateral relationships.[2] In the interpretation explored in this book, 'Europeanisation' espouses liberal-democracy, European integration and consensus-based foreign policy. As such, the process is particularly relevant for those states undergoing a political transformation, as West Germany did after the Second World War and Poland after 1989.

As often argued by both German and Polish politicians and policy experts, this rapprochement is crucial to peace and stability in East Central Europe in a similar way as the Franco-(West) German relationship was for post-war Western Europe.[3] While past conflicts and disagreements between Poland and Germany had disastrous implications for the rest of Europe, post-Cold War co-operation between these two states has already transformed the nature of international relations in Central and Eastern Europe. Crucially, with EU enlargement in May 2004 Polish–German relations became of growing importance to the future of European integration and Europe's role in the wider world.

Structure of the book

The book is divided into six chapters: one conceptual, three historical and two contemporary (focusing on questions of NATO and more specifically EU enlargement) followed by a conclusion.

Chapter 1 rethinks the concept of 'Europeanisation', by drawing upon existing applications, International Relations literature and secondary sources on Polish–German relations. Chapter 2 then provides a historical survey of bilateral relations in the era between the creation and break-up of the war-time Grand Coalition. Chapter 3 examines the course of the relationship in the years up until the end of the Cold War. Specific focus is placed here upon efforts made on the part of both states to overcome the conflictual nature of the relationship despite the prevalence of superpower rivalry. Chapter 4 then proceeds with an investigation into the relationship between 1989 and 1991, a period which was characterised by a high level of ambiguity and tension on the one hand, coupled with the emergence of consensus on the other. Chapter 5 focuses on the 1991–98 period, providing an overview of what became arguably the most important issues to the relationship in the 1990s, namely EU and NATO enlargements. The chapter also explains why and how Polish and German interests seem reconcilable and congruent in these processes. Chapter 6 looks at the 1998–2001 period which, following the beginning of EU accession negotiations, saw a transformation in the EU enlargement policies of both Germany and Poland with the ever-growing importance of numerous domestic actors and their often diverging interests in the enlargement process. The Conclusion rounds off the book by providing an overview of the study, as well as raising issues for further consideration.

Notes

1 See Rogers Brubaker, *Citizenship and Nationhood in France and Germany* (Cambridge, MA: Harvard University Press, 1994).
2 See Maria Green Cowles, James Caporaso and Thomas Risse (eds), *Europeanization and Domestic Change: Transforming Europe* (Ithaca and London, Cornell University Press 2001).
3 For example, see Friedbert Pflüger 'Polen – unser Frankreich im Osten', in W. Schäuble and R. Seiters (eds), *Außenpolitik im 21. Jahrhundert. Die Thesen der Jungen Außenpolitiker* (Bonn: Bouvier Verlag, 1996), pp. 183–92; Artur Hajnicz, *Ze Sobą czy Przeciw Sobie* (Warsaw: Presspublika, 1995).

1

'Europeanisation' and Polish–German relations

Introduction

For most of modern history Polish–German relations have been marked by enmity, hostility and intolerance. However, with the end of the Cold War there was an expectation that these two neighbours would now embark on a much-delayed process of rapprochement. The end of East–West hostilities, the collapse of communism in Poland and elsewhere in the former Eastern block, the implosion of the Soviet Union and the unification of Germany were events creating a new environment that was conducive to the emergence of new close relationship between these two historical adversaries. The broad geopolitical significance of German–Polish relations to the rest of the continent prompted academics, politicians and other commentators to promote the idea of anchoring the relationship within a European context, a move that, it has been suggested, would serve the security of the wider Europe.[1] The essence of such a notion remains far from being clearly defined, though it is possible to identify its most crucial facets which, as they appear in political debates, concern first of all consensus-based international relations, domestic democratisation and western integration.

In this context the post-Second World War transformation of West Germany was often referred to as a model to be followed by Poland – and, indeed, other East Central Europeans. It was argued that the democratisation of West Germany and its membership in western organisations proved crucial in securing peace and stability in Western Europe,[2] and consequently that with the end of the Cold War a similar 'anchorage to the West' needed to be extended to include East

Central Europe, in order that Germany, Poland and other countries of the region might establish new and consensus-based relations. It was also argued in this context that just as post-war rapprochement in Franco–(West) German relations was essential for the elimination of violence in West European relations, the post-1989 German–Polish process could have the same effect for East Central Europe.[3] Significantly here, it is the notion of 'Europe' – or, more explicitly, of 'Europeanisation' – that is being credited for overcoming past differences and moving towards a more co-operative relationship.[4] However, in these interpretations the notion is highly political and devoid of analytical, let alone theoretical, dimensions. Broadly speaking 'Europeanisation' is seen here as a label for all things desirable, whether domestically or in the broader international context.

The purpose of this chapter is to give some analytical underpining to the notion of 'Europeanisation' and discuss its meaning in the context of German–Polish relations. The chapter is divided into three principal parts. The first section introduces the notion of 'Europeanisation' as both an academic and a political concept, in the first instance referring explicitly to the EU and in the second a broader and more normative application. The chapter then moves on to discuss the concept of 'Europeanisation' through the prism of the main International Relations theories. Finally, the chapter draws from the existing literature on Polish–German relations in order to define conditions for the 'Europeanisation' of the relationship, which will form the basis for further investigation in the chapters that follow.

Varieties of 'Europeanisation'

The notion of 'Europeanisation' is not new and has been present in academic and political debates since at least the 1990s. However, as is often the case with new concepts that aim to encapsulate broad phenomena, 'Europeanisation' refers to many processes and remains under-theorised or often conceptually confused. Moreover, the political discourse of Polish–German relations is only loosely related to academic and EU-focused debates on the essence of 'Europeanisation'. It is therefore important here to distinguish between the key strands of these debates and to relate them to the Polish–German case.

There are two distinctive 'Europeanisation' debates relevant for this discussion:[5]

1   An *academic, predominantly West European debate* that mobilised the
    term to refer to the impact of EU-level policies and politics upon
    domestic processes in member states and, to a lesser extent, in the
    candidate countries.[6] For the sake of clarity, and because it remains
    explicitly EU-focused this debate will be called here '*EU-isation*'.

2   A *normative, mostly political debate* that equates 'Europeanisation'
    with political and economic transformations, pluralism and mod-
    ernisation. This debate is particularly relevant for the peripheral
    states that are either insecure about their place in Europe – such as
    East Central Europeans and Mediterranean states – or nations that
    have a problem with their own history and identity, with Germany
    being a primary case. This debate will be referred to here as either
    '*normative Europeanisation*' or simply 'Europeanisation'.

The most striking feature about these two debates is how quite unre-
lated and different they are both in substance and form. Whereas
EU-isation (usually called 'Europeanisation') has been more or less
established as a discernible research field in European studies and, to
a lesser extent, in politics and economics, the '*normative Europeanisation*' debate, which is currently mostly focused on East Central Europe,
has remained largely just a matter of political discourse. In addition,
while the 'EU-isation' debate is about dynamics that exist, or are
claimed to exist, the normative debate sees 'Europeanisation' as a desirable development and a good in itself. As it is concerned chiefly with
the 'transformation' of Polish–German relations this account will refer
mostly to the 'normative Europeanisation' debate. However, the phenomenon of 'EU-isation' will also come to have a significant impact
upon this relationship, particularly in the context of EU enlargement,
and will therefore also be outlined below together with the normative
conception.

'EU-isation'

'EU-isation' has been identified as a multifarious process of the EU
influencing, shaping or even determining the internal processes of
member states and candidate countries. This conception has been
applied to a broad range of areas, including regional policies, immigration and economic modernisation.[7] Despite this burgeoning research
agenda, the meaning of what 'EU-isation' really is and what it 'does'
remains open to interpretation. It appears that there are two broad

ways of defining 'EU-isation' as a process impacting upon domestic institutions and policy processes:

- As an *independent variable that has a direct impact upon domestic processes*. Here, 'EU-isation' is seen as the 'emergence and the development at the European level of distinct structures of governance, that is, of political, legal, and social institutions associated with political problem-solving that formalises interactions among actors, and of policy networks specialising in the creation of authoritative rules'.[8] Some other scholars referred to this process as '*Europeification*'.[9]

- As an *intervening variable*, a process which may bring about change at the domestic level. Here 'EU-isation' depicts: 'Processes of (a) construction, (b) diffusion and (c) institutionalisation of formal and informal rules. Procedures, policy paradigms, styles, "ways of doing things" and shared beliefs and norms which are first defined and consolidated in the making of the EU decisions and then incorporated in the logic of domestic discourse, identities, political structures and public policies.'[10]

In spite of their differences, both of these definitions remain exclusively preoccupied with the EU, in that they argue that policies made at the European level are capable of changing or influencing domestic interests and the overall environment within which governments make their decisions. It is thus clear that investigating 'EU-isation' at the domestic level is limited to analysis of 'top-down' dynamics between Brussels and member states and the candidate countries. As such, there are some obvious limitations on the efficacy of the concept as a tool for explaining developments in Polish–German relations. The debate is explicitly institutionally bound and explicitly interested in one-way (top-down) dynamics between the institution and its units. The normative dimension is only of interest as long as the EU is clearly identifiable as a possible source of norms and ideas that have some bearing upon member–candidate states. But even then, it is clear that the debate is more interested in the rational aspects of institutional spillover and the general bureaucratic developments involved in the domestic adaptation of EU policies and less in the normative side of these processes. True, there has been a growing body of research that purposefully incorporates ideational aspects of policy adaptation into the debate.[11] Yet, these new perspectives, though useful for some EU-related aspects of this study, are not suitable for explaining general patterns of conflict and co-operation in Polish–German relations. The other reason why 'EU-isation' is not fully applicable here has to do with the relative weakness of the EU as a viable foreign and security policy actor, which is of core importance to this discussion. It is clear that member states continue to jealously guard their sovereignty in this area, and whatever the institutional impact of the EU in foreign and security matters, it remains severely limited – as demonstrated by the EU's inability to address the conflict in the former Yugoslavia and the division that occurred between its members with regard to the war in Iraq in 2003.

However, as argued earlier, despite the limitations mentioned above, the concept of 'EU-isation' is important for any discussion that aims to address bilateral relations in a contemporary European context. In particular, it is believed here that while looking at the specific case of Polish–German relations, 'EU-isation' should be considered, since much of the post-1989 relationship has revolved around the issue of EU enlargement. Consequently, the institutional impact of the EU will be addressed in the subsequent chapters but, as argued earlier, this account is concerned with broader questions of conflict and co-operation in Polish–German relations which, although certainly affected by the EU, have been shaped by a much broader range of processes. It is in this context that this analysis is more interested in the normative notion of 'Europeanisation'.

'Normative Europeanisation' and the 'return to Europe'

As argued before, the notion of 'Europeanisation' as a normative force is relevant for those states that, for a variety of reasons, are insecure about their place in Europe and are prepared to pursue some specific policies for the sake of being considered 'European'. This definition applies to both Germany and the states of East Central Europe, Poland included. It may be also applicable to Mediterranean states, in particular those with a turbulent history such as Italy, Spain, Portugal and Greece. But outside these 'troubled' areas it is doubtful that the 'European idea' may hold the same appeal and comparable political consequence. It is, for example, unlikely that a British government would try to 'sell' a reform package designed to make Britain 'more European'. However, the nations that were deeply affected by their own or their neighbours' nationalism, which were either isolated from 'mainstream Europe' or were threatened to be so, are far more disposed to see

'Europe' as an entity of which they want to be a part. It is argued here that this historically motivated predisposition has some tangible political implications.

The (West) German case may in many respects serve as an archetype 'return to Europe', where it was a guiding principle of a fundamental transformation. The West German democratisation process, establishing the rule of law and constitutionalism, was often portrayed to the electorate – and, perhaps more so, to international opinion – as a policy of 'Europeanisation'. This was even more so the case with the foreign policy of the Bonn Republic and in particular with its enthusiastic attitude towards the notion of European integration and reconciliation with France.[12] Arguably a comparable situation emerged in East Central Europe in the wake of the end of the Cold War, with the states of the area seeking domestic reforms and an end to their isolation from western Europe. Consequently, 'Europeanisation' became a popular slogan in ex-communist East Central Europe, encapsulating the very essence of the political and economic transformation of the region and setting the standard for the nurturing of democracy, opening of the economy and radical re-direction of foreign policies. Unlike in the 'EU-isation' debate outlined above, the EU was not initially the main point of reference here, although European integration was often mentioned as a practical realisation of what 'Europe' was about. Predominantly, however, 'Europe' was not portrayed as a concrete entity but rather as a political and cultural construction, which as East Central Europeans believed, had determined the pace of developments in western Europe after 1945 and which, therefore, they wanted to emulate and be a part of.[13]

The exceptional popularity of the idea of 'Europe' during the watershed of 1989 and its aftermath can be explained by two fundamental factors. First, for many East Central Europeans 'Europe' meant western Europe, from which they felt that they had been artificially excluded by the 'non-European' Soviet Union.[14] Thus the notion of 'Europe' carried with it a very clear political message and one that was pro-western and anti-Soviet. Secondly, the idea of European integration had come to enjoy exceptionally high prestige within anti-communist dissident circles, particularly since the late 1970s.[15] Therefore, after 1989 it was self-evident to the former dissidents, who turned overnight into statesmen, that their internal reforms and foreign policies would be guided by the principle of 'Europeanisation' and the 'Return to Europe'. The practical implications of this strategy meant that these countries embarked on a number of internal reforms aimed at emulating the polices and standards of 'core Europe'.

This connection between the normative notion of a 'return to Europe' and the reform agenda in East Central Europe has inspired some scholars to define 'Europeanisation' as an actual political and transition-related process. For example, Attila Agh defined 'Europeanisation' as a process of introducing pluralism in politics and privatisation in the economy.[16] Geoffrey Pridham spoke about the 'Europeanisation' of political parties in East Central Europe as influenced by either a conscious emulation of the western-style polity or by the conditionality of EU membership criteria.[17] Both Agh and Pridham regard 'Europeanisation' as being mostly to do with domestic political issues and the politics of post-communist transformation. However, it is clear that 'Europeanisation' in East Central Europe has also had its international dimension, as manifest in the embracing of the principle of multilateralism and applying for membership in the EU, the Council of Europe and NATO by all of the countries in the region. More importantly here, the process of 'Europeanisation' also proved to have a profound effect upon the general 'posture' of foreign policies in the region which, excluding the former Yugoslavia, have been marked by consensus-seeking and a preference for solving inter-state conflicts through diplomatic means. In this context, it is important to note that in political discourse the term has often been used as a synonym for modernisation at home and benign behaviour and co-operation abroad.[18] 'Europeanisation' has often been presented as an alternative to '*Balkanisation*', with the latter notion symbolising conflict and violence.[19] It is also in this context that the term appeared in the discourse about Polish–German relations.

'Europeanisation' in the context of Polish–German relations

The 'Europeanisation' of international relations in East Central Europe can mean different things depending on the particular circumstances of the countries concerned. For example, an argument about the 'Europeanisation' of Hungary's relations with Romania or Slovakia would concentrate on the question of the Hungarian minority in these countries and their freedom to express their ethnic distinctiveness.[20] In the case of Austro-Czech relations the 'Europeanisation' discourse may focus on the question of a nuclear plant at Temelin that Prague insensitively decided to locate close to the border with Austria, thus causing a major dispute between these two countries.[21] In both these cases, the complaining parties referred to international and mostly 'European' rules and regulations, as defined by the Council of Europe, the Organisation for Security and Co-operation in Europe (OSCE) and the EU to support their arguments and to mitigate existing or emerging conflicts.[22]

It seems, therefore, that in its broad foreign policy sense 'Europeanisation' means *co-operation* in interstate relations and that *international institutions* also play a key role. Arguably, the process of achieving consensus and co-operation in Polish–German relations is dependent on an exceptionally multifaceted set of issues. This is a result of the difficult history of these relations and of their broader geopolitical importance. There are also many psychological factors to be taken into account. While in the past violence and cross-national resentment were one of the region's defining characteristics, Polish–German relations were exceptionally belligerent even by the area's poor standards. In addition, many years of communist propaganda made the Poles one of the most anti-German nations in Europe while the Germans developed a strong contempt for Polish unruliness, which inspired the pejorative saying *Polnische Wirtschaft*.[23]

On the other hand, the Polish–German 'Europeanisation' debate did not start only in 1989, but began with the reconciliation movement in the mid-1960s and developed further in the wake of West Germany's new *Ostpolitik*.[24] Two policies in particular stand out as clear manifestations of the promotion of co-operation: firstly, the call for reconciliation initiated by the Christian churches in the two countries in the mid-1960s and, secondly, the provisional recognition of the Oder-Neisse border line by the West German government in 1970.[25] Willy Brandt's *Ostpolitik* rested on the assumption that it could not be conducted in separation from the Federal Republic's broader 'European' policy. This, Brandt suggests in his memoirs, led him to recognise the Oder-Neisse border and inspired his famous *kniefall* (bended knee) at the monument of the Warsaw ghetto in 1970.[26] The link between *Europapolitk* and *Ostpolitik* was further advanced by Brandt's successor, Helmut Schmidt, who argued that the Federal Republic's deeper integration with the European Community (EC) and Poland's co-operation with it were in both states' interests. Furthermore, Schmidt argued that the future of European peace rested on Germany's co-operation with both France and Poland.[27]

Indeed, after 1989, the Franco-German relationship was often flagged as a point of comparison and a potential model for the 'Europeanisation' of Polish–German relations.[28] Two similarities were noted in this context, both of which were strongly related to issues of *co-operation* and western *institutional integration*. Firstly, as was the case between Germany and France, it was argued that the deep disagreements that existed in Polish–German relations could be overcome only through the emergence of exceptionally intimate links and even a degree of *convergence* in the future. One of the main advocates of this thesis, CDU politician Friedbert Pflüger, illustrated this connection by arguing that Poland and Germany 'could not be just casual friends but they must be like a married couple'.[29] Secondly, it was suggested that the best way to achieve such an intimate relationship was to co-operate through multilateral channels, preferably through the EU, in a way resembling the Franco-German axis. However, as will be explored later, the Franco-German model had its limitations as a point of emulation for the Polish–German relationship.

To sum up, the purpose of this section was to identify some common denominators for normative 'Europeanisation' and the notion's applicability to international relations. It was suggested here that two broad principles of the notion are 'co-operation' and the presence of some degree of 'multilateral integration'. It is, however, clear that in strictly analytical terms 'Europeanisation' is a rather 'fluffy' notion – in fact, it is questionable whether it can be researched as an actual political process or rather as a set of normative ideas and aspirations. There is little doubt that in opposition to 'EU-isation', which has been preoccupied with *identifiable processes* (i.e. where the EU affects domestic arrangements), the debate on 'Europeanisation' and international relations remains predominantly a *politically driven range of objectives*. On the other hand, there is plenty of evidence to suggest that what has been declared under the banner of 'Europeanisation' has often taken the shape of concrete policy initiatives with tangible impacts on Polish–German relations. The same is true for Franco-German relations, which may be considered an archetypical case of 'normative Europeanisation'.

It would, however, be implausible to suggest that 'normative Europeanisation' may have a similar force, instruments and tangible point of reference as 'EU-isation'. True, German, Polish, French and other statesmen continue to refer to 'European' values and norms, which suggests that, in their view, 'Europe' represents a normative entity. There is also an implicit, and sometimes explicit, understanding in these views that what is 'European' is 'good' and worth emulating. However, it is important to make clear at this point that these claims are not taken as the basis for this analysis. First of all, it is questionable that 'Europe' represents a coherent normative entity: for example, it is apparent that the difference between Scandinavian and Greek values is not smaller than between Scandinavian and Australian values. Secondly, the claim that international relations in Europe are based on consensus and 'Kantian' rules of peaceful federation of democratic states[30] may be to some degree justified in contemporary circumstances, though, the ethnic strife and wars in the Balkans seriously undermine this view. But more to the point, in the recent past Europe was home to a very 'un-Kantian' balance of power system, ethnically defined nationalism, fascism and communism. In other words, a non-European observer could easily conclude that the 'Europeanisation of international relations' stands for aggressive and belligerent foreign policies.

Consequently, the point of departure for this analysis is the claim that while 'Europeanisation' lacks a material reference point, such as the EU, it is based on an ideational reference and an 'imagined' Europe.[31] It is therefore the relationship between 'constructed' norms or rules of 'appropriate' behaviour and the *actual* political process that provides the focus of this analysis. It is therefore important here that the question of the role of *norms* in international relations be discussed and its applicability to empirical research be outlined.

Norms, 'Europeanisation' and international relations

The two mainstream theories of international relations – neorealism and neoliberalism – do not give much credence to the importance of norms. Neorealism, which is explicitly structural, either ignores the role of cultural factors or sees them as secondary phenomena resulting from a states' position in the international system or as facets deployed by governments in order to justify their actions. Neoliberalism accepts some major premises of neorealism, mainly the claim that international structure is inherently anarchical, but it argues that international institutions can mitigate its otherwise lawless nature. The theory also argues that under certain conditions institutions can affect states' *fundamental preferences* and hence co-define their interests. There is an implicit normative dimension in this claim – institutions can produce norms that may be subsequently adopted by states. But while the neoliberal stress on the role of institutions is relevant for the 'EU-isation' debate, it is less relevant for the normative notion of 'Europeanisation', which, as argued above, does not have an identifiable institutional reference point.

'Normative Europeanisation' is based on the assumption that states are informed in their actions by their specific experiences and that they enter international politics with *internally* defined norms. These norms are consequently important for the way states behave – in other words, they have *causal qualities*. These claims stand in direct contradiction with the neorealist (and, to a lesser extent, neoliberal) approaches, both of which stress the role of factors *external* to states, either the international structure or international institutions.[32] In addition, both neorealism and neoliberalism are overtly 'rational', paying attention to the material aspects of state powers – military in the first instance and economic in the second – while 'normative Europeanisation' is by definition concerned with non-material cultural factors.

While traditional international relations approaches do not provide tools to deal with 'normative Europeanisation', sociological approaches – and, in particular, social constructivism – are considerably more helpful. For example, Peter Katzenstein's sociological account of international security focuses explicitly on social factors and in particular on norms, culture and identity, all of which are essential for 'Europeanisation' discourse.[33] According to Katzenstein, there are two categories of norms that are of significance in international relations: they can be either 'constitutive' or 'regulative'. Norms may be used to 'describe collective expectations for actors with given identity'. In this instance, the concept has *constitutive* effects and norms exist to *define* actors' identity. For example, making military service optional or voluntary for citizens is an indication that a state is becoming 'liberal'; in this instance, it is the 'choice' offered to potential draftees that represents a *constitutive* norm. But norms may also represent standards for specifying 'the proper enactment of an already defined identity'. Here norms are *regulatory* as they denote what constitutes proper behaviour. For example, a liberal state cannot introduce compulsory military service without the emergence of a direct threat to its security, otherwise the disappearance of the 'choice' previously enjoyed by citizens would be a clear violation of liberal principles, which by this point act as *regulative* norms. Norms can therefore 'define (or constitute) identities or prescribe (or regulate) behaviour or do both'.[34]

Since these definitions of the types of norms used by sociological perspective are linked to 'identities', which by nature are specific rather than universal, it may appear here that these concepts are too particular. This, it may be argued, questions their applicability to 'Europeanisation', which by definition represents a claim to some sort of commonality. But it needs to be pointed out here that 'Europe' as a cultural notion is itself at best ambiguous in this respect. True, it could be claimed that when in relation to the 'other' – for example North America or Africa – 'Europe' represents some kind of community of values, at least in a fundamental sense. Yet, at the same time, it is precisely Europe's cultural heterogeneity that is considered its most enduring characteristic.

This ambivalence of the European notion is also apparent in the international dimension of 'Europeanisation'. The emphasis on *co-operation* and *institutional integration* in the 'Europeanisation' discourse indicates that there is a degree of shared understanding regarding the essence of the idea. 'Europeanisation' appears in this context as a 'Kantian' notion based on the belief that liberal-democratic government and multilateralism forge co-operation and eliminate violence in international politics. In other words, these principles act here as *constitutive norms* for the states that want to be considered European. Yet, while 'Kantian' principles provide some fundamental basis for the normative agenda of 'Europeanisation', they are insufficient to ensure that the Poles, Germans and others would have the same understanding of rules of 'appropriate' behaviour. Consequently the *regulative norms* of 'Europeanisation' are at best in the process of creation, and remain weak.

On the other hand, 'European' norms of foreign policy behaviour do not derive solely from 'Kantian' abstract principles but also from the instance of their practical application in Franco-German relations, a process which came to serve as an *informal institution*, offering a model of what is often called a '*Europeanised*' relationship. Throughout its duration the Franco-German process produced a whole set of rules and norms guiding the relationship. For example, both states refrained from stirring up nationalistic sentiments against each other for domestic consumption. They routinely worked towards presenting concerted and often joint positions in the context of the EU, other organisations and vis-à-vis third states. When, however, they happened to differ in their view of the outside world, Paris and Berlin often went to pains to cover up their divisions. Over the years these and many other practices have become rules of appropriate behaviour – in other words, they may be in the process of becoming *regulative norms*.

There is no doubt that the Franco-German process can serve as a normative reference point for states that claim to embrace 'Europeanisation', and in particular for the international relations of new democracies in East Central Europe. Importantly here, as will be seen in the following chapters, Franco-German rapprochement has featured prominently in the Polish–German 'Europeanisation' debate shaping, jointly with 'Kantian' principles, a normative agenda for the process. Clearly it was always unrealistic to expect that within a decade this relationship would achieve the same level of intimacy and co-operation as France and Germany reached after nearly half a century. But the starting point of the Franco-German rapprochement – in particular the reconciliation process and embracing of the notion of European integration – are amongst the defining points of Polish–German 'Europeanisation'. But what exactly is the content of the Polish–German 'Europeanisation' debate, and what weight is given in it to material and non-material factors? This becomes clear with an analysis of the key literature on the subject, which essentially identifies four conditions that are of key relevance for the process, as outlined in the following section.

Conditions for the 'Europeanisation' of Polish–German relations

The literature on Polish–German relations reveals the highly eclectic nature of ideas underpinning the 'Europeanisation' concept. Some of the arguments seem to confirm a neorealist thesis of the importance of the balance of power in determining the nature of relations – most authors agree that without the profound change in the international structure of 1989, Polish–German rapprochement would not have come about. Other arguments point to the impact of Germany's membership in western institutions and Poland's aspirations to join the EU and NATO as decisively shaping the relationship which, depending on the interpretation, may uphold a neoliberal or more sociological-type thesis. There are also accounts that refer to domestic sources of foreign policy or discuss issues of political culture – most importantly, the reconciliation process – that clearly seem to endorse the sociological view.

Significantly, the majority of authors do not discriminate between material and non-material sources of conflict and co-operation but stress the significance of *both* in relations between Poland and the Federal Republic. In effect, then, the literature tends to uphold the view that the causes of developments between Poland and (West) Germany came from more than one determinant and, moreover, that they were interrelated. Existing literature identifies the following issues: change in the international structure, domestic democratisation, western integration and reconciliation. These are briefly outlined and discussed below.

International–structural

The literature suggests that structural factors – in other words, the international balance of power – had considerable importance for developments between Poland and (West) Germany. As a result of postwar changes in the international system, Poland and Germany found each other involved in a deep territorial conflict over the Oder-Neisse border. The dawning of the Cold War and the division of Germany subsequently strengthened this antagonism. These changes, neither of which were initiated or even directly influenced by either of the two parties, defined the key features of the relationship until the end of the Cold War. The end of the Cold War resulted both for Poland and Germany in the return of their sovereignty and the lessening of superpower domination in their foreign policies. This has meant that German–Polish relations since have been far less determined by structural factors exogenous to both countries. But there is an implicit or explicit assumption that 'Europeanisation' would have never been initiated, and could not continue, without the existence of a conducive international environment. In other words, structural material factors are seen as an essential pre-condition for 'Europeanisation'.

Democratisation

Domestic democratisation is seen as another important factor with formative qualities for the relationship. In particular, it has often been regarded as the process actively mitigating conflict in Polish–(West) German relations.[35] This argument has both material and ideational explanations. In a material context, democratisation brings about a more peaceful state, since the decentralisation of decision-making means that policy is a result of a number of bargains, influences and positions – a process – which negates the likelihood of a state pursuing an unambiguously hostile policy towards a neighbour. For example, the fact that from its very inception the Federal Republic ruled out the use of force in its territorial dispute with Poland was in part influenced by internal differences over the issue which, arguably, could have been quite different had the Bonn Republic been undemocratic. As regards the non-material aspects of the argument, it is often pointed out that democracy frees public debates and the overall intellectual atmosphere becomes more inquisitive, multidimensional and more prone to breaking taboos. It is argued in this context that the post-war revision of German national mythology, and in particular the rejection of the *Lebensraum* concept, led for the first time in German history to the acceptance of the Polish state.[36] It is also argued that intellectual change in the Federal Republic served to constrain its post-1989 behaviour in East Central Europe and shaped Bonn's determination to stabilise the region.[37]

This 'democratic' argument also concerns Poland and its approach towards Germany. For example, some authors point to the ideational aspects of the post-1989 Polish–German 'community of interests', arguing that Germany and Poland embarked on a course of 'good neighbourly relations' (*dobre sasiedztwo*), not only because of changes in the international environment but also in the wake of Poland becoming a liberal-democracy. An important aspect of this process was Poland's new policy towards national minorities, and in particular the legal recognition of the German minority, a change which was of direct importance for the relationship.[38] In fact, some authors argue that this policy was as important for the 'Europeanisation' of the relationship as the end of the Cold War was.[39]

Western integration

Like democratisation, western integration is an argument with both material and non-material dimensions. The material argument stresses the notion of greater congruence of interests bound by institutional co-operation while the non-material explanation accentuates the ideological, liberal-democratic proximity of member states. Most authors who have written about post-1989 developments in Polish–German relations have underlined the importance of West European and Euro-Atlantic integration. Moreover, though on a much smaller scale, these issues are also seen as having importance for the relationship prior to 1989. For example, a number of authors emphasise that the Federal

Republic's *Westbindung* (Western integration of Germany) proved crucial for revising the formerly held perception of East Central Europe as Germany's power base and that this in turn enhanced Bonn's credibility in Warsaw. This was manifest in parts of the Polish opposition's stance that supported the unification of Germany long before 1989 and which was often premised on Bonn's positive record of membership in NATO and the EC since the 1950s.[40] However, as regards the relationship before 1989 generally, western integration is rarely perceived of as an explanatory variable in the course of Polish–West German relations. In contrast, it is often seen as a significant causal factor in the analysis of post-1989 developments. In fact, it is possible to say that while international structure (bipolarity) remains the most common explanation of pre-1989 developments, it is the notion of western integration that is seen as a dominant factor in German–Polish rapprochement after the end of the Cold War.[41] After all, it was in the context of EU and NATO enlargements that Germany's and Poland's interests and ideas began to converge.

Reconciliation

The reconciliation question, which falls squarely into the 'non-material' category, represents a particularly difficult and emotive issue for the relationship. It is clear that the 'Europeanisation' of Polish–German relations could never have taken place without addressing the past, as both a pre-condition and a part of the process. Dealing with the past is always difficult even in the best of circumstances, but it is particularly complex in this case, which involves millions of human casualties, threats to the very existence of a state, racism and expulsion of populations. It is thus perhaps not surprising that this question is often underlined as one of the major issues in the relationship in both the negative (the effects of the absence of reconciliation) and positive (the political implications of reconciliation) sense.[42] For example, it is often pointed out that Adenauer's general lack of historical sensitivity in relations with Poland was one of the major reasons explaining the failure of the short-lived 'armistice in exchanging insults' between Warsaw and Bonn in the late 1950s.[43] In contrast to this, the fact that the *Ostpolitik* of the Social Democrat (SPD)–Free Democrat (FDP) government between the late 1960s and 1970s was morally and historically grounded, as manifest in Brandt's *kniefall*, is often seen as paving the way for the first significant breakthrough in the relationship.

With the reconciliation process gaining a new momentum after the end of the Cold War and in the wake of the final recognition of the Oder-Neisse border line by Bonn–Berlin, the relationship advanced impressively on both the official as well as the societal level. This, for example, has been reflected in the changes in the Polish public's view of Germany, which has improved dramatically since 1991, marking the virtual extinction of the fear of German military aggression from public discourse.[44] It will become clear that Polish–German reconciliation was considerably inspired by the earlier Franco-West German process.

Evaluation

The issues underlined by specialists and writers on Polish–German relations are both material and ideational in nature, and do not fall easily into a single theoretical framework. Most authors see the end of the Cold War and the subsequent change in the international structure as pre-conditioning the improvement in the relationship and that the other vital elements of the process – democratisation, western integration and reconciliation – as following from this development. This view is conducive with structural explanations, and with neorealism in particular.

On the other hand, very little attention has been paid to structural factors in discussions about the actual 'Europeanisation' process as it developed after 1989. Here authors seem to underline institutional or normative factors which are better addressed by sociological and, to a limited extent, by neoliberal perspectives. In a sense therefore, the 'Europeanisation' argument may be supporting the thesis that whilst structural theories are suited to explain Cold War dynamics they do not adequately explain post-Cold War politics. This line of argument will be investigated in later chapters of the book. However, it is important to stress at this point that the primary purpose of this book is not to contribute to theoretical discussions by way of referring to the example of Polish–German relations, but rather the other way around. The purpose of this book is to understand the unique process taking place in Polish–German relations, a process that is often referred to as 'Europeanisation' and which is believed here to be intimately bound up with the 'Kantian' notion of international politics and the practice of west European relations during the post-1945 period.

Conclusion

The purpose of this chapter was to introduce and define the concept of 'Europeanisation' and its applicability to Polish–German relations. It was argued here that the term has been used over-generously and with reference to a broad array of political and economic processes. The chapter identified two main and distinctive 'Europeanisation' debates; the first related exclusively to the EU while the second embraced processes of transformation and referred to broader European notions. The EU-focused debate, which for this reason was renamed 'EU-isation', deals with issues of relations between EU institutions and its member states as well as candidate countries. In its most recent incarnation, this discussion applies a 'top-down' focus, looking at the EU as the source of policies and politics that are being 'exported' at the level of member–candidate states. This debate is preoccupied with issues of adaptation and convergence, looking into the dynamics and actors that obstruct or promote transfers of influence from the EU to national levels and the ways in which the process makes the receiving states more 'similar' to each other. It was argued here that the 'EU-isation' debate is of relevance for some aspects of Polish–German relations, and in particular for looking at the relationship in the context of EU enlargement.

However, it is the second, transformation-related, 'Europeanisation' debate that is considered to be more capable of explaining the nature of the Polish–German process. This debate, which is called here either 'normative Europeanisation' or just 'Europeanisation', refers to the processes of democratisation, economic reforms and consensus-based international relations. It is in the latter of these categories that this book is interested. The chapter argues that the traditional rationally bent theories of international relations, neorealism and neoliberalism are not capable of addressing the 'Europeanisation' phenomenon, which lacks an identifiable material point of reference, be it international structure or international institutions. Instead, 'Europeanisation' of international relations relates to the normative, Kantian, idea of liberal-democracy and multilateralism as factors forging co-operative relations among states. It also relates to the practical embodiment of these principles in the case of Franco-German relations, which came to serve as an 'informal institution' or a model for emulation for other states with a troubled past. This largely 'normative' character of the 'Europeanisation' debate – in particular, the claim that ideas, not exclusively material factors, may determine the course of politics – means that the notion is most compatible with sociological approaches that are concerned with the role of norms in international relations.

The chapter subsequently looked into the conditions that underpin the notion of 'Europeanisation' in Polish–German relations. Four particular issues were identified as crucial in this context: a conducive international environment, democratic government, western integration and reconciliation. A working hypothesis emerging from this preliminary examination of the four conditions is that the *international environment* serves as a 'permissive' condition for 'Europeanisation', making the process possible but only in a passive sense. It is suggested that the remaining three conditions – *democratic government, western integration* and *reconciliation* – play more active roles in actually bringing 'Europeanisation' about. This hypothesis will be examined in the chapters that follow.

Although the concept of 'Europeanisation' provides a conceptual framework for the book, it is important to point out that the book is predominantly about the issue of *conflict and co-operation* in the relationship, and it is in this context that 'Europeanisation' is discussed. Consequently, the following chapters will look at the conditions shaping the Polish–German conflict after the Second World War, attempts to overcome the conflict under the conditions of the Cold War, the ambivalent period immediately after 1989 (marked by a simultaneous launching of rapprochement and the re-opening of the border dispute) and finally developments in the relationship in the context of EU and NATO enlargements. The Conclusion will discuss the prospects of the relationship in an enlarged Europe, focusing in particular on the issue of the future of the EU.

Notes

1 See Willy Brandt, 'Der Kniefall von Warschau', in Friedbert Pflüger and Winfried Lipscher (eds), *Feinde werden Freunde* (Bonn: Bouvier, 1993), pp. 51–60, esp. 53–4, 59; Helmut Schmidt, *Die Deutschen und ihre Nachbarn* (Berlin: Siedler, 1990), pp. 513–14. Gerhard Schröder and Jerzy Buzek, 'Wspólna przyszłość ma na imię Europa', *Rzeczpospolita*, 18 November 2000.

2 For example, see Simon Bulmer and William Paterson, 'West Germany's Role in Europe: "Man-Mountain" or "Semi-Guliver?"', *Journal of Common Market Studies*, Vol. 28, 1989, pp. 95–117.

3 See an argument developed by Friedbert Pflüger, 'Polen -eunser Frankreich im Osten', in W. Schäuble and R. Seiters (eds), *Außenpolitik im 21. Jahrhundert. Die Thesen der Jungen Außenpolitiker* (Bonn: Bouvier Verlag, 1996), pp. 183–92.

4 See Bronisław Geremek and Joschka Fischer, 'Deutsch-polnische Beziehungen – Schlüssel zum Aufbau einer stabilen Europäischen Union', *Der Tagesspiegel*, 17 February 2000; Schröder and Buzek, 'Wspólna przyszłość ma na imię Europa'.

5 There is also a distinctive anthropological debate, which identifies the emergence of a more homogeneous European identity. For example, see John Bornemann and Nick Fowler, 'Europeanization', *Annual Review of Anthropology*, 26 1997, pp. 487–514.

6 See Maria Green Cowles, James Caporaso and Thomas Risse (eds), *Europeanization and Domestic Change: Transforming Europe* (Ithaca and London: Cornell University Press, 2001).

7 For example, see Thomas Conzelmann, '"Europeanization" of Regional Development Policies? Linking the Multi-Level Governance Approach with Theories of Policy Learning and Policy Change', *European Integration online Papers* (EIoP), Vol. 2, No. 4, 1998.

8 A definition by Cowles, Caporaso and Risse (eds), *Europeanization and Domestic Change*. Here quoted from Tanja A. Börzel and Thomas Risse, 'When Europe Hits Home: Europeanization and Domestic Change', *European Integration online Papers* (EIoP), Vol. 4 No. 15, 2000, p. 3.

9 See Svein S. Andersen and Kjell A. Eliassen, *Making Policy in Europe: The Europeification of National Policy Making* (London and New Delhi: Sage, 1993), pp. 3–18.

10 See Claudio M. Radelli, 'Whither Europeanization? Concept Stretching and Substantive Change', *European Integration online Papers* (EIoP), Vol. 4 No. 15, 2000, p. 3.

11 For example, Thomas Risse, 'A European Identity? Europeanization and the Evolution of Nation-State Identities', in Cowles, Caporaso and Risse (eds), *Europeanization and Domestic Change*, pp. 198–217.

12 *Ibid.*

13 For example, see the speech by Tadeusz Mazowiecki, 'Belonging to Europe', in the collection of documents edited by Adam Daniel Rotfeld and Walther Stützle, *Germany and Europe in Transition* (Oxford: Sipri and Oxford University Press, 1998), pp. 131–4.

14 See Milan Kundera, 'The Tragedy of Central Europe', *New York Review of Books*, 26 April 1984.

15 See 'Niemcy i Polska', *Kultura*, July/August 1978, pp. 123–9 (also published in German: 'Polen und Deutschland', *Osteuropa*, February 1979, pp. 101–5); Jiri Dienstbier, *Sneni o Evropie* (Prague: Lidove Noviny, 1990).

16 See Attila Agh, *Democratization and Europeanization in Hungary* (Budapest: Hungarian Centre for Democracy Studies, 1995).

17 See Geoffrey Pridham, 'Patterns of Europeanisation and Transnational Party Cooperation: Party Development in Central and Eastern Europe', ECPR Paper, Mannheim, March 1999.

18 Judy Batt and Katarzyna Wolczuk, 'Keep an Eye on the East', *Financial Times* (International edn), 23 February 2001; interview with Joshka Fischer, 'Boimy się wielkich Niemiec', *Rzeczpospolita*, 13 October 1995.

19 Marek Garztecki, 'Bałkanizacja przed europeizacją', *Rzeczpospolita*, 8 January 1994.

20 See George Schöpflin, *Nations, Identity, Power* (London: Hurst: 2000), pp. 378–410, esp. 389–90.

21 See 'Ekolodzy czekają na opinie ekspertów' *Rzeczpospolita*, 18 December 2000.

22 'Spór o elektrownie załagodzony', *Rzeczpospolita*, 14 November 2000.

23 See *Germany and Eastern Europe: Cultural Identities and Cultural Differences*, Yearbook of European Studies, 13 (Amsterdam and Atlanta, GA: Rodopi BV Editions, 1999).

24 See Pflüger and Lipscher (eds), *Feinde werden Freunde*, pp. 145–289.

25 See Jan Józef Lipski, 'Polen, Deutsche und Europa', in Józef Lipski, *Wir müssen uns alles sagen/Musimy Sobie Wszystko powiedzieć* bilingual edition (Warsaw: Deutsch-Polnischer Verlag, 1996), pp. 253–64.

26 See Willy Brandt, 'Der Kniefall von Warschau', in Pflüger und Lipscher (eds), *Feinde werden Freunde*, pp. 51–60.

27 See Helmut Schmidt, 'Schwieriger Besuch in Warschau 1966', in Pflüger and Lipscher (eds), *Feinde werden Freunde*, pp. 49–50.

28 Friedbert Pflüger, 'Polen – unser Frankreich im Osten', in Schäuble und Seiters (eds), *Außenpolitik im 21. Jahrhundert*, pp. 183–92.

29 See Pflüger, 'Polen – unser Frankreich im Osten', p. 183.

30 Immanuel Kant, 'Perpetual Peace', (ed.) Lewis White Beck (Indianapolis and New York: Bobbs-Merrill, 1957).

31 See Laura Cram, 'Imagining the Union: A Case for Banal Europeanism', in Helen Wallace (ed.), *Interlocking Dimensions of European Integration* (Basingstoke: Palgrave: 2001), pp. 231–46

32 For a neorealist account, see Kenneth N. Waltz, 'Explaining War' (pp. 130–45); for a neoliberal approach, see Robert O. Keohane and Joseph S. Nye, 'Realism and Complex Interdependence' (pp. 307–17), in Paul R. Viotti and Mark V. Kauppi (eds), *International Relations Theory*, 3rd edn (Boston and London: Allyn & Bacon, 1999).

33 Peter J. Katzenstein, 'Introduction: Alternative Perspectives on National Security', in Peter J. Katzenstein (ed.), *The Culture of National Security: Norms and Identity in World Politics* (New York: Columbia University Press, 1996).

34 *Ibid.*

35 See Anna Wolf-Powęska, 'Poszukiwanie Dróg Dialogu', in Anna Wolf-Powęska (ed.), *Polacy wobec Niemców: Z Dziejów Kultury Politycznej Polski 1945–1989* (Poznan: Instytut Zachodni, 1993), p. 371

36 Dieter Bingen, *Die Polenpolitik der Bonner Republik von Adenauer bis Kohl, 1949–1990* (Baden-Baden: Nomos, 1998), p. 1.

37 Tewes Henning, 'The Emergence of Civilian Power: Germany and Central Europe', *German Politics*, Vol. 6, No. 2, August 1997, pp. 95–117.

38 Krzysztof Malinowski, 'Asymetria Partnerstwa: Polityka Zjednoczonych Niemiec wobec Polski', in Zbigniew Mazur (ed.), *Rola Nowych Niemiec na Arenie Międzynarodowej* (Poznan: Instytut Zachodni, 1996), p. 281.

39 Bingen, *Die Polenpolitik*, p. 274.

40 'Polen und Deutschland', *Osteuropa*, February 1979, pp. 101–5.

41 See Malinowski, 'Asymetria Partnerstwa', pp. 270–302 Pflüger, 'Polen – unser Frankreich', pp. 183–92.

42 For example, see Lily Gardner Feldman, 'The Principle and Practice of "Reconciliation"' in German Foreign Policy: Relations with France, Israel, Poland and the Czech Republic', *International Affairs*, Vol. 75, No. 2, April 1999, pp. 333–57.

43 Bingen, *Die Polenpolitik*, pp. 41–78.

44 In 1999, 73 per cent of the Poles thought that reconciliation with Germany was both possible and desirable; see 'Polacy o możliwościach pojednania z Niemcami i Ukrainą – Komunikat z Badań, Centrum Badania Opinii Społecznej (CBOS), Warsaw, June 1999, p. 2.

2

An interlocking conflict of interests, 1944–48

I would like to review the basic Soviet postwar program for Germany as seen from Moscow. The first step in this program was the creation of the Oder-Neisse border. By this measure, Moscow ... made unthinkable for the foreseeable future any independent collaboration between Polish and German peoples and placed Poland in a position of total military dependence on Russia.' (Telegram by George Kennan, American *Chargé d'Affaires* in the Soviet Union, to the Secretary of State, Moscow, 6 March, 1946.)[1]

Introduction

As argued in Chapter 1, this book is interested in the emergence of co-operative relations between Poland and Germany. However, in order to understand the conditions in which the current consensus is being built it is necessary to address the severity of the conflict that dominated the relationship until the end of the Cold War. Tensions in the relationship were present from the late eighteenth century when Prussia joined Russia and Austria in dividing the Polish state.[2] Clearly the Second World War deepened the already strong perception in Poland that Germany represented a constant threat to its existence as an independent state. Yet, with the end of the war, there was a hope that the Poles and Germans could make a fresh start towards peaceful co-existence and gradual rapprochement. It was viewed in some quarters as possible that the trauma of the war could actually have a cathartic effect, facilitating the emergence of co-operative relations, as became the case with France and West Germany. In his inaugural address before the *Bundestag* Chancellor Adenauer explicitly pronounced Germany's reconciliation with Poland, alongside that with France and Israel, to be one of his policy objectives. However, circumstances prevailed which served to reinforce existing Polish–German antagonism and to deny the possibility of achieving a consensus.

This chapter posits the argument that three particular developments and issues impacted upon Polish–German rapprochement during the Cold War period and rendered the *Europeanisation* of the relationship unattainable:

- *Territorial conflict* Following the Soviet invasion of Poland in 1939, Poland lost half of its territory to the Soviet Union, which proved irrecoverable. Instead, Poland was compensated by taking over part of Prussia and other eastern territories of pre-war Germany, a move which subsequently stretched Poland westwards up to the rivers Oder and Neisse.

- *Expulsion and migration* As a result of the re-drawing of the region, mass migrations of people became inevitable. Millions of Poles who fled from the lands east of the river Bug replaced millions of Germans who were expelled from their homes east of the Oder and Neisse at the end of the war.

- *Burden of History* 20 per cent of the entire Polish population was killed and thousands of Germans perished during the transfers; this, together with the terror of the German occupation of Poland, the loss of *dom* (home) for eastern Poles and of *Heimat* (homeland) for eastern Germans served to deepen the hatred and contempt between the two neighbouring nations.

Clearly, the most important of these three elements was that of *territory*. Certainly the other two – the issue of expulsions and the historical burden – were also important, but were arguably secondary and in many ways dependent upon the territorial dispute. The expulsion and forced migration of both Germans and Poles was a consequence of changing boundaries, while the historical burden could not be successfully addressed under the prevailing condition of territorial conflict. The frontier issue thus came to dominate the relationship until its resolution in 1991. The frontier question also played a pivotal role in the broader post-war international balance of power. Crucially, as long as the West refrained from recognising the Oder–Neisse line as Poland's western frontier, there remained an element of genuine national interest for Poland in sustaining its alliance with the Soviet Union, the powerful neighbour who officially guaranteed Poland's western boundaries. Post-war territorial settlements were consequently often described in Poland as 'Stalin's trap', which determined not only Poland's foreign policy but also its domestic order.

The aim of this chapter is to identify and explain the sources of the Polish–German conflict and the ways in which it was re-defined after the Second World War. The chapter will look specifically at the period between the emergence and collapse of the Grand Alliance (1945–48), developments which, as argued here, determined the substance of the Polish–German conflict, and subsequently set the agenda for the relationship throughout the entire Cold War period. The chapter is divided into three parts. It will begin by building upon the three elements of the post-war conflict as outlined above and will then move to analyse these issues from both structural-international and domestic angles. In the third section, the chapter will seek to explain exactly why the developments of 1943–48 impacted so decisively upon the prospect of the *Europeanisation* of the relationship during the Cold War.

Facets of the Polish–German conflict of interests

The post-war Polish–German border

The Polish–German territorial conflict was undoubtedly externally determined, with all three members of the Grand Alliance playing decisive roles in this dispute. However, it is clear that the Soviet Union was the most engaged and by far the most influential in deciding the final shape of the post-war Polish–German boundary. Two developments, involving Moscow came to have a decisive impact upon the key features and final outcome of this dispute: first, the joint German-Soviet invasion of Poland in September 1939 and, secondly, the Red Army's successful campaign against German forces and its subsequent 'liberation' of Poland between 1944 and 1945.

In October 1939, Poland's territory was divided on a roughly fifty-fifty basis between Nazi Germany and the Soviet Union, in accordance with the Ribbentrop-Molotow agreements of August and September 1939 in which it was agreed that after the Polish state ceased to exist the German–Soviet border would be established along what had formerly been the internal Polish river Bug.[3] This new frontier remained the status quo until the German invasion of the Soviet Union in June 1941, a development, which made western leaders regard the Soviet Union as a potential ally and consequently led to the emergence of a favourable disposition in the West towards Soviet territorial demands against Poland. Resulting from this, the Polish government-in-exile in London became internationally isolated in its policy of wishing to see the half of Poland under the Soviet occupation returned to its pre-war status.

On the other hand, although little could be done to reverse Soviet territorial gains in eastern Poland, chances to see this loss compensated in the west, on the German–Polish border, grew considerably as the Soviet Union became engaged in the war. Subsequently, the 'compensation' argument emerged as a dominant element of the debate on the post-war territorial settlement between Poland and Germany. From the very outset of their co-operation with Moscow, it was clear that London and Washington had agreed that the Soviets would keep the half of Poland that had been under their occupation since September 1939 and that Poland would be moved westwards. As argued by Churchill, 'Poland would be a state on wheels'. The only issue open to negotiations was how far westward would the Polish wheels be allowed to roll into German territory?

The first arrangements concerning the future Polish–German and Polish–Soviet boundaries were reached at the conferences in Teheran (November–December 1943) and Yalta (February 1945). Despite the protests of the Polish government-in-exile, it was agreed here that Poland's eastern frontier would remain at the river Bug, as formerly delineated in the German–Soviet treaties, and that Poland would be compensated by taking over eastern Prussia and some other east German territories, although the actual detail of this remained unclear until the end of the war.[4] Polish opposition regarding the decisions taken in Teheran and Yalta was subsequently weakened when the Soviet-sponsored 'Union of Polish Patriots' (*Związek Polskich Patriotów*), whose core members later formed the communist-dominated 'Lublin Committee' (*Komitet Lubelski*), denounced territorial claims against the Soviets and demanded the westwards shift of the Polish–German frontier to the rivers Oder and Neisse. This subsequently became the official position of the Polish communist-dominated delegation at the post-war conference in Potsdam and, after protracted negotiations, was temporarily agreed upon by the United States, Britain and Russia, with the understanding that the final settlement of this issue would be reached at a future peace conference.[5]

However, the peace conference never happened and as Europe's division deepened so did the differences between the superpowers' positions on Poland's western frontier. By 1946, it had become clear that Poland would remain in the Soviet sphere of influence, whereas Germany's future remained to be determined. This clearly had an impact upon the policies of the western powers concerning the new German–Polish border, which was overwhelmingly unpopular in Germany. In order to ensure German loyalty to the West, Winston Churchill and the US State Secretary James Byrnes underlined soon after Potsdam the transitory character of the border and stressed that its final delineation remained to be confirmed in a future peace settlement.[6] These statements subsequently evolved into the official policies of the United States, Britain and all other states in the emerging western bloc.

Changing borders: the movement and transfer of people

The moving wheels of the Polish state were followed by massive migrations of Poles, Germans and other ethnic groups which moved away from, but also into, contested territories. Some of these movements were voluntary but most were forced, either indirectly by circumstances (escaping foreign occupation) or directly, carried out as official policy by foreign administrations through resettlements and expulsions.

As a result of the campaign of September 1939 the part of Poland occupied by Germany was divided into two entities. The most western territory was directly and fully incorporated into the *Reich*, with the remainder, the so-called 'General Government' (*Generalna Gubernia*), falling under German administration. Hitler's plan envisaged the incremental enlargement of the 'ethnically clean' *Reich* through the extermination of Jews and resettlement of Poles first from the territories that were administratively joined with Germany to the *Generalna Gubernia* and subsequently from the *Generalna Gubernia* further eastwards. Consequently, thousands of Poles from the territories incorporated into Germany were expelled to the *Generalna Gubernia* or transported to Germany to work in forced labour camps. Beginning from 1942 the so-called '*Plan Ost*', aimed at creating a German zone in the East, was launched in the *Generalna Gubernia*, resulting in the extensive resettlement of Poles from the eastern part of this territory. On the whole, however, these expulsions never reached the scale that had been intended. The major reason for this was that the migration of Poles was hindered by the low demand from Germany to replace vacated households in Poland.[7]

The movement of people on a massive scale was also taking place in the part of Poland under Soviet occupation. Some of these movements were forced transportations 'zsyłki' of ethnic Poles, Ukrainians, Byelorussians and Lithuanians into the far eastern parts of the Soviet Union. The voluntary migration of Poles from the East also ensued after the war towards what became post-war Poland; at the end of the war around 1.2 million Poles migrated westwards to replace Germans in the lands east of the Oder and Neisse.[8]

Essentially, as the war came to an end the German *Drang nach Osten* (desire to push East) was reversed, in that the Allies oversaw the transfer of over 10 million Germans from East Central Europe to Germany. Initially this was supported by both the British and Americans, described by Herbert Hoover as a 'heroic means' of achieving lasting peace and promoted by Churchill as 'the most effective and successful method of solving the problems arising from the ethnic complexity'; it was subsequently attacked by both London and Washington in the wake of the emergence of the Cold War.[9] Unsurprisingly, in Poland public support for the resettlement of Germans was overwhelming.

At the Potsdam conference, where the war-time consensus still prevailed, the Great Three (Stalin, Truman and Atlee) decided that Poland, Czechoslovakia and Hungary should go ahead with the transfer of Germans to all four occupation zones of post-war Germany. Subsequently, the Allied Control Council decided on a schedule for the relocation of 3.5 million Germans from Poland. The initial time schedule proved to be unrealistic and the organised resettlements took almost five years; during this period some 2.8 million Germans were transferred from Poland. This figure did not, however, include the 400,000 Germans who had been forced out prior to the Potsdam agreement.[10] In addition, around 1 million people moved voluntarily from Poland to West Germany in the 1970s and 1980s within the framework of the bilateral Polish-(West) German agreement of 'uniting divided families'. Those Germans resettled from Poland, Czechoslovakia and Hungary subsequently became a powerful irredentist force and exercised significant influence on the Federal government's *Ostpolitik*.

Public perceptions of German–Polish relations

The already negative public perceptions of Germany present in Poland in the wake of the war were deepened further by the re-drawing of national frontiers; likewise in Germany, Nazi propaganda which had portrayed Poles as an 'inferior race' maintained much of its resonance. The masses of Germans migrating from East Central Europe, whose resettlement was rarely conducted in the 'humanitarian spirit' pre-scribed at Potsdam, also strengthened the sense of bitterness and injustice that prevailed in the German attitude towards Poland for much of the Cold War period.

Nazi crimes in Poland were widespread and more atrocious than anywhere else in Europe, with the possible exception of the Soviet Union. Poland was the key site of the Holocaust. Polish citizens were exposed to special regimes, deportations, slave labour and concentra-tion camps. Over 6 million Poles, a fifth of the entire population, were killed during the war; the death toll was so high that the national cen-sus in 1946 showed the same population figure as in 1910.[11] Moreover, the thousands of Polish soldiers who migrated with the Polish armed forces to France and Britain were often not allowed to return home and many of those who managed to come back were imprisoned and often executed. As a result of the war, Poland lost 180,000 km² in the east and although it was compensated by 103,000 km² in the west, the country's overall size was reduced by one-fifth.[12] Finally, although officially Poland was among the victors in the war, its sovereignty was lost as it fell under Moscow's rule.

A profoundly negative perception of Germany thus prevailed in Poland, leading to extreme behaviour, often sanctioned by law, towards ethnic Germans in the early post-war years. For example, Polish sol-diers were prohibited from shaking hands or sharing meals with Germans; Germans and the so-called *Volksdeutsche* (former Polish nationals who became Germans during the war) were prohibited from various forms of employment. The very word: *Niemcy* (Germany) was deliberately spelt with a lower-case first letter: *niemcy*. There were also some incidents of public executions of war criminals, for example of the staff of Majdanek's concentration camp.[13]

Anti-Germanism in Poland was also reflected in political writings of the time and even in some policy proposals coming from the Foreign Office. For example, a book entitled *Criminal Nation* (*Naròd-Zbrod-niarz*), published by a member of the National Supreme Court, Emil Stanisław Rappaport, developed an argument in favour of the collec-tive responsibility of the entire German nation for Nazi crimes. To eradicate the inherent aggression of the Germans, Rappaport suggested that the country should be turned into a purely agricultural land and that its industry should be limited to simple craftsmanship. Even more extreme views originated from the Foreign Office. Stanisław Nahalik, a civil servant who was involved in the preparation of the Polish position for the negotiations on a peace settlement, proposed to amend a future treaty with a secret 'negative denazification programme' clause. This programme would promote alcoholism, abortion and strict contraception in Germany, as well as active depopulation through encouraging emigration from Germany.[14]

Although clearly much of this voraciously anti-German mood died down with time, one of its key elements – seeing Germans as an inherently aggressive and anti-Polish nation – continued to impact heavily on all subsequent debates. This perception was additionally fired by the rise of territorial claims in Germany against the Oder-Neisse border – a policy, which came to support the claims of the so-called 'historians', Polish academics who argued that western Slavs had always been threatened by Germanic tribes and that the Polish state had never been accepted by its western neighbour. Consequently, the school argued, Polish national interests were best served if Germany remained weak, divided and checked by external powers.[15]

Anti-Polonism in (West) Germany, although not as decisive as anti-Germanism in Poland, also came to be a significant factor in the construction of Bonn's official policies towards Warsaw. There were three main sources of this. First, historically, German irredentism in the East had a long tradition, and even before Hitler had constituted a central element of the German 'national idea'. Significantly even Gustav Stresemann the Weimar Republic's Foreign Minister, and Nobel Peace Prize winner, generally perceived by the West as a peaceful liberal, actively worked towards the demise of the '*Saisonstaat*' (transitional state) Poland.[16] Therefore, just as the Weimar Republic had never accepted the loss of 10 per cent of its pre-1914 territory on behalf of Poland it could not be realistically expected that post-1945 (West) Germany would not protest against the loss of 25 per cent of its pre-1937 lands. In addition, unlike in 1918 the lands that were taken over by Poland in 1945 were undoubtedly ethnically German.

Secondly, the sheer number of Germans forced to resettle from the lands east of the Oder–Neisse line to Germany (3.4 million by 1950) constituted a considerable political force that remained bitter about the way they had been treated by the Polish authorities. While waiting for transfers, the living conditions of ethnic Germans were poor, not to mention the labour and the prisoner-of-war (POW) camps where the mortality rate was high and even executions were carried out; for example in the camp 'Lambieniowice', forty prisoners were executed on 4 October 1945.[17]

Thirdly, the German population felt humiliated and victimised by the post-war settlement. These feelings could not be wholly directed towards the occupying powers, owing to their position as 'administrators' of Germany; moreover, it was actually in Germany's interests to become reconciled with their occupiers, even with the Russians who remained the traditional focus of Germany's Eastern policy. With regard to Poland none of these considerations played a role, at least not in the first years after the end of the war; also, unlike in the Russian case, there was no history of friendly relations with Poland. In the first elections after the war not a single German party, in the West or East, not even the Communists, refrained from posing territorial demands against Poland.[18]

Interlocking conflict of interests

With the end of the Second World War, prospects for Polish–German reconciliation looked very thin, the relationship remained burdened by the past and locked in a severe territorial conflict. This antagonism was heightened and sustained by the negative perceptions held by both nations of each other, which were ingrained in Polish and German national historical memories. As argued above, at the end of the war German–Polish relations were set in a severely antagonistic framework wherein an international conflict was bolstered by hatred between the two societies. The dawning of the Cold War only increased the existing discord in Polish–German relations. Clearly by supporting and raising hopes for territorial revisionism in Germany, western leaders aimed to ensure the latter's loyalty to the West. At the same time, such appeals served to strengthen calls in Poland for an alliance with the Soviet Union which, paradoxically, came to be promoted even by those who did not sympathise with the communist regime.

As a result, the Polish–German conflict came to play a significant role in international as well as in the domestic politics of Cold War Europe. In international politics, it became apparent by the late 1940s that the positions of individual countries towards the conflict had become polarised strictly along the lines of their allegiance to either the East or West, with all of the people's democracies and none of the western states recognising the Oder-Neisse rivers as Poland's western frontier.

But the issue had also far-reaching domestic implications in both Poland and Germany. The Polish writer, Bronisław Pasierb argued that the conflict came to serve the ruling communists by consolidating their power and being a useful weapon against domestic opposition. Pasierb distinguished between the *instrumental* and the *integrationist* role of the issue. The *instrumental* role, he argued, was carried out through exaggerating the extent of anti-Polish revisionism in post-war Germany and in the West's tolerance for this policy. This role was, for example, apparent during the 1946 elections in Poland when the communist press was full of headlines such as: 'German Social-Democrats demand the return of Silesia, English authorities let them do it.' This served to strengthen public support for the anti-German but also anti-western communist party. The *integrationist* role aimed at consolidating the communists' hold on to power, by capitalising upon the deep anti-Germanism in post-war Poland that ran through all sectors of society. In this situation it became useful for the government to accuse the anti-communist opposition of having pro-German or even pro-Fascist sympathies. Any possible criticism of Poland having 'too close a relationship with the USSR' was immediately acquainted with support for the German revisionists.[19]

As regards Germany, it is clear that before the actual division of the country fully materialised, the Oder-Neisse border line was probably the only issue on which all political parties agreed. After its inception the GDR did recognise the Oder-Neisse, line but this happened only through strong pressure from the Soviet Union.[20] In West Germany, not only did a domestic consensus on the issue prevail until the early 1960s but German re-settlers also became a significant political force, forming their own party, the *Block der Heimatvertriebenen und Entrechteten* (BHE), which co-governed in coalition with the CDU between 1953 and 1957.

It is evident that the key determinants of Polish–(West) German relations in the post-war period were related to both countries' positions in the international system, their allegiance to confronting military and political blocs and to internal developments and domestic arrangements in Poland and Germany. An 'interlocking conflict of interests' best describes this multifaceted and mutually dependent discord, which in essence prevailed until the end of the Cold War.

The remainder of this chapter will concentrate upon the Oder-Neisse border issue which, as argued earlier was the main feature of the conflict. The emergence of the conflict will be tracked through the prisms of first a structural explanation and secondly at the level of domestic politics.

Explaining the emergence of the territorial conflict

With the end of the Second World War, both Polish and German territories were considerably transformed. The cradle of German nationalism, Prussia, ceased to exist and the eastern Polish borderlands (*Kresy*), became the western periphery of the Soviet Union; the whole of Poland literally moved 300 km westwards. Significantly, the predominant paradigm of Polish–German relations of the previous 200 years – the Prussian *Drang nach Osten* – was replaced by Poland's *Drang nach Westen* (desire to push to the West). As noted above, these profound changes in the Polish–German conflict did not originate from either of these two countries. The Polish–German territorial settlement was agreed between the Soviet Union, the United States and Britain. This being the case, any investigation of the Oder-Neisse debate during the war and up until the split of the Great Alliance needs first of all to address the policies of the Great Powers. However, the influence of domestic factors and developments in both Germany and Poland also require attention in order to ascertain the extent to which they influenced, colluded with or went against the grain of the perspectives of the Great Powers.

Structural explanation of Western policy
towards the Polish boundaries

It can be argued that the Great Powers approached the issue of the Polish–German frontier on a purely instrumental basis. Initially thought of in terms of compensation for the Poles, it then became a bargaining factor as part of various package deals first serving to strengthen the coalition and later dividing the Powers' respective areas of influence. Most importantly here, it is clear that the question of Poland's boundaries become a vital issue in the emerging East–West power struggle.

From Teheran to Potsdam
The Soviet annexation of eastern Poland, as agreed in Teheran, placed territorial compensation for Poland on the agenda. Had Churchill and

Roosevelt not assented to Stalin's demands, the continuation of the war-time coalition would have been doubtful. However, the notion of Poland's westwards shift was actually conceived of by Churchill who, as part of his obligation to the Polish government-in-exile, sought compensation for Poland's lost territories.[21] Both Russian and American statesmen agreed in principle, although Roosevelt reserved the right not to participate in any decision regarding Polish boundaries until after the presidential election in America in November 1944. Although he personally agreed upon the principles of the settlement he sought not to commit himself to a decision, which he feared could possibly lose him 6 million US voters of Polish ancestry.[22] For Stalin, who already at the time of Teheran planned to install a Communist government in Warsaw, the idea of moving Poland westwards meant expanding the Soviet sphere of influence. The Soviet leader was therefore highly disposed to the plan, though he still placed conditions upon his agreement that north-eastern Prussia, including Königsberg, be transferred to the Soviet Union.[23] Crucially, all three leaders agreed upon the principle of 'compensation' as conceived of at Teheran.

By the time of the Yalta conference in February 1945, Soviet demands regarding Poland had gone beyond territorial claims and had begun to focus upon the composition of a future Polish government. The key issue to be decided at Yalta was consequently no longer Poland's future borders but rather whether or not it would become a Soviet satellite state.[24]

According to Churchill, Poland 'had been the most urgent reason for the Yalta Conference, and was to prove the first of the great causes which led to the breakdown of the Grand Alliance'.[25] Poland was discussed at seven out of the eight plenary sessions at which the allies were mostly concerned with two key issues: firstly, the composition of a single Provisional Government of Poland to be followed by free elections and secondly, the issue of Poland's frontiers, in both the east and the west. During the conference, it became clear that Stalin had abandoned the idea agreed upon earlier of establishing a Provisional Government from the existing government-in-exile in London and its rival communist government established by the Soviets in Lublin. Instead, Stalin favoured a simple enlargement of the Lublin government by a few non-communist politicians plus two others from vaguely defined Polish émigré circles, thus without incorporating any members of the London-based government-in-exile. After lengthy negotiations Stalin's formula was agreed upon and Roosevelt and Churchill remained satisfied with the Soviet pledge of holding free elections in Poland at the earliest possible date.[26]

In other words, to save the coalition, Britain and America agreed that the non-democratic Soviet Union would guarantee democracy in Poland. Yet, as Churchill argued: 'What would have happened if we had quarrelled with Russia while the Germans still had two or three hundred divisions on the fighting front? Our hopeful assumptions [free elections in Poland] were soon to be falsified. Still, they were the only ones possible at the time.'[27] Whether Churchill and Roosevelt could have done more for Poland than to rely on Stalin's word remains debatable; what, however, seems certain is that Yalta merely confirmed that Poland was becoming a Soviet protectorate. Thus, the 'package deal' of binding support for Poland's territorial gains in the west to the issue of establishing a western-friendly government in Warsaw, which both the British and the United States hoped to achieve in Yalta had largely become redundant.

Subsequently, when the question of the Polish–German frontier was raised, Churchill appeared significantly less generous towards the Poles than he had been in Teheran. The British premier cautioned: 'It would be a great pity to stuff the Polish goose so full of German food that it would die of indigestion.' He argued against moving Poland's boundaries further west beyond the river Oder (in the south), which would have meant the acquisition of less territory for Poland by around one-third. On this point, Churchill was supported by Roosevelt, who agreed that Poland should receive compensation at the expense of Germany; however, as he argued, 'there would appear to be little justification for extending it up to the Western Neisse'. Stalin remained non-committal at this stage, although he clearly preferred more substantial gains for Poland in the West. Eventually, a joint declaration over Poland issued at the end of the conference drew a precise line for the Polish–Soviet border referring to the so-called 'Curzon line' (although in fact it was a line agreed in the 1939 Ribbentrop-Molotow pact) while the provisions for the Polish–German border remained undefined.[28]

With hindsight, it is clear that Yalta was a turning point in the West's policy towards the Oder–Neisse line. During the conference the British and Americans realised that their battle over Poland as their future ally was lost, which subsequently led to scepticism regarding Poland's territorial compensation in the west. Now it was Stalin who advocated further concessions for Poland. What motivated this change in

Churchill's policy was the fact that while at Teheran it had been the Polish government-in-exile in London that had been the addressee of the Alliance's policies, by the time of Yalta it was the communist 'Lublin government'. There was little doubt, then, that Poland would become pro–Soviet, while the future of Germany was still to be determined. In this context, any further extension of Poland on behalf of Germany began to be considered by the West as more to do with the expansion of the Soviet sphere of influence.

The Potsdam conference merely confirmed that a shift in western policy towards Poland's western frontier had occurred. When the three leaders met in Potsdam, the West was essentially confronted with a *fait accompli* that Poland, with Soviet encouragement, had annexed that part of Germany still under dispute at Yalta. Unsurprisingly, both the British and Americans argued that this annexation effectively denied them possible reparations and sources of food for the German population in the western zones of occupation. Most importantly, however, it meant that the Soviets had gained control over huge chunks of Germany prior to securing any formal arrangements with the British and Americans and without having given anything away.

The early resolution of this question, and Poland's withdrawal from the lands between the Oder and western Neisse, was one of Churchill's biggest preoccupations at Potsdam. He feared that the mines of Silesia would provide resources for the Soviet Union's military potential and further that millions of German refugees expelled from the territories east of the Oder–Neisse line would cause unrest in the western occupation zones, leading possibly to the rise of pro-communist tendencies in Germany. He thus remained consistently critical of granting any further territorial concessions to Poland than what had already been agreed to at Yalta. However, in the middle of the conference Churchill flew back to London, to find out that he had been voted out of office. Consequently, he was never given a chance to finish his campaign against the Oder-Neisse border line to which, as he claimed in his memoirs, he would have never agreed.[29]

When the new British Prime Minister, Attlee, and his Foreign Minister, Bevin, reached Potsdam on 28 July 1945, the Americans and Soviets were already well advanced in making a deal over the Polish western frontier and reparations for Germany. Neither President Truman nor his State Secretary Byrnes appeared, at this point, to see American national interests as affected by territorial settlements in Europe. Truman thus accepted the western instead of the eastern

Neisse as the Polish–German frontier, provided that the Russians took reparations only from their own occupation zone. In contrast, Bevin sought to secure an agreement with Moscow for free elections and respect for civil liberties in Poland, offering in return considerable concessions regarding reparations.[30]

Unsurprisingly, the American offer was more attractive to Moscow. As a result, the only option left for Bevin was to dispute the percentage of reparations awarded to the Soviets from the western zones and gain assurances that free elections in Poland would be held in 1946, which would be observed by the West. Finally, the three powers reached an agreement that Poland would administer the disputed territory in the interim period until the peace conference.[31] The lack of a final peace conference assured the endurance of the status quo.

As Churchill's policy in Yalta and Bevin's in Potsdam demonstrated, had Poland found itself on the other side of emerging the East–West division, British and probably US policies would have been more sympathetic to Polish demands. However, since Poland was falling into the Soviet sphere of influence it was not London nor Washington but rather Moscow who argued in Potsdam in favour of the Polish national interest and was even prepared to offer considerable concessions on reparations in order to secure larger territorial gains for Warsaw. This situation clearly deepened Poland's dependence on the Soviet Union.

The emergence of bipolarity

Already by the end of 1945 the establishment of puppet governments in Eastern and East Central Europe was being met with growing concern in the West. At the beginning of 1946 the West became aware that Poland, too, was being drawn under Soviet tutelage.[32] What now seemed to be the inevitable fate of Poland prompted concern in the West that a 'domino effect' might take place with the establishment of Soviet-style people's democracies throughout the entire continent. In this scenario, the German question became an imperative for both sides of the emerging divide. In this context, and bearing in mind that elections in Germany were imminent, neither the Soviet Union nor Britain and America could ignore the almost unanimously critical attitude of the German population towards the new border with Poland.[33]

Attempting to influence the forthcoming elections, the West's position on the border became openly critical of the provisions established in Potsdam, while the Soviets sent mixed signals on the issue throughout 1946. Both of these positions had, of course, bigger goals: the ultimate allegiance of Germany was now at stake, and the border issue was now being overtly framed within the prism of bipolar conflict. The broadening of the issue was apparent in Churchill's Fulton speech in 1946: 'The Russian-dominated Polish Government has been encouraged to make enormous and wrongful inroads upon Germany, and mass expulsions of millions of Germans on a scale grievous and undreamed-of are now taking place.'[34] The wider significance of the border issue was also becoming evident to the hitherto indifferent United States. Washington's apparent lack of concern about Soviet aspirations in Europe thus far was now changing. It was the speed at which communist take-overs in East Central Europe were taking place which forced this reconsideration in Washington's policy, a shift which was considerably influenced by the new US Chargé d'Affaires in Moscow, George Kennan. Kennan's perspective was grounded in the belief that the previous British and American consent on the Oder–Neisse line in Potsdam had been a mistake, and that it could eventually lead to the Soviet take-over of the whole of Germany and consequently of the rest of western Europe which, he judged, was Stalin's ultimate aim. According to Kennan, Moscow had already secured the Soviet strategic border along the shortest line possible between the Carpathians and the Baltic; this, he argued, made any collaboration between Poland and Germany impossible. Moreover, it confirmed Poland's military dependence upon Russia. The secession of eastern Germany to Poland would in addition severely reduce the likelihood of Germany being able to exist and function as a national entity.[35]

Kennan's convictions led him to argue against the unification of Germany which, he believed, would have made Germany vulnerable to Soviet penetration and influence. Consequently, he argued that the 'possibility of a united sovereign Germany, fitted constructively into patterns of western European life as an independent self-respecting unit, bound by ties of mutual confidence and common ideals to the countries of the Atlantic community, *was effectively disposed of the day we and the British assented to* [the] *Oder–Neisse line as the future boundary of Germany* (my emphasis)'. Thus he recommended that in the current situation (March 1946) America should advocate the partitioning of Germany and the sealing of the western zones from the East.[36]

The strategy advocated by Kennan was to begin with America's withdrawal from the Potsdam agreement, particularly from the provisions regarding the Oder–Neisse Line. Secondly, the United States should propose the economic unification of Germany 'not only within the Oder-Neisse boundary but also generally within the old boundaries, excluding East Prussia'. Such a move was meant to serve several purposes: it would disarm French claims for the Rheinland and the Ruhr (which was often put forward by the French in the framework of the 'Oder-Neisse' issue), and it would complicate the situation for the Russians, who would be faced with the necessity of making a choice between cutting the ground out from under the Polish communists (should they accept) or losing the possibility of posing as the champions of a united Germany (should they decline). Most importantly, however, America would be free to proceed with the organisation of western Germany, independently of the Soviets, without being seen as the opponent of unification. Otherwise, argued Kennan, the Russians, who placed tremendous value on communist successes in Germany, might undertake a revision of the Oder–Neisse Line themselves. This, however, would have occurred only if the Russians 'were sure that such a revision would mean [a] Communist victory, and that only in that way could such a victory be obtained'.[37]

Similar indications of the possible shift in Soviet policy towards Poland's western frontier came from Robert Murphy, the US Political Advisor on Germany. In his official correspondence, Murphy spoke of a possible change in Soviet attitudes in favour of a revision of the Oder-Neisse frontier which, he warned, might be used to swing votes in favour of the communists.[38] He also observed that the pro-merger group in the eastern Social Democratic Party (SPD) not only had a 'pro-Russian' orientation, it also advocated a revision of the border. According to Murphy, in March 1946 a prominent member of the SPD (and subsequently SED), Grotewohl, emphasised that any final determination on the Polish–German border would be made by the Soviets who stood alone in support for the retention of the Ruhr for Germany and might in the nearest future consider the revision of the Oder-Neisse frontier.[39]

These policy proposals and observations by American civil servants soon impacted upon official US policy towards Germany. In September 1946, State Secretary Byrnes addressed a gathering in Stuttgart with a speech regarding policy on Germany in which he advocated the economic unification of all four zones and also mooted the possibility of a future revision of the frontier with Poland. However, contrary to Kennan's suggestion, Byrnes did not declare the Potsdam agreement not binding for America but chose to employ a strictly legalistic interpretation of the agreement's provisions which, indeed, prescribed eastern German territories to Poland only until a 'Peace Settlement'.[40]

At the Moscow conference, in April 1947, the American delegation tabled an official proposal regarding a possible revision of the German–Polish border. The new Secretary of State, George Marshall, proposed to limit Poland's territorial gains to south-eastern Prussia and Upper Silesia. Had this notion been accepted, Poland's territorial accession in the west would have been less than 50 per cent of what had been agreed in Potsdam. In addition, Marshall proposed establishing provisions to ensure that the coal and other resources of Upper Silesia should fall under international supervision in order to 'sustain the economy of Europe'.[41] Although neither of these propositions found the support of the other conference participants (including the French and British) they nevertheless raised hopes in Germany and contributed to the policy of revisionism that heavily influenced relations between Bonn and Warsaw.

Within a year after the Moscow conference the quadripartite control of Germany finally broke down. In February 1948 Britain, France and the United States convened a conference in London without inviting the Soviet Union. When the Allied Control Council met on 20 March 1948, the Soviet delegation demanded full information concerning the London conference and proposed discussion over the so-called 'Prague declaration' (issued by the Foreign Ministers of Poland, Yugoslavia and Czechoslovakia concerning the disintegration of Germany and violation of the Potsdam agreement in the western zones, including the Oder-Neisse debate[42]). When the latter proposal was declined by the western delegates the Council practically disintegrated, which meant that the division of Europe became official. The final attempts of Polish diplomacy to address the Oder-Neisse issue independently of Russia through the revival of the earlier American suggestion of a forty-year four-power German demilitarisation plan with a subsequent settlement of the border question was rejected by Washington, which suspected that the Polish Foreign Office was acting on instructions from Moscow.[43]

Domestic developments and the border issue

The previous section laid out the broader structural factors at play; we will now present a survey of domestic developments within both Germany and Poland. Two questions, in particular, will be dealt with here: the Polish government-in-exile's policy towards the borders in the East and the West and the implications of post-war developments in Germany and Poland for British and American policies on the issue.

The Polish government in-exile and the question of borders
The Polish government-in-exile in London never accepted the loss of eastern lands to the Soviet Union. It did, though, raise unspecified territorial demands against Germany (East Prussia and Silesia), but they were far more moderate in scope than the extent of the actual territorial corrections established in Potsdam. These claims were not grounded in the frame of territorial compensation, but rather as a form of reparations for Germany having started the war.[44] Essentially, the exiled government opposed all major territorial settlements concerning Poland's borders maintained by the allies.[45]

There are several reasons explaining why the Polish government in London rejected territorial concessions in the east, in spite of the offer to be generously compensated in the west. Firstly, there were a number of issues related to what might be called the 'national idea'. Clearly, it would not be easy for any government to accept changes that would reduce Poland by one-half. Nearly one-third of the entire Polish population remained east of the so-called 'Curzon line', many of whom lived in Wilno/Vilnius and Lwów/Lviv, two cities which were as closely related to Polish history and culture as Cracow and Warsaw. Clearly, had the London Poles gone along with the Yalta agreement, their position and legitimacy would have been seriously undermined at home.

Secondly, the government had to take account of the position of the Polish armed forces on the issue. The majority of Polish soldiers were recruited from the eastern parts of Poland and were naturally eager to see these lands returned from the Soviet Union to Poland after the war. Significantly here, after the publication of the Yalta conference documents which spelled out the West's consent to the Soviet annexation of eastern Poland, the intervention of the government-in-exile was needed to prevent a mutiny by Polish troops.[46] Thirdly, the existence of the rival communist government called first the 'Union of Polish Patriots' and then the Lublin committee, served to strengthen the London government's resolve on the border issue. The pro-Soviet Lublin committee renounced claims for the return of pre-war eastern Poland while demanding far-reaching compensation in the west.

Lastly, and most importantly, the government-in-exile did not believe that Russia's ambitions concerning Poland would end at the annexation of its eastern lands. Moscow's demands to reconstruct the Polish government through the inclusion of communists and the pressure it placed on the West to terminate arms supplies to the Polish Home Army (AK) (the domestic arm of the London government) seemed to confirm that Stalin was seeking to turn Poland in to a Soviet-style people's republic.[47] In addition, when under Mikołajczyk's premiership the London government temporarily bent under British and American pressure to accept the principle of territorial compensation and to negotiate the change of borders both in the east and west, the Soviets only raised their political demands.[48] This led to a governmental crisis; Mikołajczyk, who was ready to accept the so-called 'Curzon line' and form a government with the communists resigned and the London government returned to its former position on the eastern border.[49]

Clearly none of these developments could be the most decisive factor in determining the policies of the Grand Coalition. Since at least Teheran, Churchill, Stalin and Roosevelt had agreed upon the so-called 'Curzon line' as the future boundary between Poland and the Soviet Union. When the Polish Prime Minister Mikołajczyk protested to Churchill over the idea of transferring Poland's eastern territories permanently to the Soviet Union, he was told that 'it is unthinkable that Britain would go to war with the Soviet Union over Poland's eastern frontier, and the United States would certainly never do so'.[50]

However, at the same time, London and Moscow were hosting two rival Polish governments whose popularity at home would clearly be affected by their patrons' policies towards the borders. In addition, the US government could not ignore the voting preferences of some 6 million Americans of Polish ancestry. Consequently, as much as the Great Powers agreed on the question of Poland's eastern borders, they also had strong interests in facilitating their respective Polish lobbies with the prospect of territorial compensation in the west. However, their calculations on this matter differed greatly. Churchill accepted the Soviet annexation of eastern Poland out of a desire to ensure Moscow's place in the coalition against Germany, but at the same time he sought not to undermine the Polish government-in-exile, hence his proposal of compensation in the west. Stalin, on the other hand, was convinced that a Poland that was forced to surrender its eastern half to Russia and take German territory in compensation would fear Germany and depend on Moscow for its security.[51]

While Stalin had no problems with convincing his Polish protégés that Teheran was a great success for Poland, Churchill failed to impress the government-in-exile with his compensation scheme. The Polish government in London did not really aspire to great territorial concessions in the west and certainly was not prepared to give up on the whole of eastern Poland. Churchill argued that Poland would be better off losing its rural lands in the east and gaining the more developed eastern Germany and when Mikołajczyk raised the population question he was assured that all unwanted Germans would be transferred out of the acquired areas and the United Nations would safeguard Poland against possible German vengeance.[52]

After the Yalta conference Britain and the United States withdrew their recognition of the government-in-exile and subsequently acknowledged the so-called 'provisional government' (with Mikołajczyk as its Deputy Premier) as the only representative of Poland. The communist-dominated Provisional Government fully adhered to the principle of compensation and anything else it was told by Stalin. However, in the meantime the Western Powers had become cautious, if not sceptical, concerning the extent of Polish territorial gains in eastern Germany.

Poland and Germany after the war and the West's policy towards the Oder–Neisse line

As noted above, in spite of the Potsdam agreement, the question of the Polish–German border remained open at the end of the War. In this situation, the course of internal developments in both Germany and Poland became important for the construction of British, Soviet and American policies towards Poland's western frontier.

In the Soviet zone, the well-organised Communist Party (KPD) was quick to secure a number of prominent positions in local administrations. Only eleven months after political parties had been re-invented, the KPD managed to forge a merger with the eastern Social Democrats into a single party, the SED (*Sozialistische Einheitspartei Deutschlands*). A similar attempt in the western zones of Berlin failed as the SPD Congress voted overwhelmingly against the merger.[53] The West's take on this development was that the Soviets were aiming to turn east Germany into a sphere of influence, and would then seek to establish a Soviet-style people's republic in all of Germany. As suggested in Kennan's telegram, the United States reacted to this by taking a position on the division of Germany. When, in his Stuttgart speech in

September 1946 State Secretary Byrnes confirmed that American troops would remain in Germany indefinitely, it was apparent that a formal division of Germany had become inevitable.

As regards Poland it was also becoming clear that internal developments were taking the same course as events in other countries now under Soviet tutelage. The situation in Poland had come to the attention of the British and US governments after the Polish government broke its obligation to hold free and unfettered elections, as dictated by the terms of the Yalta and Potsdam agreements.[54] In the meantime, evidence of political terrorism and abuses of power in Poland were reported in the House of Commons, the House of Representatives and even at the United Nations.[55] Furthermore, as observed by the American Embassy, the 'Stalinisation' of Poland was also occurring in the economic sphere, where Warsaw was believed to be following the Soviet model.[56]

In response to Warsaw's violation of the provisions of Yalta and Potsdam, the British and American governments warned that should Poland continue its coercive practices it should expect, in return, an unsympathetic attitude towards its political and economic requirements.[57] Implicit in this warning was the suggestion that unless broad policy reversals were implemented in Poland, the West would alter its position on the border issue in the run-up to the forthcoming peace conference.

At the same time, developments in Germany confronted the occupying powers with the need to make clear their policies on the frontier issue. The 'Sovietisation' of the Russian zone was progressing rapidly and with the German communists advocating unification they appeared to be the champions of the national cause. In this situation, the British and Americans needed to respond with an equally attractive position on the German national question.

The border issue and the revision of existing territorial provisions was the only point on which all German political forces agreed. In the western zones, both the SPD and the Christian Democrats (CDU) dismissed out of hand the idea of granting Poland any territorial concessions. It was significant, for example, that the issue made Konrad Adenauer consider neutrality in the event that the Western Powers agreed that the former German territories would become permanently Polish.[58] The leader of the eastern CDU, Jakob Kaiser, made his opposition to the new frontier his key electoral plank during the 1946 campaign. The communist SED addressed the frontier question during the elections by arguing that only through its victory and alliance with the Soviet Union would the revision of the border become possible.[59]

Faced with a choice between a communist Poland, with no chances of victory for the pro-western opposition and a divided Germany with a western part, which could still become the West's ally, Britain and America decided to support the latter. As apparent in Churchill's Fulton speech, Byrnes' Stuttgart address and Marshall's proposal at the Moscow conference, Poland's inclusion in the Eastern Bloc was viewed as inevitable. Significantly, all of these declarations met with opposition from US and British diplomats based in Poland. The American Ambassador in Warsaw, Bliss Lane, criticised Byrnes' speech (which had underlined the idea that the territorial provisions of the Potsdam agreement were temporary) on the basis that it undermined American interests in Poland and had given the communists a chance to discredit the United States. Lane also noticed that the timing of the speech, just three months before the elections in Poland, had hurt the pro-western Polish Popular Alliance (PSL) and its president Mikołajczyk politically.[60] A similar reaction came from Lane's successor, Stanton Griffis. In response to Marshall's proposal in Moscow (to reduce the amount of Poland's gains in the west by nearly 50 per cent), Griffis had no doubt that this would result in an increase of Soviet influence and the decline of America's prestige in Poland.[61] It is evident, therefore, that the Western Powers were abundantly aware of the possible detrimental effect their policies would have upon Poland, but by this time they were resigned to the idea that Poland's place in the West had already been lost.

Assessment

As argued earlier, both the Polish and German governments could not impact considerably upon the outcome of the Oder-Neisse debate, which was almost entirely determined by the Soviet Union, Britain and the United States. As seen in Churchill's memoirs, British policy towards Poland's borders was motivated by broader structural considerations. In order to win the Second World War London agreed to the so-called 'Curzon line' and proposed compensation for Poland at the expense of Germany. The subsequent shift in British policy, as demonstrated in the far cooler attitude towards the scope of compensation for Poland, came out of a desire to tame the rise of Soviet influence in Central Europe. The same motivation held true for the United States, although, as

argued before, America was slow in showing an interest in Central European affairs. For the Soviets, after securing territorial gains and installing
a puppet government in Poland, the next stage of expansion was to
ensure generous territorial compensation for Warsaw, which was by
now perceived as an ally.

Conflict between the Great Powers led to a further polarisation in
their positions towards the Polish western border; the issue thus became
one of the main focal points of the emerging bipolar division. With
America's greater involvement in European affairs it found itself
increasingly at odds with the Soviet Union, while its policy towards
the Oder-Neisse border grew steadily more sympathetic towards the
German position. At the same time, however, America did not really
believe that any considerable revision of Poland's western frontier was
possible, or that it was even desirable. Yet, according to George Marshall, to argue in favour of such a policy would give the West a strong
bargaining position against Soviet claims in the Ruhr as well as being
a useful instrument to put pressure on the Polish government. When
Marshall was warned by the US ambassador in Warsaw, Bliss Lane,
that the policy of supporting Germany's demands would bring about
resentment on the part of the Polish people, the State Secretary
responded with a parallel between Lane as a theatre commander during the war and himself as a chief commander dealing with the picture
as a whole.[62]

In sum, there is a mass of evidence which points towards a structural account of British, American and Soviet motivations towards the
border issue. Domestic explanations of these policies, as outlined above,
do not contradict but rather 'interlock' with the 'balance of power'
explanation. Internal developments in Germany and Poland clearly had
some impact upon the Great Powers' policies on the Oder–Neisse Line,
predominantly because the domestic politics in these two countries
were in fact in a state of interlocking dependency with international
developments.

Conclusion

The defining questions in Polish–German relations in the post-war
period were tightly connected with the emergence and subsequent disintegration of the Grand Alliance. As a result of the decisions taken in
Teheran, Yalta and Potsdam, Poland and Germany found each other

in conflict over the Oder–Neisse line and the expulsion of Germans. This conflict only deepened with the emergence of the Cold War, when the frontier issue became one of the core arguments which re-opened historical discussions and delayed the reconciliation process. Consequently, while the end of the war provided the conditions in which the 'Europeanisation' of French-German relations could begin, the same was not true for Polish–German relations.

Of the four defining conditions of 'Europeanisation', as identified in Chapter 1: international-structural, domestic democratisation, western integration and reconciliation – none appeared in a form conducive enough to promote congruence in relations in this period. International-structural conditions acted against rapprochement in Polish–German relations and decisively impacted upon the other conditions necessary for the emergence of 'Europeanisation'. International-structural conditions were, then, the key factors responsible for the division of Germany and subsequently for the establishment of incompatible regimes in Poland and West Germany. Consequently a common democratic basis was missing from the relationship. Similarly, western integration, as an outcome of the Cold War, led only to further divergences in Polish–(West) German relations. As to the reconciliation process, it is apparent that this could hardly begin while West Germany held claim to a third of Poland's territory and while East Germany emancipated itself from any responsibility for wartime crimes by declaring itself a Nazi-free land. In addition, the communist government of Poland had no interest in abating anti-German hostility in Polish society, which remained one of the key elements legitimising its hold on to power.

The overriding international-structural conditions of Polish–German relations, as established at the onset of the Cold War remained largely unchanged until 1989. They continued as the major hurdle in the 'Europeanisation' of the relationship. In spite of this, during the Cold War attempts to alleviate the detrimental impact of bipolarity upon the relationship were made. The most significant of these attempts were the small *détente* between Bonn and Warsaw that followed de-Stalinisation in Poland in the late 1950s and West Germany's *Ostpolitik*, which began in the late 1960s with the election of the SPD/FDP government. These will be discussed in Chapter 3.

Notes

1 See *Foreign Relations of the United States 1946 (FRUS)*, Vol. V (Washington, DC, Department of State Publication, 1969), p. 516.

2 See Norman Davies, 'One Thousand Years of Polish–German Camaraderie', in Roger Barlett and Karen Schönwälder (eds), *The German Lands and Eastern Europe* (Basingstoke: Macmillan, 1999), p. 261.

3 See the following documents: 'Secret Additional Protocol to German-Soviet Treaty of Nonaggression', 'Soviet Statement to Poland, September 17, 1939', 'Confidential Protocol to German-Soviet Treaty, September 18, 1939', in George F. Kennan, *Soviet Foreign Policy 1917–1941* (Princeton: D. Van Nostrand, 1960), pp. 178–82.

4 See 'Passages from the Resolutions of the Crimea Conference regarding Poland. Yalta, February 11, 1945', in *Documents on Polish-Soviet Relations 1939–45, Volume II 1943–45*, (London: The Sikorski Institute, 1967), Doc. No. 308, p. 520.

5 See 'Potsdam Agreement – Article IX b. Western Frontier of Poland', in *Documents on Germany* (Washington, DC: United States Department of State, 1985), p. 63.

6 For the speech by Byrnes, see *Documents on Germany* (Washington, DC: United States Department of State, 1985), pp. 97–8.

7 Krystyna Kersten, 'Stulecie Przesiedleńców: Przymusowe Przemieszczenie Ludności – Próba Typologii', in Klaus Bachmann and Jerzy Kranz, *Przeprosić za Wypędzenie?* (Cracow: Znak, 1997), pp. 106–7.

8 The figures quoted above are from Kersten, 'Stulecie Przesiedleńców', pp. 106, 108.

9 The statement by Herbert Hoover quoted in Kersten, 'Stulecie Przesiedleńców', p. 109. For the statement by Winston Churchill, see Albrecht Tyrell, *Großbritannien und die Deutschlandplanung der Alliierten 1941–1945* (Frankfurt am Main: Bundesmimsterium für Innerdeutsche Beziehungen A. Metzner, 1997), p. 394.

10 Bernadetta Nitschke, 'Położenie Ludności Niemieckiej na Terenach na Wschód od Odry i Nysy Lużyckiej w 1945 roku', *Przegląd Zachodni*, No. 3 (Poznan: Instytut Zachodni 1997), p. 89.

11 Wolfgang Pailer, *Na Przekór Fatalizmowi Wrogości: Stanisław Stomma i Stosunki Polsko-Niemieckie* (Warsaw: Wydawnictwo Polsko-Niemieckie, 1998), p. 52

12 All the above figures quoted from Pailer, *Na Przekór Fatalizmowi Wrogości*, p. 52.

13 See Mieczystaw Tomala, *Patrząc na Niemcy: Od Wrogości do Porozumienia 1945–1991*, (Warsaw: Polska Fundacja Spraw Międzynarodowych, 1997) pp. 28–31.

14 *Ibid.*, p. 33.

15 See Zygmunt Wojciechowski, 'Polityka Wschodnia Niemiec a Katastrofa Współczesnej Cywilizacji', in *Przegląd Zachodni – Antalogia Przeglądu Zachoniego 1945–1990*, No. 2 (Poznań: Instytut Zachodni, 1995), pp. 123–35.

16 See Stanisław Stomma, *Czy Fatalism Wrogości?* (Cracow: Znak, 1980), pp. 158–60.

17 See Nitschke, 'Położenie Ludności Niemieckiej', pp. 71–91.

18 On this point, see Włodzimierz Borodziej, *Od Poczdamu do Szklarskiej Poręby: Polska w Stosunkach Międzynarodowych 1945–1947* (London: Aneks, 1990), p. 298.

19 See Bronisław Pasierb, 'Funkcje Problemu Niemieckiego w Pierwszym Okresie Polski Ludowej', in Bohdan Jałowiecki, and Piotr Przewłocki (eds), *Stosunki Polsko-Niemieckie. Integracja i Rozwój Ziem Zachodnich i Północnych* (Katowice: PIW, 1980), pp. 95–108.

20 See Borodziej, *Od Poczdamu do Szklarskiej Poręby*, p. 306.

21 As Churchill recalls in his memoirs: 'I then demonstrated with the help of three matches my idea of Poland moving westwards. This pleased Stalin, and on this note our group parted for the moment'; see Winston S. Churchill, *The Second World War: Closing the Ring*, Vol. V (London: Cassell & Co., 1952), p. 320.

22 See Louis Fisher, *The Road to Yalta* (New York and London: Harper & Row, 1972), p. 134.

23 See Churchill, *The Second World War*, Vol. V, p. 357, Fisher, *The Road to Yalta*, p. 138.

24 See Churchill, *The Second World War: Triumph and Tragedy*, Vol. VI, (London: Cassell, 1954), pp. 209–10.

25 *Ibid.* p. 320.

26 See 'Passages from the Resolutions of the Crimea Conference, Doc. No. 308, p. 520.

27 Churchill, *The Second World War*, Vol. VI, p. 352.

28 See 'Passages from the Resolutions of the Crimea Conference, Doc. No. 308, p. 520.

29 See Churchill, *The Second World War*, Vol. VI, pp. 560–82.

30 See Alan Bullock, *Ernest Bevin, Foreign Secretary 1945–1951* (New York and London: W. W. Norton, 1983), pp. 23–8.

31 'The three Heads of Government reaffirm their opinion that the final delimitation of the western frontier of Poland should await the peace settlement'; see 'Potsdam Agreement – Article IX b. Western Frontier of Poland', in *Documents on Germany*, p. 63.

32 See 'Memorandum of Transatlantic Telephone Conversation Between the Chairman of the American Delegation to the United Nations (Stettinius) in London and Secretary of State (Byrnes) in Washington', *Foreign Relations of the United States 1946 (FRUS)*, Vol. VI (Washington, DC: Department of State Publication, 1969), pp. 387–92.

33 See Borodziej, *Od Poczdamu do Szklarskiej Poręby*, pp. 291–314.
34 See Winston S. Churchill, 'The Sinews of Peace. March 5, 1946. Westminster Collage, Fulton, Missouri', in Robert R. James (ed.), *Winston S. Churchill. His Complete Speeches*, Vol. VII 1943–1949 (New York and London: Chelsea House Publishers, 1974), p. 7290.
35 See 'The *Chargé* in Moscow (Kennan) to the Secretary of State. Moscow, March 6, 1946', *1946 (FRUS)*, Vol. V, pp. 516–20.
36 *Ibid.*
37 See 'Memorandum by Mr. George F. Kennan to Mr. Carmel Offie. Paris, May 10, 1946', *1946 (FRUS)*, Vol. V, pp. 555–6.
38 *Ibid.*, p. 729.
39 *Ibid.*, p. 712.
40 See *Documents on Germany* (United States Department of State, 1985), pp. 97–8.
41 See 'Speech by Secretary of State Marshall, Moscow 9 April 1947', in Julian Makowski, *Zbiór Dokumentów*, No. 5(20) (Warsaw: Drukarnia Automa, May 1947), p. 213–20.
42 See 'Prague Conference on Germany', in *Poland, Germany and European Peace. Official Documents 1944–1948* (London: The Polish Embassy Press Office, 1948), pp. 74–7.
43 See *Foreign Relations of the United States 1948 (FRUS)*, Vol. II (Washington, DC: Department of State Publications, 1973), pp. 341–2.
44 See *Documents on Polish–Soviet Relations 1939–45, Volume II 1943–45*, Doc. No. 34, p. 49; Doc. No. 41, 42, pp. 61–8; Doc. No. 51, pp. 83–6.
45 See *Documents on Polish–Soviet Relations 1939–45, Volume II*, Doc. No. 309, p. 521.
46 See *Documents on Polish–Soviet Relations 1939–45, Volume II*, Doc. No. 310, p. 522.
47 For examples of Soviet pressure to change the composition of Polish government see *Documents on Polish–Soviet Relations 1939–45, Volume II*, Doc. No. 97, p. 171; Doc. No. 99–100, pp. 173–6.
48 See *Documents on Polish–Soviet Relations 1939–45, Volume II*, Doc. No. 99–100, pp. 173–6.
49 On Mikołajczyk's resignation see *Documents on Polish–Soviet Relations 1939–45, Volume II*, Doc. No. 272–6, pp. 476–85.
50 See Fisher, *The Road to Yalta*, p. 160.
51 See *ibid.*, pp. 128–38.
52 See Stanisław Mikołajczyk, *Polska Zgwałcona* (Chicago: Wici, 1981), p. 67; Fisher, *The Road to Yalta*, p. 160.
53 Borodziej, *Od Poczdamu do Szklarskiej Poręby*, pp. 274–9.
54 See *1946 (FRUS)*, Vol. VI, pp. 485–7. In protest against the fraudulent elections the American Ambassador to Warsaw, Bliss-Lane, resigned; See

Foreign Relations of the United States, 1947 (FRUS), Vol. IV (Washington, DC: Department of State Publications, 1969), pp. 411–14.

55 See *1946 (FRUS)*, Vol. VI, pp. 387–92.

56 *Ibid.*, pp. 376–8, 462–4.

57 *Ibid.*, pp. 420–2.

58 Hans-Peter Schwarz, *Konrad Adenauer: From the German Empire to the Federal Republic, Vol. 1: 1876–1952* (Oxford and Providence: Berghahn, 1995), p. 383.

59 See Borodziej, *Od Poczdamu do Szklarskiej Poręby*, pp. 304–7.

60 See *1946 (FRUS)*, Vol. VI, pp. 494–9.

61 See *1947 (FRUS)*, Vol. IV, p. 445.

62 *Ibid.* pp. 427–9.

3

'Europeanisation' despite the Cold War? 1956–88

There are no answers in isolation, only European answers. That, too, has brought me here. (Extract from a speech by Willy Brandt given in Warsaw on 7 December 1970 after signing the (West) German–Polish border treaty)[1]

We had no choice; the key to normal relations [with Poland] lay in Moscow. (Willy Brandt on *Ostpolitik*'s priorities)[2]

Introduction

Both the external and internal conditions of Polish–(West) German relations continued to deteriorate throughout the late 1940s and for most of the 1950s. Warsaw reacted strongly against the creation of the Federal Republic, which was portrayed by the communist-controlled press as the successor state of Nazi Germany, with its leaders depicted as Hitlerites.[3] The West German view of Poland was also unfavourable at the time; it remained dominated by self-pity and territorial revisionism, which was particularly apparent amongst expellees. Consequently, reconciliation between these nations which, as argued in Chapters 1 and 2, was one of the key conditions for the relationship's *Europeanisation*, remained a remote prospect.

With Stalin's death in 1953 East–West tensions began to relax, which had profound implications for Poland's domestic politics and consequently for Bonn-Warsaw relations. As the de-Stalinisation of Poland began, the new Communist leadership moved in 1956 to 'normalise' relations with West Germany. Although these policy initiatives proved to be unsuccessful, in 1968–70 further attempts to alleviate the prevailing conflict were being pursued. This time it was the West German government, under the leadership of Willy Brandt, that took the first steps towards what was subsequently called, the 'normalisation' of relations with Poland. This policy, which became known as new *Ostpolitik*, succeeded in bringing about the partial settlement of bilateral disputes, including a temporary agreement on the border issue.

This chapter is interested in the possibility of realising 'Europeanisation' in Polish–(West) German relations despite the prevalence of external East–West conflict. In other words, the major question here is: is 'Europeanisation' possible without the existence of a conducive structural-international environment? It is in this context that both policy initiatives mentioned above (1956 and 1968–70) will be discussed. The chapter is divided into two main parts with the first considering the failed post-1956 episode and the second concentrating on new *Ostpolitik*. As was the case with Chapter 2 these developments are considered from both domestic and international angles.

'Polish October 1956' and the implications for Bonn–Warsaw relations

Background

In response to the creation of two German states in 1949, Poland established radically different relations with each one of them. While Warsaw was among the first to recognise the communist German Democratic Republic (GDR) it boycotted the Federal Republic of Germany (FRG). The GDR recognised the Oder–Neisse line in its first-ever international document; meanwhile the FRG immediately declared this treaty as invalid and the expulsion of Germans from eastern territories as unlawful.[4]

Consequently, from its very inception, the Federal Republic's relations with Poland were confrontational, if not openly hostile. Unsurprisingly, then, Adenauer's early calls for reconciliation with Poland failed to have any resonance in Warsaw, where they were received as insincere and cynical.[5] This situation prevailed until 1956 when Poland reappraised its policy towards West Germany, while the latter found itself under international pressure to respond to these new initiatives.

The 'Polish October 1956' and Bonn–Warsaw relations

Throughout the second half of 1956 Poland underwent profound internal changes. On 28 June 1956 an anti-communist uprising broke out in Poznań and in October, after a series of domestic upheavals the Stalinist leadership of the communist party resigned and was replaced by the 'nationally-minded' Władyslaw Gomułka and his team. A number of domestic freedoms were subsequently introduced, including the immediate release of political prisoners, a relaxation in censorship, decollectivisation of agriculture and a halt on the repression of the Catholic church.[6]

The introduction of domestic freedoms and a degree of independence in the international arena encouraged western leaders to look at Poland with a fresh attitude. In addition, the Polish communists, isolated in the Eastern Bloc after the collapse of the Hungarian uprising (November 1956) and unsure of Soviet intentions, were keen to establish closer links with the West. It was clear, however, that it would be against Poland's interests to relax its ties with the Soviets as long as it remained in conflict with the Federal Republic. The establishment of diplomatic relations with Bonn was therefore regarded by Warsaw as a first and necessary step towards its rapprochement with the West. In order to achieve this, Warsaw was even initially prepared to commence with official relations with Bonn without expecting that West Germany would recognise the Oder–Neisse line.[7]

However, Bonn remained cautious on account of its assessment of the international situation and domestic considerations, which remained influenced by the expellees. In addition, the Federal Republic was also self-constrained by the 'Hallstein doctrine', according to which, Bonn was prevented from establishing official relations with the countries that recognised the GDR, as was the case with Poland. It was not, therefore, until the Berlin crisis of 1961 that Adenauer changed his mind and started to consider introducing diplomatic relations with Warsaw, but leaving the Oder-Neisse border unrecognised. Yet, by this time it was too little and too late, and Adenauer's offer was rejected by Gomułka.[8] Consequently the first post-war attempt to achieve some degree of co-operation in the relationship failed.

The 1956–60 period is often viewed as a lost chance for genuine rapprochement in Polish–(West) German relations.[9] After his initial flirt with the Federal Republic, Gomułka turned towards the GDR and strengthened Poland's alliance with the Soviet Union. It appears that there were two key reasons explaining Adenauer's failure to respond sufficiently quickly and generously to Warsaw's new policy initiatives. Firstly, Adenauer proved unable to construct an innovative policy towards Poland, continuing to see Bonn-Warsaw relations as just a part of his overall policy towards the Soviet Bloc. Secondly, he let the relationship be considerably influenced by domestic interests, and in particular by his concerns about the expellees. These two factors are discussed in later sections of the chapter.

East–West relations and Adenauer's policy towards establishing diplomatic relations with Poland

In the immediate wake of the 'Polish October' it seemed almost inevitable that greater convergence would begin to emerge in Bonn–Warsaw relations. This impression was also confirmed in official declarations. For example, during his speech in the *Bundestag*, Adenauer addressed the new Polish situation by expressing his government's desire to resolve differences and to 'normalise' relations with Warsaw.[10] Although the obvious obstacle to such a 'normalisation' was the Hallstein doctrine, Foreign Minister von Brettano argued in 1956 that this rule did not apply to Poland since it had come into the world 'with a congenital defect'. In other words, the Federal Republic recognised that realistically Poland did not have any other choice but to maintain diplomatic relations with the GDR. As mentioned earlier, Gomułka's government at first approached the issue with an open mind, as was apparent in the government's statement that Warsaw was prepared to establish official relations with Bonn without any pre-conditions, including West German recognition of the Oder–Neisse line.

It appears therefore that the failure to establish official relations between the states was not exclusively related to the frontier question nor to Warsaw's relations with the GDR. Rather there is strong evidence to suggest that Adenauer's policy on this issue was primarily motivated by his caution with regard to the Soviet Union and his overall assessment of East–West relations. Adenauer declared that the whole question of relations with Warsaw must be approached with prudence and that Moscow should not be irritated in its own sphere of influence.[11]

Adenauer's caution on the issue was additionally exacerbated by the Soviet intervention in Hungary and the possibility of a repetition of this scenario in Poland, which indeed was considered by Moscow in autumn 1956. Arguing in February 1957 to his CDU colleagues, 'we must do nothing that Gomułka, for instance, believes to be tactically incorrect', Adenauer remained convinced that the time was not ripe for initiating a more active policy towards Poland.[12]

Ironically, as seen in Adenauer's conversation with the Soviet deputy Prime Minister Mikoyan, in which the latter prompted the Chancellor to begin negotiations with Poland, it appears that Adenauer stuck to his position in spite of Soviet encouragement to act otherwise. However, as argued by the Chancellor's biographer, Hans Peter Schwarz, the conversation with Mikoyan 'did not deflect Adenauer from using the argument that every effort must be made to avoid irritating Russia in its own sphere of influence by a too active Polish policy'. Because of the same concerns, Adenauer rejected the opinion of some members of the government who argued in favour of developing more active economic co-operation with Poland.

After a short period of moderate improvement in Bonn-Warsaw relations, Adenauer's policy towards Poland became more reticent at the end of 1957, as a reaction to two developments: Yugoslavia's recognition of the GDR and the publication of an international peace plan by the Polish Foreign Minister Adam Rapacki. In September 1957, after Gomułka's much-heralded trip to Yugoslavia, Tito recognised the Oder–Neisse line as Poland's western frontier. A month later the Yugoslav President went further and announced the establishment of diplomatic relations with the GDR. This posed a serious problem for the Federal Republic, which was now faced with the choice of either renouncing its 'Hallstein doctrine' or breaking relations with Belgrade. Adenauer, who finally decided in favour of the latter option, was furious and blamed Poland for creating this awkward situation.[13]

Further increasing Adenauer's irritation with Warsaw was Rapacki's plan, the main point of which was a proposal to create a nuclear-free zone covering Poland, Czechoslovakia and both German states.[14] The Chancellor rejected the plan on the basis that it would break up NATO without getting anything in return, and that it would go against American plans to equip their troops in West Germany with nuclear weapons. Crucially, Adenauer feared that should the plan go ahead, the Federal Republic's *Westbindung* would be undermined. The plan was never realised, but it came considerably to complicate Adenauer's own position both at home and abroad. Most importantly, Rapacki's initiative was popular with significant segments of the West German public, as seen in a number of street demonstrations organised in support of it. The plan was also received with interest in France, which subsequently proposed a similar initiative.[15] Adenauer's uncompromising rejection of Rapacki's initiative was thus a further factor contributing to the growing perception of the Chancellor as a Cold War warrior and an obstruction to international *détente*. A side effect of this was Adenauer's increasing inflexibility towards Poland.

However, with tensions escalating in East–West relations in the late 1950s and early 1960s, the Federal Republic found itself under international pressure to improve its relations with Poland and other Eastern Bloc countries. It also became clear around this time that the West was no longer supportive of the Federal Republic's position on the Oder–Neisse line, which it was increasingly inclined to recognise.[16] For example, in March 1959 Adenauer learned from de Gaulle that France would not support the unification of Germany unless the Federal Republic moved towards the recognition of the Oder–Neisse line.[17] Meanwhile, in response to the Berlin crisis, Eisenhower's administration began to exercise pressure on the Federal Republic, first to commence diplomatic relations with Warsaw and subsequently to go a step further and recognise the Oder–Neisse line.[18] These Western pressures intensified after Kennedy won the presidential election in the United States in 1960. Aware of the pro-Polish tendencies in the new US administration, Adenauer finally decided in favour of establishing diplomatic relations with Warsaw, but only with the pre-condition that Poland would leave the frontier question aside.[19] However, by this point it was too late and Gomułka did not agree to the 'normalisation' of relations without at the same time solving the border question. This consequently became the official and persistent position of Polish diplomacy, which signified the end of its post-1956 flexibility. In effect, therefore, Polish-West German relations returned to their pre-1956 unco-operative status.

This account has emphasised the prevalence of external international-structural considerations in Adenauer's policy towards establishing diplomatic relations with Poland. However, it was not intended here to totally refute the role of domestic factors in the policy formation of the West German Chancellor. Quite clearly, it would be difficult to deny that concerns such as the possible strong reaction of the German expellees against the establishment of relations with Warsaw were of some importance in Adenauer's policy on this issue.

It is argued here that domestic concerns came to play a more decisive role in shaping Bonn's policy towards the Oder-Neisse border. It is to this issue that the chapter will now turn.

Domestic factors in Bonn's policy towards the Oder–Neisse line

As argued above, in the late 1950s there was a possibility that the process of 'normalising' Polish–(West) German relations could have begun irrespective of the frontier question. To be sure there is little doubt that rapprochement without West German recognition of the Oder–Neisse line as Poland's western border would have been limited. Unlike the establishing of diplomatic relations with Warsaw discussed above, the Federal Republic's policy towards the frontier question was almost entirely determined by domestic factors. As seen in Chapter 2, after the end of the Second World War there was an overwhelming domestic consensus in the whole of Germany, including the Soviet zone, against Poland's annexation of the lands east of the Oder and western Neisse. The new border was so unpopular that, as indicated in public opinion polls conducted in the American zone, in late 1945 more than 50 per cent of Germans would not accept losing the eastern lands as a condition for unification and a peace agreement.[20]

By the mid-1950s West German society had grown less defiant; but the border question continued to raise considerable emotion in the Federal Republic and the political consensus on the border's non-recognition continued. In this context, it is important to note that the 1957 *Bundestag* elections, during which all parties kept a cautious eye on refugee voters, took place at the height of the debate about establishing new relations with Poland. Clearly, revisionist rhetoric, which prevailed in the programmes of all major parties, affected the chances for the improvement of the relationship.

It is significant here, that although privately Adenauer had given up on the eastern lands in the mid-1950s, (as seen in his conversation with the leader of the SPD, Ollenhauer, during which he said: 'Oder-Neisse Ostgebiete, die sind weg! Die gibt's nicht mehr!'), in public he remained a consistent revisionist,[21] and this policy was also followed by his successors. Consequently until the late 1960s the Federal Republic let its foreign policy towards Poland be shaped by the principle of territorial revisionism.

Undoubtedly Bonn's policy was related to the powerful position of the German expellees, who made-up about one fifth of the entire West

German population. It is often argued in this context that revisionism was the only policy available to ensure the integration of expellees into West German society without undermining the fragile process of transition to democracy. Adenauer was also faced with the task of convincing the expellees of his pro-western foreign policy; on several occasions he did not hesitate to instrumentalise their feelings about their lost *Heimat*. For example, during an expellees' rally in July 1960, Adenauer called for further solidarity with the West and NATO which, if fulfilled, he promised, should lead to the return of East Prussia to Germany.

Remarkably, in opposition to the issue of establishing diplomatic relations between Bonn and Warsaw discussed above, in its Oder-Neisse policy the Federal government proved to be largely immune to external considerations. For example, in the case of his declaration at the expellees' rally it is clear that Adenauer had received no mandate from his western allies to raise the hopes of possible western help in revising the border. In fact, in response to the strong reaction from Poland, NATO clearly distanced itself from the Chancellor's speech.[22] Nevertheless, Bonn remained extraordinarily persistent in questioning the border, and this policy did not even change under American and British pressure during the Berlin crisis. Faced with Soviet demands for the neutralisation of Germany, the termination of the special status of West Berlin and recognition of Poland's western frontier, Adenauer did not agree to give up on the border question, although it was clear to him that he lacked western support. Even under direct pressure from President Kennedy, who himself was strongly in favour of the border's recognition, all that Adenauer was prepared to offer was a renunciation of the use of force.[23] In conclusion, it is apparent that domestic concerns proved to be a powerful factor in determining West Germany's policy towards the border issue.

Assessment

The 1956–60 period in Polish–(West) German relations was marked by the emergence of the first genuine chance to initiate a rapprochement. There were a range of favourable conditions in place to prompt warmer relations between Bonn and Warsaw, the most important being the onset of *détente* between the two superpowers and domestic liberalisation in Poland after the events of October 1956. The change in Poland brought to power new leaders who were initially eager to manifest their 'own way to socialism', by introducing some domestic freedoms and by pursuing a more nationally flavoured foreign policy which was less bound to Moscow.

One of the most significant outcomes of the changes of October 1956 in Poland was the greater freedom of expression and association. Relaxed censorship permitted freer discussion on issues of Polish foreign policy, while the legalisation of semi-political non-communist structures, most importantly the 'Catholic Intelligentsia Clubs' (KIK), provided a framework for the expression of alternative visions of Polish national interests. Furthermore, a limited number of representatives from the non-communist opposition were allowed to sit in the national parliament and to form a small Catholic group (Znak). Significantly, these new independent structures became identified as pro-German lobbies. Although clearly not all Polish non-communist politicians wanted reconciliation with West Germany, the desire to remove 'the threat of a belligerent Germany', which the communists used to justify their hold on to power, became increasingly popular in dissident circles.

A more favourable disposition towards West Germany also became apparent at this time within the communist party itself. Gomułka became First Secretary during a period of conflict with the Soviet leadership and against Khrushchev's personal wishes, and in the absence of international support from the Soviet Bloc Poland seemed almost compelled to enact a rapprochement with the West. However, at the same time, it was clear that closer relations with the West would not be possible while Poland's western frontier remained recognised only by the Eastern Bloc countries and questioned by the Federal Republic. It became apparent that 'Stalin's trap' had really worked: Poland remained locked in the Soviet sphere despite having a more nationally minded leadership which had demonstrated the capacity to improve relations with Bonn. In order to overcome Poland's dependence on the Soviets, Warsaw needed to reconcile with West Germany, which was to prove elusive, principally because Adenauer was unable to deliver a consistent *Ostpolitik*.

It seems that in this particular instance, Adenauer's foreign policy was considerably influenced by his personal image of Poland and of the whole of East Central Europe. Born and brought up in Wilhelmian Germany, Adenauer saw Poland as 'God's Playground', an area where external powers meet and divide up their interests.[24] For the last 200 years it had been Russia and not Poland which had remained the main addressee of German *Ostpolitik*, so there was no tradition which could guide Adenauer otherwise. When faced with the possibility of improving relations with Warsaw, Adenauer's response was thus geared towards the Soviet Union and the western allies.

The failure of the Federal Republic's policy towards Poland was also partly due to the lack of knowledge about and interest in Poland which was consistently displayed by the *Auswärtiges Amt* (Foreign Office) and the Chancellery.[25] This was particularly evident in the way Adenauer mishandled historical sensitivities: it was in the middle of the dispute about establishing official relations that Adenauer was invested as an honorary knight by the Grand Master of the Knights of the German Order, whose major achievement had been the colonisation of the lands East of Germany. The German Chancellor was proudly photographed dressed in a white cloak with the black cross of the Order. There were few other symbols more likely to incite Polish anti-Germanism, with an obvious detrimental effect upon the relationship.

Another example of Adenauer's disregard for feelings in Poland was his rejection of the speech, prepared in the Foreign Office, commemorating the twentieth anniversary of the outbreak of the Second World War, which explicitly referred to the theme of reconciliation with Poland. In the end Adenauer gave the speech, but made little reference to Poland and did not issue the apology which was included in an earlier version of the text.[26]

The failure of a Polish–(West) German rapprochement had far-reaching implications for the general direction of Warsaw's international relations. Polish foreign policy returned to its previous style of mirroring Soviet diplomacy. The disagreement with the GDR (which was initially concerned with the possible spread of 'anti-socialist' ideas resulting in the banning of Polish newspapers and the end of official exchanges with Warsaw) had ended by the late 1950s, leading to intensified co-operation and the emergence of the anti-western 'iron-triangle' (Prague-Warsaw-Berlin).

Even the promoters of the 'return to Europe through Germany' became disillusioned with the Federal Republic. For example, pro-West German *Znak* MPs, such as Stanisław Stomma and Tadeusz Mazowiecki (who, in 1989, was to become the first post-war non-communist Premier), became resigned to the view that Poland's alliance with the Soviets was a necessity and that the continued existence of the GDR was in Poland's interest. This perception of the German question and of Poland's international relations remained unchallenged until the 1970s. In fact, it may be argued that some elements of it were still present in the policy of the first Polish non-communist government, which in response to the reappearance of the border question in 1989–90 was once again willing to balance the 'German threat' by strengthening its relations with the Soviet Union.

The fact that the anti-German line was not discredited following the events of October 1956 continued to have strong international and domestic implications for Warsaw and for the rest of the Eastern Bloc. In the area of foreign policy it tied Poland closer to the Soviet Union and consolidated its dependence on Moscow's guarantees. Domestically it strengthened the position of the communist party as the 'true defender of national interests' and undermined the pro-western elements within as well as outside the party. It was not until the emergence of new *Ostpolitik* that the casting of West Germany in this role in Polish foreign policy began to lose its resonance.

New *Ostpolitik* and its reception in Poland

Background

As argued above, during the Berlin crisis Adenauer had compromised on none of the significant demands that were put forward by Moscow. However, as the East German authorities moved to erect the wall in Berlin on 13 August 1961, the Chancellor's strategy looked flawed and Bonn's *Ostpolitik* came under fire from domestic opposition. It was argued that the events in Berlin showed that the Federal Republic's reliance on the West had proved insufficient to protect its fundamental interests and bring about German unification.[27]

In response to these pressures Bonn started to pursue a more active eastern policy. As far as Poland was concerned, this led to the completion of a trade agreement and establishment of official economic relations. In March 1966, Bonn initiated the renunciation of force agreements with all East Central European states, including Poland, in the form of the so called 'peace note'.[28] However, the basis of this proposal remained unacceptable to Poland, since it stressed that in international law Germany continued to exist in the frontiers of 31 December 1937. Needless to say, none of these initiatives achieved the desired breakthrough in West Germany's relations with East Central Europe.

It was not until the SPD and FDP forged a governing coalition in 1969 that an entirely new conception of *Ostpolitik* began to be pursued. Conceived of and led by Willy Brandt and his Foreign Minister Walter Scheel, West Germany's new *Ostpolitik* was based upon it's acceptance of the post-Yalta status quo. The Oder-Neisse frontier line was recognised and confirmed through a bilateral treaty signed between both states in December 1970. Although the significance of this development was subsequently weakened by the *Bundestag's* resolution of 1972 and the ruling of the Constitutional Court in 1975 (both of which reasserted that the frontier with Poland remained provisional until a future government of a united Germany decided otherwise)[29] for the time being the border issue remained secured. In this new context, 'Stalin's trap' became largely redundant, as Poland was no longer reliant upon Soviet guarantees.

This policy also had profound domestic implications. The communist party's use of the 'German threat' argument in order to justify its hold on to power lost much of its appeal. Although the communists never tired of propagating anti-Germanism, this had become increasingly less effective, and popular attitudes towards West Germany were improving.[30] On the other hand, many dissidents were disappointed with West Germany's prioritisation of the Soviet Union and the communists in Poland. It was questioned, in some quarters, whether Bonn was interested in developing democracy in Poland. Most significant in this respect was Bonn's 'non-reaction' to the introduction of martial law in Poland in December 1981.

In the field of economic relations *Ostpolitik's* record also seems ambivalent. Although throughout the 1970s West Germany spent billions of deutschemarks (DM) on economic assistance and cheap credits for Poland, it was argued that these served to sustain rather than to reform the communist regime. In addition, it was mainly due to the mismanagement of foreign credits (most of which were West German) by the Gierek government that Poland fell into a debt trap and faced an economic crisis at the end of the decade.[31]

At the point of collapse of the communist regime in Poland, Polish–(West) German relations were rather mixed. On an official level there appeared to be very few problems, indeed the Federal Republic had already become Poland's major western political and economic partner before 1989. However, at the same time as successive communist governments were reaping the benefits of cheap West German loans, their official propaganda maintained the myth that Germans were

inherently anti-Polish, and exaggerated the significance and belliger-
ence of the expellees' movement. Consequently, although by the late
1980s the notion that (West) Germany was a threat was becoming
increasingly redundant, the Polish communists remained opposed to
reconciliation between the two societies.

In sum, it seems that the new *Ostpolitik* contributed to the emergence
of conditions conducive with the 'Europeanisation' of Polish–(West)
German relations but it failed to achieve a qualitatively new relationship. It appears that while the sources of the new *Ostpolitik's* success
were related to a favourable climate inside both countries, the policy's
failure to achieve a real congruence of interests was mostly caused by
developments outside both states. The subsequent sections of this chapter will look at the rationale behind the emergence of new *Ostpolitik*
and its role in mitigating elements of conflict in Polish–(West) German relations. An attempt will also be made to explain why the new
Ostpolitik could not bring about a truly co-operative relationship until
after 1989.

The emergence of new Ostpolitik: *reconciliation, economic co-operation and Polish–(East) German relations*

The successes of Bonn's policy would not have been possible without
favourable domestic conditions in West Germany and Poland. In particular, two kinds of internal developments contributed to the change
in Polish–(West) German relations: first in the wake of the events of
13 August 1961 *Ostpolitk* became increasingly popular with West German voters. This subsequently awakened public awareness regarding
Nazi policy in Eastern and East Central Europe during the Second
World War: calls for reconciliation with East Central Europe became
an integral part of the West German political landscape. At the same
time rapprochement with the Federal Republic became a crucial element in the attitude of the pro-western part of the Polish opposition.
Secondly, the Polish government's expectation of profiting economically from closer co-operation with West Germany clearly fuelled its
enthusiasm for *Ostpolitik*, the latter reason being additionally related
to East Germany's inability to offer an attractive alternative.

The pro-reconciliation movement had already emerged in West
Germany in the early 1960s. In the so-called 'Tübinger Memorandum'
of 1962, a group of prominent CDU politicians (including Richard
von Weizsäcker, Klaus von Bismarck and Karl Heisenburg) had

declared themselves in favour of recognising the Oder–Neisse line. The group called for a normalisation of relations with West Germany's eastern neighbours which, according to the memorandum, had been burdened by history and by the fact that Bonn was pursuing a policy of unrealistic demands without international support.[32] A further landmark was reached by the organisation of the Protestant Church of Germany (all-German at that time) with its memorandum on 'the situation of the expellees and the relationship of the German nation to its eastern neighbours'. The authors of the memorandum supported the recognition of the Oder–Neisse line and although they rejected the Polish historical claim to the disputed territories, they pointed out that Poland should be compensated for the loss of its eastern lands.[33]

In response to these West German initiatives, the Polish Catholic Episcopate addressed their German counterparts in November 1965 with a gesture of reconciliation, underlined in the following words 'we forgive and ask for forgiveness'. This came to provide the focus for domestic political discussion in Poland and served to infuriate the communists. The bishops were subsequently accused of non-patriotic behaviour and of acting against Poland's interests. Through their actions, the Church – the most powerful non-communist organisation in Poland – laid the foundations for an alternative, pro-western vision of national interests[34] and the communists' monopoly on designing Poland's foreign policy was decidedly weakened. Although the government continued to oppose the idea of reconciliation it had nevertheless to adjust its policies to the fact that the Church had urged its followers to move away from distrust of their western neighbours.

However important the position of the Catholic Church was in forcing a change in the government's perspective, it was the prospects of economic benefits that ultimately convinced Warsaw of the merits of *Ostpolitik*. Poland badly needed to acquire access to western technologies and Gomułka, who was increasingly politically isolated, was himself in need of a success. The process of normalising relations with West Germany, Gomułka believed, would provide him with both political and economic achievements. Politically it was important that Poland's western frontier would be finally secured and economic success, it was assumed, would be facilitated through a stream of cheap loans arranged by Bonn.

In this context, it is important to note that Warsaw's attitude to the new *Ostpolitik* was significantly influenced by its failure to strengthen economic co-operation with East Germany. Initially, however, Warsaw joined East Berlin in rejecting Bonn's new initiative, which at the time increasingly began to attract other members of the Eastern Bloc. In order to counter-balance this growing influence of Bonn, the GDR and Poland in March 1967 concluded a bilateral 'friendship and mutual assistance' treaty, which included extensive provisions for economic co-operation. For the GDR, the main value of the treaty was political, as an argument serving to strengthen its position vis-à-vis the Federal Republic; Poland on the contrary hoped to develop closer economic links with East Germans. After a while East Berlin withdrew from the economic measures of the treaty and its deputy Prime Minister, Julius Balkow, was even dismissed for promising the Poles deeper integration of both economies.

The GDR's rejection of the development of economic co-operation with Poland was the breakthrough point in Gomułka's attitude towards the new *Ostpolitik*.[35] Disappointed with East Berlin, the Polish communists began to perceive the Federal Republic as their prospective key economic partner, and also one willing to treat Poland on favourable terms. This attitude subsequently led to an instrumental perception of new *Ostpolitik*, which prevailed in Warsaw's policy towards Bonn until the end of communism. Illustrating this was the deal known as 'cash for people', secured by Chancellor Schmidt and Gomułka's successor, Edward Gierek. The deal, agreed during the Helsinki Conference in August 1975, included West German loans on favourable terms and financing of a mutual pension agreement in exchange for Poland agreeing to the resettlement of ethnic Germans to the Federal Republic.[36] A similar approach prevailed in the 1980s, as emphasised in a speech delivered in 1988 by Polish Foreign Minister, Marian Orzechowski, in which he linked the opening of the 'expellees debate' with an appeal for the re-structuring of the loans owed by Poland to the Federal Republic.[37] Clearly, this instrumental attitude postponed genuine reconciliation, and it subsequently hindered the prospect for the relationship's *Europeanisation*. However, the major reason blocking the rapprochement process remained related to disadvantageous external conditions and the prevalence of the Cold War.

As argued above, new *Ostpolitik* was based on an acceptance of the existing status quo yet, it aimed at 'overcoming it'. This policy proved, however, to have clear limitations, as in spite of international *détente*, bipolarity, and with it the division of Europe, persisted. This factor continued to impact decisively on Polish–(West) German relations. In addition, Bonn's policy of 'overcoming the status quo' was based on pursuing a 'Russia-first' approach, which clearly remained problematic from the point of view of the Polish–(West) German *Europeanisation* project.

'Overcoming' the status quo and the 'Russia-first' principle

New *Ostpolitik's* key objectives – the preservation of world peace and the unification of Germany – were undoubtedly dependent on external developments in East–West relations. The two most outstanding features of the new *Ostpolitik* – the overwhelming priority given to the Soviet Union in its policy towards the Eastern Bloc and, as a result of this, a restriction on developing dialogue with the satellite states through other than official channels – seem to confirm the salience of external determinants.

Change was meant to come from 'above'; *Ostpolitik's* objectives were to be met through co-operation with governments that, as hoped by the policy's architects, would gradually become more liberal. In other words *Ostpolitikers* did not want to change but to 'overcome the status quo', which meant that Bonn had to avoid treading on Moscow's toes, as argued by Brandt's foreign policy advisor, Egon Bahr: 'The preconditions for reunification are only to be created with the Soviet Union. They are not to be had in East Berlin, not against the Soviet Union, not without it.'[38]

Thus compared with Adenauer's eastern policy, new *Ostpolitik* was marked by elements of both change and continuity. While it radically departed from Adenauer's inability to embrace international *détente*, it continued along a traditional 'Russia-first' path. New *Ostpolitik's* first international document was thus a treaty signed with the Soviet Union which regulated a number of contentious issues including the Oder-Neisse border line. Poland's western frontier was, for the first time, recognised in a treaty between a German state and Russia. The fact that Warsaw was practically ignored in this agreement caused resentment not only among the Polish people but even in the communist government.[39]

A far more significant clash between Polish national aspirations and West German new *Ostpolitik* occurred in the wake of the Polish revolution of August 1980 followed by the emergence of the '*Solidarność*' (Solidarity) movement and its subsequent underground retreat. It was clear during this period that West German leaders were surprised and disoriented by the events in Poland and unsure about its implications for European *détente*. It was often argued in this context that the Polish democratic movement was in conflict with new *Ostpolitik's* key priority to moderate tensions in East–West relations. 'World peace is more important than Poland' were reportedly Egon Bahr's words while he was urging caution following the introduction of martial law in Poland in December 1981. The Polish opposition was also deeply disappointed by the official reaction of Chancellor Helmut Schmidt, who was visiting the GDR when events in Poland took an authoritarian turn. When asked during a press conference hosted by East German leader Erich Honecker about his assessment of the Polish situation, Schmidt's comment seemed to smack of appeasement: 'Herr Honecker was as dismayed as I was, that this has now proved necessary.'[40]

West Germany's reluctance to support dissidents in East Central Europe was illustrated in its reticence to assist such movements materially or morally. West German politicians went to great pains to avoid meeting representatives of the Polish opposition. Even at the time when '*Solidarność*' was a fully legal organisation, Foreign Minister Genscher declined to meet its representation and Brandt refused to meet it's leader Lech Wałęsa during his visit to Poland in December 1985.[41]

The reasoning behind this West German reserve towards Polish dissidents was, according to the SPD's Secretary General in the 1980s, Peter Glotz, ideologically motivated. The Solidarity movement in Poland, and Wałęsa especially, argued Glotz, were not considered ideologically compatible with the SPD.[42] Glotz's argument, however, neglected the fact that there was a social-democratic wing within the Polish underground movement.

Certainly the SPD's and Solidarity's interests were divergent, but not for reasons of ideology. The SPD's concern about Polish domestic politics and the role played by dissidents was based upon a profound fear of the potential external repercussions of the events in Poland for both German states. Bonn's cautious behaviour was grounded in the belief that should the Soviets be further provoked by Solidarity, this might lead to the collapse of the entire *détente* process, and with it the indefinite delay of German unification.

Assessment

On the whole, it appears that new *Ostpolitik* proved to be a useful instrument in minimising conflict and bringing an amount of reciprocity between both states. Most importantly both communist Poland and the Federal Republic had mutual interests in sustaining *détente*, which served their external security and political interests. For Bonn, rapprochement with the Eastern Bloc enhanced chances for uni-fication, while it diminished prospects for a global conflict in which Germany would have become a major battlefield. In order to achieve these objectives Bonn was prepared to recognise the Oder-Neisse bor-der. The reason why it had not been ready to offer this concession in the late 1950s was clearly internal and related to the prominent posi-tion of the expellees within the CDU, as well as the predominantly reticent attitude of the West German population towards the question. These domestic pressures were considerably weakened by generational change and after the erection of the Berlin wall a change in Bonn's policy towards the frontier issue became possible.

For Poland new *Ostpolitik* offered security for its western frontier, which also led to its greater independence from the Soviet Union. After a period of emphasis on East Berlin, led by Gomułka's hopes regard-ing the deeper integration of the GDR within the Eastern Bloc, the latter proved to be a reluctant partner. As a result, Gomułka became convinced that the unification of Germany was just a matter of time in which case Poland would return to its pre-war position of a coun-try between a mighty Soviet Union and an ever-more powerful Germany which would immediately raise the territorial question. If this black scenario was to happen, and Gomułka was here a pessimist, he had no doubts that the Soviet guarantees regarding the Oder–Neisse line would no longer stand.[43]

Therefore, in the absence of East Berlin being persuaded that in order to survive the GDR had to integrate its economy with Poland and Czechoslovakia, Gomułka made another U-turn and accepted the West German offer of rapprochement. This greater flexibility on the part of Warsaw was additionally helped by the domestic problems associated with Gomułka's regime and its expectations of economic and political rewards offered by the new *Ostpolitik*.

Although in many respects successful, new *Ostpolitik* did not deliver a breakthrough in West Germany's relations with Poland and other East Central European countries. Most importantly, in spite of the unofficial societal initiatives discussed above, new *Ostpolitik* did not facilitate a genuine rapprochement between both nations. This, it could be argued, was not achievable anyway, since Bonn's policy was exclusively addressed to the communist government and because the communists had the means and the will to prevent open interaction between societies and peoples on either side of the Iron Curtain.

Conclusion: détente or 'Europeanisation'?

This chapter has looked into two policy developments which were attempts to alleviate some elements of the conflict between Bonn and Warsaw during the Cold War. The international-structural conditions of the relationship remained disadvantageous for the process of consensus-building throughout this period. As long as the East–West conflict prevailed, the basic security interests of Warsaw and Bonn were bound to be discordant. Bipolarity also infringed upon West German and Polish domestic arrangements, which resulted in the incompatibility of both governments and economies. The international and domestic background against which the relationship was developing was thus qualitatively different from the parallel French-(West) German process.

These generally unfavourable external conditions and their domestic implications impinged decisively upon the post-1956 attempt at rapprochement which, as argued above, failed after a short period. On the other hand, the post-1956 episode demonstrated that in spite of the prevailing conflict a return to the pre-1945 severe state of hostilities could be prevented. It is argued here that this happened because of the domestic 'Europeanisation' of West Germany, in terms of its internal democratisation and its integration with the western community. These two factors led to the dropping of belligerent methods from the repertoire of West Germany's policies towards Poland: the Federal Republic renounced the use of force as an option in solving its conflicts with Poland. Unlike the Weimar Republic, it also refrained from sponsoring sabotage activities of the German minority in Poland. Therefore, although Bonn's Polish policy remained heavily influenced by the notion of territorial revisionism this never went beyond the level of rhetoric. The Federal Republic's domestic 'Europeanisation' also helped nurture a pro-German lobby in Warsaw which started to perceive Poland's 'return to Europe' as pre-conditioned by a rapprochement with Bonn.

These developments and conditions laid the foundations for the beginning of the reconciliation process, which was initiated by the Protestant and Catholic Churches in both countries in the mid-1960s. It also prepared the ground for rapprochement at the governmental level, which was finally achieved in the wake of West Germany's new *Ostpolitik*. By the end of the 1980s the Federal Republic had become one of Poland's most important economic partners, the first in the West and the second after the Soviet Union.[44] At the political level, Bonn also demonstrated a greater closeness with Warsaw than any other country in the West. The relationship between Poland's communist leader Edward Gierek and Chancellor Helmut Schmidt, for example, was described by both statesmen as personal and friendly.[45] In the 1980s Bonn gained the gratitude of the Polish communists for its muted reaction to the imposition of martial law and its objection to US-led economic sanctions.

The success of new *Ostpolitik* in 'normalising' relations with Poland raises a number of questions as to whether it can be compared with the Federal Republic's *Westpolitik* (Policy towards the West). Essentially, did Bonn apply to Poland a similar policy approach as it did with its western partners, characterised by the building of a dense network of economic ties and institutionalised co-operation? Finally, did Bonn's aim of achieving *Wandel durch Handel* (change through trade) bring about any degree of 'Europeanisation' in Polish–(West) German relations?

It is true that the policy instruments of new *Ostpolitik* were mostly economic and that an explicit articulation of its interests was carefully avoided by Bonn. For example, according to Gierek's account, at no time during his frequent meetings with Helmut Schmidt was the issue of German unification discussed.[46] It is also true that Bonn aimed to build a web of interdependence which would lead to an intertwining of interests between East and West. In other words, it is probably correct to say that new *Ostpolitik* was intended as an eastern version of 'Europeanisation'.

However, it seems that although largely successful at the governmental level, new the *Ostpolitik* failed to achieve a genuine rapprochement between the German and Polish peoples. In fact, as often argued, West German unwillingness to distinguish between state and society was perceived as immoral in dissident circles of democratic opposition in Poland. This was particularly the case with Bonn's (non-) reaction to the introduction of martial law in December 1981. As a result, new *Ostpolitik*'s record remains somewhat ambiguous: successful in 'normalising' official relations, promoting *détente* and stabilisation, it remained out of synchronisation with Polish democratic forces. Consequently, by the end of the 1980s Polish–(West) German reconciliation had made only marginal progress. In effect, although new *Ostpolitik* clearly contributed to a lower threat perception of Germany in Poland it failed in its task of bridging both societies which, as argued earlier, remains one of the defining factors of 'Europeanisation'.

In sum, both policy developments discussed here appear to confirm that 'Europeanisation' is not attainable in a situation of prevailing international conflict. As far as Poland and West Germany were concerned this was true not only because of international constraints but also as a result of the externally imposed incompatibility of domestic orders in both countries. Here, the ambiguities of new *Ostpolitik* seemed specifically to prove the point. Even after both governments had managed to alleviate their main differences in the 1970s this did not lead to a genuine congruence of interests, due to the dearth of a democratic platform for their agreement. Consequently, both internal democratisation and reconciliation were still missing from the relationship. As regards the latter, it has been sometimes suggested that Willy Brandt's kniefall at the monument of the Warsaw Ghetto in 1970 had a profound effect upon the Polish perception of Germany.[47] In reality, however, the impact of this incident was limited in Poland to official circles. The reason for this was simple: no Polish newspaper was allowed to publish a picture of the kniefall, which in effect remained unknown to a broader public.[48] This event seems to illustrate in a crude way that in order to build a genuine rapprochement with West Germany, Poland had to undergo internal 'Europeanisation', by way of democratisation. This, however, was not attainable until the end of bipolarity in 1989.

Notes

1 Willy Brandt, *My Life in Politics* (London: Hamish Hamilton, 1992), p. 199.
2 *Ibid.*, p. 196.
3 See Jadwiga Kiwerska, 'W Atmosferze Wrogości (1945–1970)', in Anna Wolf-Poweska (ed.), *Polacy Wobec Niemców: Z Dziejów Kultury Politycznej Polski 1945–1989* (Poznań: Instytut Zachodni, 1993), pp. 61–5.
4 See Hans Georg Lehmann, *Der Oder-Neisse - Konflikt* (Munich: Beck, 1979), pp. 171–2.
5 See Władysław Gomułka, *O Problemie Niemieckim: Artykuły i przemówienia* (Warsaw: Książka i Wiedza, 1971), pp. 165–81.
6 Zbigniew Brzeziński, *The Soviet Block, Unity and Conflict* (Cambridge, MA: Harvard University Press, 1960), pp. 245–53.

7   See Dieter Bingen, *Die Polenpolitik der Bonner Republik von Adenauer bis Kohl, 1949–1990* (Baden-Baden: Nomos, 1998). p. 54, n. 57.

8   Hans-Peter Schwarz, *Konrad Adenauer: A German Politician and Statesman in a Period of War, Revolution and Reconstruction, Vol.2: The Statesman: 1952–1967* (Oxford and Providence: Berghahn, 1995), pp. 560–1.

9   See Bingen, *Die Polenpolitik*, pp. 49–58.

10 See 'Bulletin der Presse', 9 November 1956.

11 See Schwarz, *Konrad Adenauer, Vol. 2*, p. 306.

12 *Ibid.*, p. 304

13 *Ibid.*, pp. 304–8.

14 See 'Der Rapacki Plan Memorandum der Regierung der Volksrepublic Polen zur frage der Abschaffung eines atomusaffenfreien zone vom 14. Februar 1958,' in Hans Ester, Hans Hecker and Erika Poettgens (eds), *Deutschland, aber wo liegt es? Deutschland und Mitteleuropa: Analysen und historische Dokumente*, (Amsterdam Studies on Cultural Identity, 3 Amsterdam and Atlanta, GA; Rodopi, 1993), pp. 207–11.

15 See Schwarz, *Konrad Adenauer, Vol. 2*, pp. 308–9.

16 See *Foreign Relations of the United States 1958–1960 (FRUS)*, Vol. IX (Washington, DC: Department of State Relations, 1993), p. 259.

17 See Bingen, *Die Polenpolitik*, p. 65.

18 See *1958–1960 (FRUS)*, Vol. IX, pp. 25, 34, 100–1, 220.

19 See Schwarz, *Konrad Adenauer, Vol. 2*, pp. 560–1.

20 See Włodzimierz Borodziej, *Od Poczdamu do Szklarskiej Poręby:, Polska w Stosunkach Międzynarodowych 1945–1947* (London: Aneks, 1990), p. 292.

21 Quoted from Timothy Garton Ash, *In Europe's Name: Germany and the Divided Continent* (London: Vintage 1994), p. 225.

22 Mieczysław F. Rakowski, *Dzienniki Polityczne 1958–1962* (Warsaw: Iskry, 1999), pp. 212–16.

23 Schwarz, *Konrad Adenauer, Vol. 2*, pp. 559–60, 576.

24 See Bingen, *Die Polenpolitik*, pp. 22–6.

25 See Pailer, *Na Przekór Fatalizmowi Wrogości: Stanisław Stomma; stosunki Polsko-Niemieckie* (Warsaw: Wydawnictwo Polsko-Niemieckie, 1998), p. 78.

26 Bingen, *Die Polenpolitik*, p. 67.

27 See Brandt, *My Life in Politics*, p. 4.

28 See Hans-Adolf Jacobsen und Mieczysław Tomala (eds), *Bonn-Warschau 1945–1991. Die Deutsch-Polnischen Beziehungen, Analyse und Dokumentation* (Cologne: Verlag Wissenschaft und Politik, 1992), pp. 145–9.

29 *Ibid.*, pp. 239–40, 256–7.

30 See *Młodzież o Służbie Wojskowej, Komunikat z Badań* (Warsaw and Listopad CBOS, 1988), pp. 13–14.

31 See Kazimierz Poznański, 'Economic Adjustment and Political Forces: Poland since 1970', *International Organization*, Vol. 40, No. 2, 1986.

32 See Jacobsen und Tomala (eds), *Bonn-Warschau 1945–1991*, pp. 114–15.

33 *Ibid.*, pp. 125–35. Also see Helmut Hild, 'Was hat die Denkschrift der EKD bewirkt?', in Friedbert Pflüger and Winfried Lipscher (eds), *Feinde werden Freunde* (Bonn: Bouvier Verlag, 1993), pp. 90–103, 106–10.

34 See Jacobsen und Tomala (eds), *Bonn-Warschau 1945–1991*, pp. 135–42; Hanna Suchocka, 'Znaczenie Orędzia Biskupów Polskich z 1965 rdla Budowania Tożsamości Nowej Europy', *Przegląd Zachodni*, 96/1, February–March 1996, pp. 17–29.

35 See Mieczysław Tomala, *Patrząc na Niemcy: Od Wrogości do Porozumienia 1945–1991* (Warsaw: Polska Fundacja Spraw Międzynarodowych, 1997), pp. 165–72.

36 See Ash, *In Europe's Name*, p. 237; Tomala, *Patrząc na Niemcy*, pp. 319–21.

37 See Bingen, *Die Polenpolitik der Bonner Republik*, p. 239.

38 Quoted in Ash, *In Europe's Name*, p. 65.

39 See Tomala, *Patrząc na Niemcy*, pp. 269–70.

40 See Timothy Garton Ash, 'Mitteleuropa?', *Daedalus*, Vol. 119, 1990, pp. 16–17.

41 Brandt, *My Life in Politics*, pp. 440–1.

42 Interview with Peter Glotz, 12 May 1998, Erfurt.

43 See Tomala, *Patrząc na Niemcy*, pp. 169–72.

44 See Zdzisław Puślecki, *Polska w Okresie Transformacji a Zjednoczone Niemcy* (Warsaw and Poznan: Wydawnictwo Naukowe PWN, 1996), p. 143.

45 See Edward Gierek (interviewed by Janusz Rolicki), *Przerwana Dekada* (Warsaw: Wydawnictwo Fakt, 1990), pp. 100–1.

46 *Ibid.*, pp. 101–2.

47 See Adrian Hyde-Price, 'Building a Stable Peace in Mitteleuropa: The German–Polish Hinge', in www.bham.ac.uk/IGS/DiscussionPapers.htm, pp. 7–8.

48 See Bingen, *Die Polenpolitik*, p. 134.

4

Between conflict and co-operation, 1989–91

I strongly hope that together with Poland we can make a crucial step ahead, as we had done in our relations with France and Israel ... The Federal government and the Federal Chancellor could not recognise Poland's western border as definite, and they would not lead any negotiations on this matter, as long as there is no sovereign government of United Germany. (Helmut Kohl, Federal Chancellor, on his first visit to Poland, November 1989)[1]

Like every nation we would prefer that there were no foreign armies on our territory, but like every nation we must also look at our security realistically, from the perspective of the balance of forces, from the perspective of alliances, and we must assess from that perspective the continued presence of the Soviet forces. (Tadeusz Mazowiecki, Polish Prime Minister, on Gorbachev's offer to discuss the departure of the Soviet troops from Poland, Press Conference, 21 February 1990)[2]

Introduction

The end of the Cold War transformed both the external and internal conditions of relations between Warsaw and Bonn in a way potentially conducive to the relationship's 'Europeanisation'. The overarching structural context that had defined Polish–German relations after 1945 fundamentally changed as the international system established in Yalta came to an end. Communism was collapsing, Germany was heading for unification and Poland was moving towards a liberal-democratic model of government and integration with the West.

It seemed as if for the first time in modern history Poland and Germany were in a situation where their interests could truly converge. After decades of being a *Frontstaat* (a 'front-line' state) exposed to the threat from the East, the Federal Republic was keen to see its eastern environment integrated into a West European context, which was exactly what the new Polish elite also desired. However, although international-structural and ideological reasons for the Polish–German conflict of interests disappeared with the end of bipolarity, the bilateral disagreement over the Oder-Neisse issue remained in place. In fact, after the years of détente based on Bonn's acceptance of status quo, the border issue was re-opened in the run-up to German unification. This was legally possible because in the border treaty, signed in 1970, Bonn recognised the Oder-Neisse frontier in its own name but not on behalf of a united Germany. In the context of unification the successor German state was not, therefore, automatically bound by the existing agreement and the West German Chancellor, Helmut Kohl, did little to address this legal ambiguity. This provoked a diplomatic offensive from Warsaw that for a moment posed a serious threat to the unification process. Consequently, Bonn-Warsaw relations remained ambivalent during the 1989–91 period. On the one hand, they were marked by a mixture of a 'new' congruence of interests and ideologies and, on the other, by the re-opening of an 'old' quarrel over the border. Elements of both change and continuity or, respectively, of co-operation and conflict, were therefore present in the policies of both governments during this transitory period.

This chapter will analyse the strategies employed by both governments between 1989 and 1991 which, reflecting the ambivalence of the relationship, fall into two categories: 'non-institutionalised' and 'institutionalised'. This chapter will demonstrate that, while the latter form of strategy, implying multilateralism, fits best with the notion of Europeanisation, in this early phase of post-Cold War relations both types of strategy were employed by Poland and Germany. Despite the overriding success of West Germany's multilateral foreign policy style and the high hopes held by Polish elites to integrate into western institutions, historically rooted mistrust and the uncertainty of a new situation produced a number of obstacles that dogged the rapprochement process during this transitory period. This often meant that, when dealing with some vital security issues, Warsaw reversed to traditional and non-institutional diplomatic techniques rooted in a balance of power philosophy, as apparent in its policy towards the border question. At the same time the policy of the Federal Republic, though never failing to emphasise its institutional and multilateral aspects, was often an example of a European solution being used to pursue specific self-interests.

The following sections will discuss this persistent ambiguity of the relationship by focusing first on traditional non-institutionalised strategies and than moving to the institutional approach.

Non-institutionalised strategies

After a short period of a successful rapprochement in (West) German–Polish relations between the election of the non-communist government in Poland and the publication of the ten-point plan by Kohl (August-mid November 1989), Bonn-Warsaw relations came once again to be determined by the old issue of the Oder-Neisse frontier. In its handling of the dispute, Polish diplomacy displayed a strong preference to pursue unilateral and bilateral policies rather than to see the issue addressed within the broader context of European and Euro-Atlantic integration. The following sections examine the development of the conflict and discuss the strategy employed by Poland to secure the final recognition of its western border.

The unification of Germany and the border conflict

By mid-1989 it was still by no means certain that relations between Bonn and Warsaw would turn sour in the near future. On the contrary, there was a fair amount of optimism on both sides, based on the presumption of a new commonality of values and congruence of interests. Indeed, much of this optimism seemed justified, clearly both countries' interests were relatively compatible, to a degree unprecedented not only in post-war history but also for the previous two centuries. Bonn supported Poland's democratic transition and believed that its success would make the prospects of German unification more likely. This view was expressed by Helmut Kohl who said that 'the changes in Poland and Hungary were in the German national interest' and that the 'Polish experiment' was directly connected with the prospect of unification'.[3] By the same token, the new Polish government knew that it could not remain an independent island in a 'sea of communism' and consequently, the democratisation of the GDR and unification of Germany was in its vital interest. Therefore, in the summer and autumn of 1989, the West German and Polish governments were at one in seeing the benefits of the Polish reforms and the unification of Germany.

Where the first disappointment occurred was in the apparent rupture in the relationship between these two processes (unification and Polish reforms), which resulted from the unexpected opening of the Berlin wall by the East German authorities on 9 November 1989. As the border opened, unification seemed inevitable regardless of the success of Poland's democratic transition. Symbolically, Kohl was in the middle of a carefully prepared first-ever state visit to Poland when the news of the events in Berlin reached him, and the excited Chancellor left Warsaw immediately.

At this point, it was clear that Poland's support for German unification was no longer required. In addition, Poland was clearly losing the advantage of being the leader of democratic change in the Eastern Bloc, which led to anxiety in Warsaw as to whether the West, and the Federal Republic especially, would continue to support Polish reforms. For example, the leader of Solidarity and future President, Lech Wałęsa, stressed that although he was happy that the wall was coming down he was afraid that 'Poland will pay for it'. Kohl's advisor Horst Teltschick agreed that Wałęsa's concerns were indeed justified.[4]

In the wake of the Polish–German 'reciprocity of interests' becoming 'water under the bridge' Warsaw reacted with increased insecurity. It was feared that as the events in Europe were taking a new shape, history might repeat itself and Poland would find itself excluded from vital decisions that would impact upon its security. The phrase that was often used in Warsaw during this period was 'Poland would not agree to another Yalta'.[5] This, of course, was a direct reference to the policy of establishing spheres of influence and changing borders in East Central Europe over the heads of the nations concerned, a policy to which, as it was believed in Warsaw, Poland had been subjected since the nineteenth century.

During this particularly sensitive period in Polish–German relations it was essential that Bonn give no reason to show that Warsaw's anxiety was justified. Unfortunately for both parties, the opposite happened. Just two weeks after his trip to Poland Helmut Kohl published his plan for German unification, the so-called 'ten-point plan', which although mentioned a number of security initiatives failed to address the Oder-Neisse frontier question.[6] The plan was consequently received with apprehension in Warsaw, which indeed had reasons for concern, since according to the official West German position the 1970 border treaty, signed between Poland and the Bonn Republic, was not binding for the successor German state.[7] Until 1989 West Germany had insisted that its border with Poland could be established only by an international peace settlement (*Friedensregelung*), as in fact had been envisaged in article IXb of the Potsdam agreement. This in practice meant that the border dispute could not be finalised before unification come about. However, after the events of 9 November 1989 it was becoming apparent that the unification process would not take the shape of a peace settlement involving all parties engaged in the war (including Poland). Instead it was clear that the German question would be decided in the framework of the '2 + 4' negotiations involving both German states and the former occupying powers (the United States, the United Kingdom, France and the USSR), excluding Poland. In addition, arguments were raised in the Federal Republic that a future Germany would not need to abide by the border treaties that had been signed in the past between Poland and both German states.[8] This all meant that for the Poles a repetition of Yalta began to look dangerously possible.

The Polish response to this ambiguous situation was to link the progress of unification with the settlement of the border issue. As argued by the Polish Foreign Minister, Krzysztof Skubiszewski, 'there should be no border question at the onset of German unification'.[9] Polish diplomacy maintained that the final border treaty should be signed prior to the completion of the unification process and be only ratified by a future government of a unified Germany. Warsaw also embarked on a diplomatic offensive to ensure its participation in those parts of the '2 + 4' negotiations that concerned its borders.[10] In response to this, Bonn applied a 'tit-for-tat' strategy, rejecting the Polish demands and linking the settlement of the frontier dispute with a demand that Poland refrain from pursuing reparation claims against Germany and that it grant extensive rights to its German minority.[11] As a result of this manoeuvring, Polish–German relations returned to the pre-1989 low point characterised by a dominance of conflict over co-operation. During this period, Polish foreign policy often reverted to traditional non-institutional balance of power strategies. In order to check Germany's external behaviour, Warsaw moved to reinvent its traditional *entente cordiale* with Paris as well as attempting to exploit its ties with the USSR.

French and Soviet support for the Polish position

All the former occupying powers (the United States, the United Kingdom, France and the USSR) made it clear to Kohl that they considered the Oder-Neisse borderline as final and non-negotiable.[12] However, while London and Washington did not always wish to become involved in the German–Polish dispute, both Paris and Moscow promoted specific Polish positions throughout the conflict.

While the Soviets traditionally portrayed themselves as the guarantors of Poland's western borders, the French, uneasy about Germany's looming unification, were quick to establish themselves as Warsaw's main advocate in the West. Thus it was mainly due to French and Soviet backing that Poland was involved in those parts of the '2 + 4' negotiations relating to its borders. The Soviet delegation even made a motion establishing Warsaw as a venue for this part of the talks. This was subsequently supported by the French, but in the end it fell through because of Bonn's objection and British and American lack of interest. Finally, it was decided that the meeting, with the participation of a Polish representative, would take place in Paris, which was welcomed by Warsaw, who by this stage perceived France as an ally.[13]

Soon after these decisions were taken, Mazowiecki and Poland's President Jaruzelski (a former communist general who acted as President until 1991) paid an official visit to France, where they received full backing from President François Mitterrand. Mitterrand supported the broad participation of Poland in the '2 + 4' process, beyond discussing the frontier issue, as well as Warsaw's demand to have the border treaty signed before the unification process was completed.[14] The fact that these positions had been backed earlier by the Soviets was received in Bonn without surprise but the French declaration of support for Warsaw came as a shock to Helmut Kohl. In a telephone conversation with the French President, Kohl asked whether the Franco-German special relationship was being reconsidered and whether Paris had lost its trust in 'European' Germany. In interviews and in his memoirs the German Chancellor complained that as Mazowiecki and Mitterrand were set on reintroducing an anti-German small *entente*: they plotted to 'play with each other a table-tennis game over the German net.'[15]

But in spite of these German reactions, the French continued to promote Poland's position. As the host of the '2 + 4' negotiations with Poland's participation (which were enthusiastically renamed by the Polish press as the '2 + 5' talks) France was able to set the agenda in such a way that Poland was involved not only in discussing the Oder-Neisse issue but also on some broader security questions concerning the new Germany. In addition, before the Paris meeting took place the French Foreign minister, Roland Dumas, considered whether the cancellation of the rights of the Four Powers in Germany (the final settlement) should not wait until the final resolution of the Oder-Neisse issue. This suggestion, which was widely perceived as an attempt to postpone German unification, was subsequently raised during the trilateral negotiations between Poland and both German states prior to the '2 + 4' meeting in Paris.[16] Eventually, however, Warsaw found itself under strong domestic and international pressure to withdraw from the position suggested earlier by the French.[17]

Beside its attempts to exercise pressure on Bonn through seeking diplomatic coalitions with France and the USSR, Warsaw sought much more serious ways of balancing the perceived 'German threat'. Until the border treaty was signed, Poland proved reluctant to support the dissolution of the Warsaw Pact. In addition, it postponed the withdrawal of Soviet troops from its territory.

Soviet troops in Poland

As argued in earlier chapters, there was an element of genuine national interests in Poland's alliance with the Soviet Union throughout the Cold War. Following the territorial changes after the Second World War, the new Polish–German border was not recognised by the western powers while it was officially guaranteed by the Soviets. The Soviet Union thus became in effect an official guarantor of Poland's security and any government, communist or not, had to take this fact into consideration. The Polish–(West) German treaty of 1970 weakened this argument, as the border was temporarily recognised by Bonn; however, as argued above, with unification looming, the question was reopened. Paradoxically, then, the first ever non-communist government in East Central Europe continued to rely on Soviet guarantees and, for the time being, did not object to the Soviet military presence in Poland. While Czechoslovakia and Hungary concluded agreements on the withdrawal of Soviet troops in February and March 1990, respectively, Poland waited to open negotiations on this issue until the border treaty with Germany had been signed in November 1990.

Although few in Poland thought that a reunified Germany would actually challenge the existing border, still Poland's historical experience with a unified German state had been mostly difficult and traumatic. Confused by Helmut Kohl's ambiguous statements, Warsaw proved reluctant to remove its existing security arrangements that rested on the continuing presence of Soviet troops in Poland and its membership in the Warsaw Treaty Organisation (WTO).[18] When Polish Premier Mazowiecki was asked at a press conference in February 1990 about Gorbachev's offer to discuss the terms of the troops' departure, if Warsaw expressed such a desire, he indicated that Poland's security situation was not yet ready for the Soviets to leave. Consequently the government held that the troops should remain until 'military blocks were no longer necessary'.[19]

Already evident in various governmental statements, the German theme was explicitly brought up in an article by Janusz Reiter who soon after this publication became Poland's ambassador to Germany.[20] His article '*Po co te wojska?*' (What Are These Troops For?) was published just as Poland was lobbying to participate in the '2 + 4' negotiations. It posed a thesis that while the function of the Soviet troops to enforce the communist order had came to an end, they were still required as 'part of the balance of power in Europe', which had been challenged and undermined by German unification. Reiter also argued that the remaining Soviet troops could be an asset to Poland as a counterbalance to the new, powerful Germany and a useful bargaining chip for negotiations on future European security issues.

By early 1990 Warsaw embarked on a path of balancing Germany and appeasing Moscow. This not only kept 'the Russians in', but also prolonged the existence of the Warsaw Pact. Resisting pressures from Hungary, which wanted to dismantle the Soviet-led alliance as soon as possible, the Poles argued that although the Warsaw Pact should be reformed, it nevertheless remained a valuable instrument in a very unstable security environment.[21]

At the same time, however, Polish public opinion began to split with regards to the speed of reforms, including the general direction of foreign policy. The future President, Lech Wałęsa, whose views at the time were representative of the part of public opinion that wanted to accelerate reforms, was of the view that a reunited Germany posed no threat to Poland and that the Soviet troops should be withdrawn 'as soon as possible'.[22] Despite these voices, the government maintained its position until the treaty with the united Germany had been signed. However, when in November 1990 Skubiszewski asked the Soviet government to begin negotiations for the withdrawal of troops from Poland, Moscow was unable to facilitate Warsaw's request. As a result, negotiations dragged on for much longer than was the case with the Hungarians, Czechs and Slovaks, and it was not until September 1993 that the last Soviet troops finally left Poland.

This issue continued to dog Bonn-Warsaw relations even after the border treaty had been completed. At the end of 1990 and beginning of 1991 the situation was further complicated by the task of transferring 400,000 Soviet soldiers back home from East Germany through Poland. The transit was agreed between the German and Soviet governments without the input of Poland; Warsaw became afraid that not only would it need to cope with a massive transit operation but also that it might become the last country in the former Eastern Bloc with Soviet troops. This led the Foreign Office to adopt a hard-line 'no departure – no transit' position that made Warsaw's agreement on transporting Soviet forces through its territory conditional upon the earlier withdrawal of all Red Army units from Poland.[23]

The Polish strategy did not bring about the results it aimed at, essentially because the Soviets were also not eager to withdraw from the former GDR; the 'no departure – no transit' position proved to be misguided. The main effect of Poland's position on the matter was to embitter its relations with Bonn shortly after they had moved on the right track following the resolution of the border question. At the end of 1991 the problem was resolved: the Soviets agreed to begin withdrawing their forces from Poland, Warsaw departed from its previously unco-operative stance and Bonn agreed to ship a proportion of Soviet troops via its own ports in Mecklenburg.

The two policies discussed above are clearly rooted in a traditional perception of international relations, where states are seen as self-interested and potentially belligerent actors. It is not international institutions but an effective balance of power that is seen as capable of ensuring security and stability. In response to Bonn's ambiguous position towards the territorial question Warsaw moved on to check Germany's position by ensuring the support of Paris and Moscow. Warsaw was even prepared to slowdown the dismantling of the Cold War system, as apparent in its position on the continuing presence of Soviet troops and its initial reluctance to dissolve the Warsaw Pact. While this strategy proved effective in exercising pressure on Bonn and arguably contributed to the swifter solution of the border issue, it was not risk-free. The drawbacks of the non-institutional strategy became apparent when Warsaw finally asked the Soviet troops to leave and found out that this was not immediately possible. This showed that balancing behaviour may produce a dangerously enduring effect, which may continue even when the initial reason for employing the strategy has become redundant. The other apparent weakness of these policies was their damaging impact upon trust-building in the relationship, which arguably undermined the government's 'return-to-Europe-through Germany' policy.

However, though in its policy towards the border issue Warsaw undoubtedly applied a non-institutional strategy this was, arguably, an exception rather than a rule. In all other major areas it was apparent that both Warsaw and Bonn saw institutional solutions as best suited to the re-ordering of their relationship. This was definitely the case with the question of Germany's alliance status, where both Bonn and Warsaw rejected the notion of neutrality. Another example was the approach that the two governments took in establishing the legal bases for their new relationship, as apparent in their 'Good Neighbourly Relations and Friendly Co-operation' treaty signed in 1991, which was modelled on the 1963 Franco-German agreement, and as such contained some strong institutional elements.

Institutionalised strategies

The end of the Cold War and the forthcoming unification of Germany created a new security situation in Europe. Soviet troops were withdrawing from most of East Central Europe, the Warsaw Pact was being dismantled and NATO faced an uncertain future. As the role of 'old' alliances was increasingly questioned, new ideas for creating a pan-European security system, embracing both NATO and Warsaw Pact members, were gaining ground. It was clear that, as often in the past, the key to the emerging security system lay in Germany. There were three routes that Bonn could pursue in this new situation. A future Germany could be neutral, it could withdraw from NATO but throw its weight behind the creation of a pan-European system based on the existing Conference for Security and Co-operation in Europe (CSCE) and could continue to be a NATO member while supporting the CSCE process. The issue was a vital interest for Warsaw as it was clear that Germany's security alignment would not only be of direct importance for Poland's position vis-à-vis its western neighbour but also because it would define the future security system in Europe.

While the question of military alignment was important, it was clear that in order to redefine their relationship Bonn and Warsaw needed to look beyond immediate security issues and explore possibilities of closer co-operation in economic, environmental, societal and other spheres relevant to establishing good relations between direct neighbours. Here again, the choice faced by Bonn and Warsaw was either to pursue a strictly intergovernmental path to co-operation or to set on a route to rapprochement based on creating a net of institutions and marked by a pronounced role for the EC/EU. The first of these methods would be less complex but also rather shallow and vulnerable to political influences. The second was modelled on the Franco-West German process and as such promised much deeper integration, but would be more complex and hence more difficult to achieve.

It is argued here that in both of these questions – the issue of Germany's security alignment and the rapprochement process – Poland and Germany opted for *institutional* solutions. The strategies of Bonn and Warsaw came to be highly congruent in these areas and as such they laid down the foundations for the emerging 'Europeanisation' of the relationship. The following sections outline the development of Bonn's and Warsaw's policies in these areas and address the often painful process of reconciling their strategies.

The question of Germany's security alignment

Kohl's 'ten-point plan' left open the question of the united Germany's security alignment. The plan did not explicitly envisage Germany's membership in NATO; instead, it referred to Gorbachev's idea of a 'common European home' and the CSCE as a 'central element of pan-European security architecture'. The CSCE process was also underlined by Kohl's advisor, Horst Teltshick, after the Chancellor presented his ten-point plan to the *Bundestag*.[24]

However, a week after Kohl's speech, American president George Bush made it clear that a future Germany *must* remain a NATO member. British Prime Minister Margaret Thatcher stressed the same.[25] Urged by its key allies, Bonn moved on to declare that it wished to retain its membership in NATO after unification. The Soviets, on the other hand, were at the time firmly opposed to the idea of a united Germany being a NATO member and Gorbachev asserted on 9 December 1989 that the GDR must remain a strategic partner of the USSR and a member of the Warsaw Pact. Soon after Gorbachev's declaration, East German Prime Minister Hans Modrow, apparently acting under instruction from Moscow, put forward a plan of gradual unification which envisaged 'military neutrality for both the GDR and FRG' with effect even before completion of the unification process.[26]

During Kohl's visit to Moscow in February 1990 Gorbachev softened his position on this issue in as much as he stressed that he could not conceive of the idea of NATO expanding eastwards, while also declaring that he was open to other suggestions.[27] After Kohl's visit, Gorbachev gave an interview to the Russian daily *Pravda* in which he again objected to a future Germany's membership in existing military alliances, either NATO or the Warsaw Pact which, he argued, would disrupt 'the military balance of these two organisations'. He also stressed that German unification had to be linked with the formation of 'a fundamentally new structure of European security which will replace the one based on military-political blocks'.[28] Gorbachev began therefore to lobby for a pan-European solution which would include both the United States and the USSR. Clearly, neither NATO nor the Warsaw Pact were suited to fulfil this role, so the emphasis in the Soviet argument was placed on the CSCE and disarmament regimes.

In an article in March 1990 'Too fast and too slow', Gorbachev argued that while German unification was taking 'too fast' a pace, the process of European unification, meaning East–West unity, was 'too slow'. This disparity was, in Gorbachev's opinion, a hindrance to both NATO and the Warsaw Pact transforming themselves from military into political organisations. To address this predicament Gorbachev suggested the synchronisation of the progress of the German question with that of developing the CSCE.[29]

The Polish position on this issue remained non-committal until the meeting of Warsaw Pact Foreign Ministers in April 1990, at which Poland, Hungary and Czechoslovakia expressed their support for a unified Germany to remain in NATO. Despite arguments made in the Polish literature, however, it is not wholly accurate to say that Poland consistently supported Germany's NATO membership from the election of Mazowiecki's government in Autumn 1989.[30] It is, nonetheless, true that at no point did Poland endorse the notion of a neutral Germany and that Warsaw always opted for an institutional solution to the question of Germany's military alignment.[31] Initially, however, Warsaw argued that the future Germany should be embedded in a kind of organisation conducive with Gorbachev's pan-European ideas.

In his January 1990 speech before the Council of Europe, Mazowiecki put forward a proposal for creating a new security organisation, to be called the 'Council of European Co-operation'. The idea of the Council, which drew from Gorbachev's 'common European home' and Mitterrand's 'European confederation', was meant to embrace the whole of Europe. The Council was designed as a permanent part of the CSCE process, and as such it was intended to enhance the institutionalisation of the organisation.[32] The notion of creating a new European security system that 'should reflect the concept of a single Europe' was also called for by Foreign Minister Skubiszewski in his speech at an extraordinary session of the Assembly of the Western European Union (WEU) in March 1990. While relating implicitly to the German question, Skubiszewski defended Poland's membership in the Warsaw Pact, which would be 'dissolved the moment an all-European system of security becomes a reality'.[33]

Clearly, therefore, Polish ideas for a future European security system remained strikingly similar to Gorbachev's. This can be explained in two ways. Firstly, Warsaw saw its genuine interests in supporting Gorbachev because after all he was the one who had denounced the Brezhnev doctrine (named after the Soviet leader who had ordered the Warsaw Pact's invasion of Czechoslovakia in 1968) and subsequently permitted the Polish democratic experiment. Secondly, the support demonstrated by Moscow for the Polish position during the border dispute illustrated to Poles the continued salience of the Soviet 'security guarantee'. Both of these points shaped Mazowiecki's position on Germany's NATO membership as seen during his visit to Washington in March 1990. After discussing at length the border issue with President Bush, Mazowiecki unexpectedly suggested a proposal of his own. For the sake of Gorbachev's survival, he argued, would not it be for the best if the 'forces of both the East and the West remained in Germany'. In other words, Mazowiecki was presenting a proposal for the indefinite retention of Soviet troops in Germany. At the same time, however, Mazowiecki argued that 'Poland did not believe in a neutral Germany'.[34]

Soon after the Polish Premier's visit to Washington the tensions in Polish-West German relations began to abate. Following Bush's mediation between Kohl and Mazowiecki a compromise was reached and on 8 March 1990 the *Bundestag* voted in favour of a resolution confirming the Oder–Neisse line as Poland's western frontier.[35] Clearly, these developments encouraged Poland to support the united Germany's membership in NATO which, as argued earlier, Warsaw endorsed in April 1990. Thus by May 1990 the Soviet Union was isolated in opposing Germany's continuing membership in the Alliance.

Warsaw's behaviour between November 1989 and April 1990 demonstrated a strong preference for the continuing multilateralisation of Germany's security policy. Initially Warsaw did not speak out in favour of Germany's membership in NATO, instead Mazowiecki promoted the strengthening of the CSCE as a way of tackling the German question. After the border issue had been resolved, Warsaw was freer to take on a more pro-western stance, which was immediately reflected in its position towards Germany's NATO membership. When commenting on this particular development, Chancellor Kohl remarked bitterly that Warsaw chose to support Germany's membership in the Alliance not because it was concerned about the Federal Republic's well being, but because it saw Germany's membership in NATO as the best guarantee of its own security.[36] Kohl's cynicism notwithstanding, Poland's support for Germany to remain in NATO demonstrates the overall congruence in the policies of the two states and that both had opted for an institutional solution as the best way of securing their interests.

As argued earlier, the institutional strategy was also apparent in the process of laying down the legal foundations for Polish–German rapprochement. In particular, it was clear from the very outset that the Poles and the Germans were in agreement in seeking to introduce a strong 'European' element in their relationship.

Promoting integration with the EU

Between the end of communism and the border treaty
The desire to include a strong 'European' aspect in the shaping of post-Cold War Bonn-Warsaw relations was apparent in both capitals after the collapse of communism. Drawing from its experience of relations with France, West Germany promoted the framing of the relationship within a multilateral context. The new Polish government was also committed to pursuing a multilateral route and based its foreign policy philosophy on the notion of a 'return to Europe', which to a large extent was conditional upon achieving rapprochement in Polish–German relations.

On the other hand, it was apparent that there were some obvious inconstancies, if not contradictions, both in the Polish and West German positions. Poland's new foreign policy was built on a rejection of Yalta, implying support for German unification and with it a strong preference for a European solution. But at the same time, Warsaw remained insecure and suspicious of the intentions of its powerful western neighbour. This tendency was seemingly strengthened by Kohl's failure to address the border question in his ten-point plan. As regards the Federal Republic it is beyond doubt that Bonn believed integration into the web of western institutions and bilateral arrangements to be the best framework for establishing new relations with Poland. At the same time, however, Kohl did not hesitate to don the mantle of nationalist as he portrayed himself as defender of national interests during the border conflict.

The initial period of relations, that lasted between the election of Mazowiecki's government and the publication of the ten-point plan, was marked by strong efforts on both sides to reconcile their differences and to take the relationship 'in to Europe'. Mimicking its behaviour with Western partners, France in particular, the Federal Republic established a variety of agreements with Warsaw. Eager to move closer to what it considered as western norms, the new Polish government welcomed the principle of reconciling with (West) Germany 'through Europe'.

A first move towards the implementation of these policies was made during Kohl's visit to Poland in November 1989. A joint declaration was signed between Kohl and Mazowiecki which envisaged the embedding of the relationship in the context of European integration. This broad goal incorporated many spheres of bilateral relations including economic co-operation, security, national minorities and cross-border co-operation.[37] To add a 'European' gesture to this rapprochement Mazowiecki and Kohl attended a bilingual mass in the former property of Prussian aristocrat and member of the anti-Nazi resistance James von Moltke. Subsequently, a picture of Kohl and Mazowiecki embracing each other became recognised as one of the most popular images of the watershed of 1989–90. The declaration and symbolism surrounding Kohl's visit were a conscious imitation of the spirit of Franco-German relations, and as such they were intended to take the relationship onto another level with a strong European dimension.

Two weeks after his visit to Poland, Kohl addressed the Council of Europe in Strasbourg. He stated firmly that Warsaw, Budapest, Leipzig and other cities in East Central Europe were just as European as London, Rome and Paris.[38] It was also in this context that Kohl said 'German and European unity are two sides of the same coin' which, incidentally, did not refer to West European integration, as popularly acknowledged, but to the process of uniting eastern and western Europe.

A few days later, the German Chancellor presented his ten-point plan, which deeply disappointed the Poles because of the omission of the border question. This development caused the Polish side to effectively freeze the process of rapprochement through institutional means, which was postponed until after the border question had been finally resolved. Instead, Warsaw focused on pursuing a bilateral and noninstitutional solution. As argued before, since the publication of the ten-point plan Warsaw had demanded from Bonn a strictly bilateral treaty that would finally close the frontier question. The treaty, Warsaw argued, should be completed before the unification process.

This contradicted Kohl's policy of finalising the border question as part of an extensive document that would regulate a large range of issues and which would bring the context of European integration into Polish–German relations.[39] Although in principle Mazowiecki was supportive of such a grand treaty, he wanted to address the border issue separately. This policy was largely motivated by Poland's anticipation that negotiating a larger 'European' treaty would be a lengthy process which would delay solving the frontier issue indefinitely.[40] Finally, the Polish position of decoupling the border regulation from a comprehensive 'Good Neighbourly Relations' treaty was agreed to by Bonn, and while the first was signed almost immediately after unification the second was completed only some nine months later.

However, even during the tense period between the publication of the ten-point plan and the resolution of the territorial conflict Warsaw was careful not to completely abandon the European theme in relations with Germany. Thus, for example, it was at the end of February 1990, during one of the lowest ebbs in Bonn-Warsaw relations (when Warsaw successfully lobbied for international support in the border dispute) that Skubiszewski spoke about the German–Polish 'community of interests' and posed the question: *Was können wir gemeinsam für Europa tun?* (What can we do together for Europe?). Skubiszewski's notion probably helped to improve the atmosphere between Bonn and Warsaw yet, it could not be pursued at that moment in time. In fact, it was not until the 'Good Neighbourly Relations' treaty of November 1991 was finalised that a genuinely 'new' Polish–German relationship could begin to be built.

The treaty of good neighbourly relations and friendly co-operation

The treaty was a fundamentally different document than the earlier border settlement. It introduced strong normative elements: human rights, the rule of law and the condemnation of discrimination of people on religious and political grounds.[41] It also brought into the relationship multilateral-institutional elements, most importantly a German promise to support Poland's membership in the EC and in the Council of Europe. A number of international regulations were also incorporated, principally to address the question of the German minority in Poland, questions of environmental degradation in the border region and cross-border co-operation.

The successful implementation of the treaty's provisions was reinforced by the creation of a number of bilateral initiatives. In a deliberate imitation of the Franco-German Elysée treaty of 1963, the agreement established a number of bilateral institutions, most importantly a biannual summit meeting between the heads of governments, foreign, defence and other ministers as well as top civil servants from both countries. As was the case with the Franco-German document, the treaty established a youth exchange organisation as well as a joint council for environmental protection and a number of regional cross-border bodies.[42] The treaty also actively promoted reconciliation through the setting up of cultural institutes and a joint schoolbooks' commission. Finally, the treaty provided a framework for co-operation between parliaments, political parties, churches and various non-governmental organisations (NGO).

On the whole the 'Good Neighbourly Relations and Friendly Co-operation' agreement rested on the assumption of a normative congruence, which needed to be empowered through a number of multilevel institutions. In particular, special emphasis was put on the importance of European integration. During the subsequent ratification debate in the *Bundestag*, Helmut Kohl stressed three levels of institutional co-operation envisaged in the treaty. These were: *multilateral* – Poland's future membership in the EC and its links with NATO; *bilateral-intergovernmental* – various consultative bodies; and *bilateral-non-governmental* – cross-regional co-operation and youth exchange. The German Chancellor also emphasised Germany's 'special responsibility' for the success of the Polish reforms which, according to Kohl, had led Bonn to become Warsaw's advocate in the West. In this context Bonn had lobbied for the re-scheduling of Poland's foreign debt and for the introduction of visa-free travel for Polish citizens in EU Schengen countries (the EU common immigration area). Most importantly, however, according to Kohl, Germany's 'special responsibility' meant that Bonn would support Poland's bid to join the EC/EU.

Interestingly, from the onset of Germany's support for Poland's integration with the EC/EU, a split emerged among German elites between the supporters of a quick enlargement and the proponents of a deepening of European integration prior to expanding the Community's membership. While during the ratification debate Hans Koschnick (SPD) urged for a swift opening of the Community to Poland and criticised the notion of 'deepening before enlarging', Karl Lamers (CDU) stressed exactly the opposite.[43] The argument 'deepening versus widening' – clearly a critical issue for Polish–German relations during the 1990s – indicated that a profound qualitative change in the nature of the relationship had occurred. It was no longer merely questions of security threats and territorial issues that were to shape Bonn-Warsaw relations, but rather more nuanced and complex differences regarding the nature and detail of Poland's integration with the EC/EU were now framing the relationship. In short, bilateral relations were now an integral part of broader European developments.

This new complexity did not mean that with the treaty coming in to force difficult issues of the past had disappeared from German–Polish relations. In fact, just as most German CDU/CSU Members of Parliament (MPs) were, from the very outset, supportive of Poland's future membership in the EC/EU, they also clearly imagined that the Germans who had been expelled from Poland at the end of the war would be given a chance to return as Poland drew closer to the Community.[44] In other words, the European solution to relations with Poland was not only about addressing Germany's 'special responsibility' but also the CDU's domestic interests. However, the Polish side remained reluctant to help the German Chancellor on this issue and although some promises to allow German citizens to resettle in Poland were articulated in the letter attached to the treaty, no mention of such a possibility could be found in the document itself.[45]

Mixed outcomes

With the end of the Cold War both Poland and Germany underwent profound transformations. The international bipolar framework that had ultimately shaped their relationship before 1989, disappeared with the collapse of the USSR. In the meantime Germany was heading towards re-unification and Poland departed from communism and moved swiftly towards liberal-democracy.

This new situation opened up the possibility for establishing peaceful neighbourly co-existence between Bonn and Warsaw and the creation of a 'special relationship', akin to that of the Franco-German axis. Despite these opportunities this new context disoriented both Poland and (West) Germany, whose bilateral relations had in the past been determined by a structurally and externally determined conflict. While both Kohl and Mazowiecki quickly moved to build a new relationship, they also very soon stumbled into a number of obstacles. Significantly, when dealing with difficult issues both the Polish Prime Minister and West German Chancellor reverted to methods that they were familiar with rather than to a new 'European spirit' as was espoused in their declaration.

In practice, this meant that when dealing with the frontier issue Poland chose non-institutional solutions marked by forceful diplomacy, which included elements of balancing Paris and Moscow against Bonn. Warsaw also preferred a strictly bilateral settlement of the border question irrespective of the larger 'European' treaty on 'Good Neighbourly Relations and Friendly Co-operation'. The Federal Republic, on the other hand, pushed for an institutional approach in this instance as apparent in Kohl's preference to sign just one 'European'-style agreement also to include the border regulation. However, as argued earlier, Bonn's use of an institutional strategy was in this instance instrumental, serving its self-interest.

These divergent strategies demonstrate that the relationship suffered from a lack of mutual trust and inexperience in 'practising reciprocity'. While Warsaw had to learn to conceive of and conduct a new and independent foreign policy, Bonn failed to adjust its approach to the specifics of the Polish situation. Thus, Mazowiecki initially displayed a fair amount of naïveté in his apparent belief that his democratic credentials and will to reconcile with Germany would be enough for Bonn to recognise the Oder-Neisse border. When these assumptions turned out to be false, Mazowiecki became excessively insecure and sceptical about Kohl's intentions while the latter felt offended for not being trusted.[46]

This importance of 'knowing each other' was also illustrated in the striking difference that emerged in Poland's relations with Bonn and East Berlin. During the debates on the border question, a former dissident and subsequently East German Foreign Minister, Marcus Meckel, sided with Mazowiecki rather than with Kohl. While explaining his position Meckel argued that he simply had a better understanding and empathy towards Poland, which had come about through his involve-ment in the East German dissident movement.[47] Clearly, no such factors existed in Warsaw's relations with Bonn.

In sum, (West) German and Polish strategies employed between 1989 and 1991 gave rise to a complex relationship marked by prevailing mis-trust alongside efforts to build firm foundations for future close co-operation in Europe. In spite of this rather mixed outcome, the qual-ity and extent of the changes that emerged during this period took the relationship on to a higher level in the 1990s. The relationship did not only simply improve, its dynamics were transformed in such a way that first, domestic factors and secondly, western international institutions were brought to centre stage.

On the matter of domestic factors, as policy developments of 1989–90 demonstrated, democratic identity was of central importance for new Polish–German relations. For example, the 'Good Neighbourly Relations and Friendly Co-operation' treaty went beyond addressing problems of bilateral relations in that it envisaged the Federal Repub-lic's assistance in building democratic institutions and the social market economy in Poland.[48] Clearly, the completion of this treaty would not have been possible had Poland not embarked on internal democrati-sation. In all other spheres – for example, the border issue – it would be difficult to imagine that Poland would have received comparable support from the western community, and indeed from Germany itself, had it not pioneered democratic change in East Central Europe.

Another crucial innovation was the recognition by both sides of the role that institutions could play in their relationship. As argued before, both Bonn and Warsaw perceived European integration as the frame-work most suited to construct their new neighbourly relations. This was expressed in the Federal Republic's political and technical support for Poland to join the Community. But a number of European Council reg-ulations were also chosen to redress some specific issues in this rela-tionship; for example, the minority question. How Warsaw handled the issue of Germany's NATO membership was also of great significance. Despite initial hesitations, Mazowiecki and Skubiszewski finally decided against the policy of balancing the USSR against Germany. Instead, Warsaw adhered to the view that its own security would be best guar-anteed if Germany remained tied to the North Atlantic Alliance.

These points notwithstanding it is argued strongly here that both democratisation and the growing importance of western institutions to the relationship did not lead instantly to a full congruence of interests between Poland and (West) Germany. Indeed, the case of the border dispute demonstrated that the presence of democracy could also serve to aggravate conflict, since both German and Polish foreign policies were responsive to conflicting domestic pressures. While Kohl was constrained by a need to mollify the expellees in his own party, Mazowiecki was faced with a very unstable domestic environment marked by growing discontent with the rapprochement with Germany.

A similar conflict existed between France and West Germany in the 1950s, with regard to the Saar region. These tensions were successfully alleviated through both countries participation in western integration, which facilitated the solution of the question. Poland's aspiration to join western institutions certainly served as a congruence-promoting factor; however, since Poland was outside of the EC/EU, the possibility of a Polish–German axis emerging, akin to the Franco-German model, remained elusive at this stage.

Conclusion: 'Europeanisation' after the end of the Cold War

With the end of the Cold War all four pre-conditions for the 'Europeanisation' of Polish–German relations – structural-international, democratic government, western integration and reconciliation – had begun to exist, making a genuine rapprochement possible for the first time since the eighteenth century. Most significantly, the structural-international conditions of the relationship were transformed, thus removing a major obstacle to the relationship's 'Europeanisation'. The chapter nevertheless demonstrated that the relationship was by no means free from controversy and conflict. It is argued here that this was the case principally because of the novelty of the new situation and the fact that Poland continued to be an outsider in western institutional structures. It is true that Poland was becoming a democratic state and that the reconciliation process had been set in motion after November 1989. However, in the absence of an international institutional framework to the relationship, in the form of the EC/EU and NATO, the relationship was often constructed through reflexive or even knee-jerk policy manoeuvres, sometimes geared towards meeting the demands of domestic interest groups.

The conclusion of this argument is that the 'Europeanisation' of Polish–German could not be fully launched during this period. The observations made in this chapter suggest that subsequent investigation should concentrate on EU and NATO enlargements, which became the main foci of the relationship throughout the 1990s. By adopting this focus the book no longer needs to devote as much attention to the structural-international conditions of the relationship, which have remained largely favourable since 1989–90. In turn, the prospect of the institutionalisation of the relationship – in bilateral terms and in the form of EC/EU and NATO memberships – necessitates a greater focus upon domestic factors and developments. In short, as both Poland and Germany have pursued the goals of NATO and EU enlargements the momentum towards 'Europeanisation' has become increasingly dependent on a growing number of domestic issues, both economic and political. These will be investigated in Chapters 5 and 6.

Notes

1 Helmut Kohl (interviewed by Kai Diekmann and Georg Reuth), *Pragnąłem Jedności Niemiec* (Warsaw: Politeja, 1999), pp. 68–9; for the German edition, see Helmut Kohl, *Ich wollte Deutschlands Einheit* (Berlin: Propyläen Verlag, 1996).

2 Quoted in Louisa Vinton, 'Domestic Politics and Foreign Policy, 1989–1993', in Ilya Prizel and Andrew A. Michta (eds), *Polish Foreign Policy Reconsidered: Challenges to Independence* (New York: St Martin's Press, 1995), p. 40.

3 See Kohl, *Pragnąłem Jedności Niemiec*, pp. 67–9.

4 Horst Teltschik, *329 Tage: Innenansichten der Einigung* (Berlin: Siedler Verlag, 1991), p. 16.

5 Adam Daniel Rotfeld and Walter Stützle (eds), *Germany and Europe in Transition* (Oxford: Sipri and Oxford University Press, 1998), pp. 130, 135.

6 See 'Der Zehn-Punkte-Plan zur Überwindung der Teilung Deutschlands und Europas', *Europa Archiv*, No. 24, 1989, p. D 728–30.

7 See Jan Barcz, *Udział Polski w Konferencji '2 + 4': aspekty prawne i proceduralne* (Warsaw: PISM, 1994), pp. 20–4.

8 For example see J. Abr. Frowein, 'Rechtliche Probleme der Einigung Deutschlands', *Europa Archiv*, No. 7 1990, pp. 325–6.

9 See Krzysztof Skubiszewski, 'Die völkerrechtliche und staatliche Einheit des deutschen Volkes und die Entwicklung in Europa', *Europa Archiv*, Bonn, 7 February 1990.

10 See Rotfeld and Stützle (eds), *Germany and Europe in Transition*, pp. 135–7; Barcz, *Udział Polski w Konferencji '2 + 4'*, pp. 114–16.

11 See 'Bulletin des Presse- und Informationsamtes der Bundesregierung', No. 32, 1990, p. 268.

12   See Teltschik, *329 Tage*, pp. 147–211.

13   Barcz, *Udział Polski w Konferencji '2 + 4'*, pp. 30–1.

14   See Teltschik, *329 Tage*, pp. 164–75.

15   Kohl, *Pragnąlem Jedności Niemiec*, p. 190.

16   Barcz, *Udział Polski w Konferencji '2 + 4'*, pp. 43, 57.

17   *Ibid.*, pp. 152–3.

18   This is how the government's spokesperson Małgorzata Niezabitowska described the USSR at the press conference organised during Mazowiecki's meeting with Gorbachev in November 1989; see: Thomas Urban, *Süddeutsche Zeitung*, January 1990.

19   Quoted in Vinton, 'Domestic Politics and Foreign Policy, 1989–1993', p. 40

20   Janusz Reiter, *Gazeta Wyborcza*, 14 February 1990.

21   See Richard Weitz, 'Pursuing Military Security in Eastern Europe', in Robert O. Keohane, Joseph S. Nye and Stanley Hoffmann, *After the Cold War: International Institutions and State Strategies in Europe, 1989–1991* (Cambridge, MA and London: Harvard University Press, 1993), p. 358.

22   See Vinton, 'Domestic Politics and Foreign Policy, 1989–1993', p. 42.

23   See Arthur Hajnicz, *Ze Sobą czy Przeciw Sobie* (Warsaw: Presspublica, 1995) pp. 120–3.

24   Teltschick, *329 Tage*, p. 55.

25   Teltschick, *329 Tage*, p. 64–7.

26   Teltschick, *329 Tage*, pp. 123–4.

27   See: Teltschick, *329 Tage*, p. 138.

28   See 'History Made us Neighbours. Interview given by President Mikhail Gorbachev to *Pravda*, Moscow, February 1990', in Rotfeld and Stützle (eds), *Germany and Europe in Transition*, pp. 101–4.

29   See 'Too fast and too slow. Interview given by President Mikhail Gorbachev, Moscow, 6 March 1990', in Rotfeld and Stützle (eds), *Germany and Europe in Transition*, pp. 105–6.

30   For example, see Hajnicz, *Ze Sobą czy Przeciw Sobie*, pp. 56–62.

31   For example see Teltschick's account on Kohl's conversation with Skubiszewski: Teltschick, *329 Tage*, p. 132.

32   For this speech, see Rotfeld and Stützle (eds), *Germany and Europe in Transition*, pp. 130–4.

33   *Ibid.*, pp. 135–7.

34   See Philip Zelikow and Condoleezza Rice, *Germany Unified and Europe Transformed: A Study in Statecraft* (Cambridge, MA: Harvard University Press, 1995), p. 221

35   See Rotfeld and Stützle (eds), *Germany and Europe in Transition*, p. 123.

36   Kohl, *Pragnąlem Jedności Niemiec*, p. 218.

37   See 'Hans Adolf Jacobsen und Mieczysław Tomala (eds), *Bonn-Warschau 1945–1991, Die Deutsch-Polnischen Beziehungen, Analyse und Dokumentation* (Cologne: Verlag Wissenschaft und Politik, 1992), pp. 501–10.

38 Kohl, *Pragnąłem Jedności Niemiec*, pp. 86–8.
39 Kohl, *Pragnąłem Jedności Niemiec*, p. 262.
40 Barcz, *Udział Polski w Konferencji '2 + 4'*, pp. 66, 69–70.
41 See Jacobsen und Tomala (eds), *Bonn-Warschau 1945–1991*, pp. 552–64.
42 See Alistair Cole, *Franco-German Relations* (London: Longman, 2001), pp. 49–51.
43 For this debate see Jan Barcz and Mieczysław Tomala, *Polska-Niemcy, dobre sąsiedztwo i przyjazna współpraca* (Warsaw: Polska Fundacja Spraw Międzynarodowych, 1991), pp. 52, 61, 63.
44 *Ibid.*, pp. 49–57, 62–5, 75–8.
45 See Jacobsen und Tomala (eds), *Bonn-Warschau 1945–1991*, pp. 564–5.
46 Kohl, *Pragnąłem Jedności Niemiec*, pp. 190, 262.
47 Interview with Marcus Meckel, Bonn, 12 April 1998.
48 See articles 9, 10 and 34.

5

Fostering strategic congruence: the politics of NATO and EU enlargements in Polish–German relations, 1991–98

We have lived with our neighbour Germany for 1000 years, but always back to back. Never face to face. (Edward Pietrzyk, Polish Military Officer, on his nation's admission to NATO)[1]

Introduction

The discord over the border question in 1989–90 recreated some of the deep strategic divergences that had plagued Polish-West German relations during the Cold War. Once again, the vital interests of the two countries appeared irreconcilable and Warsaw came to act as if Germany might pose a real danger to its security. However, with the final confirmation of the Oder-Neisse border and with the completion of the 'Good Neighbourly Relations and Friendly Co-operation' Treaty in 1991 the relationship became marked by a growing congruence of strategic objectives. For Poland, Germany represented a powerful ally in the EU and NATO where Berlin lobbied in favour of eastern enlargements, constantly stressing the primacy of Poland's application. For Germany, Poland's membership in these organisations and in particular the EU, would mean greater stability in its eastern neighbourhood and potential economic benefits resulting from Germany's privileged position in the region. It is therefore unsurprising that the relationship dramatically improved throughout most of the 1990s being fostered on the one hand by the efforts of governing elites in both countries and, on the other by a number of institutions set up by the 1991 treaty and other subsequent agreements.

As argued in Chapter 4, by the early 1990s the general conditions of the relationship has started to take a shape conducive with

'Europeanisation'. The Cold War had ended, Poland was democratising, the reconciliation process was becoming dynamic and both countries supported Poland's integration with the West. As seen earlier in the case of Franco-(West) German relations the first and most essential step towards 'Europeanisation' was to achieve a congruence of strategic aims and objectives. A clear manifestation of such a congruence between those two countries was an agreement to set up the European Coal and Steel Community (ECSC) in 1951 and, a decade later the Elysée treaty, establishing a uniquely close relationship verging on a political union. It was always clear that in the Polish–German case a common project would be to secure Poland's integration with the West by promoting its membership in NATO and the EU. The period between the completion of the bilateral treaty in 1991 and the beginning of Poland's EU membership negotiations in 1998 was the time when such a congruence was being discovered, defined and successfully pursued. It is the purpose of this chapter to discuss this process.

The chapter is divided into four sections. The first two look, respectively, at key developments during the political phases of NATO and EU enlargements, which arguably ended in 1998. The third discusses some specific materially and culturally defined interests of the two countries and considers their congruence as well as their continuing divergence. In the final section, the chapter examines the case of Franco-(West) German relations while considering the prospects for German and Polish policies becoming not only reconcilable but also being redefined through their partnership in the enlarging EU.

NATO enlargement

In support of pan-European security structures

In the immediate wake of German unification, Berlin's security policy towards Poland remained guided by its traditional 'Russia-first' policy, partly because there were still 400,000 Russian troops on German territory. At this point, Berlin was not yet prepared to consider the prospect of actual NATO membership for Poland and other East Central Europeans; instead, it focused on promoting the development of pan-European security structures, particularly in the form of the CSCE. Until the end of 1991, this policy was generally in line with the expectations of East Central Europeans who, still formally Warsaw Pact members, were at the time preoccupied with dismantling the remaining divisions and hence well disposed towards the development of pan-European security structures composed of both Eastern and Western Bloc countries. Such a view was voiced by the Polish Foreign Minister, Krzysztof Skubiszewski, who during his first visit to NATO, did not suggest the possibility of Poland applying for membership in the alliance, speaking instead of the benefits of establishing a pan-European security system.[2] A similar view prevailed in Prague, which at this point argued against maintaining the 'alliances of the past', including NATO, and in favour of a more robust CSCE.[3]

Besides the CSCE, Bonn also emphasised the security role of the EU as a suitable instrument for replacing Cold War-style alliances. The most immediate security problems of the region, Berlin argued, were to do with market access and 'soft' security issues – the environment, migration and criminal trafficking.[4] These new 'soft' security problems, Bonn argued, could not be addressed by NATO but rather only by EU enlargement. However, external developments were soon to put NATO back at the centre. In August 1991, just over a month after the formal dissolution of the Warsaw Pact, Soviet Vice-President Yanayev and his conservative colleagues staged a *coup* aimed at overthrowing Gorbachev and restoring the Soviet empire. The *coup* failed after just two days but the message for East Central Europe and the West was chilling – there was no guarantee that the ongoing demise of Soviet imperialism would be sustained. Reacting to the events in Moscow, German Foreign Minister Hans-Dietrich Genscher and American State Secretary James Baker initiated a new organisation called the North Atlantic Co-operation Council which was to bring together members of NATO, East Central Europe and the Soviet Union.[5] But, this initiative did not satisfy the Poles and others in the region. The leaders of the Visegrád group (Poland, Hungary and Czechoslovakia), met at an emergency summit in Cracow where, for the first time clearly and unambiguously, they expressed their nation's desire to join NATO. To strengthen this call, the Polish President Lech Wałęsa spoke about the multiple security threats resulting from the emergence of a 'grey security sphere' in East Central Europe after the break-up of the Warsaw Pact and following the events in the Soviet Union.[6]

The road to NATO enlargement

These pressures from Poland notwithstanding, the real possibility of NATO membership was strengthened by a number of mutually reinforcing factors, most crucially the dissolution of the Soviet Union and the war in Yugoslavia. Meanwhile in the West, the Maastricht treaty failed to establish a meaningful common foreign and security policy, and the EU lost credibility by its inability to address the Yugoslav crisis. These events bolstered the Visegrád Four's resolve to become NATO members and henceforth their diplomatic efforts focused on this goal.

However, the response from the West was not very encouraging. In its early days, the Clinton administration's view on the matter was influenced by Strobe Talbott, the President's advisor on Russia and, initially a critic of NATO enlargement. A similar view emanated from London, with Defence Secretary Malcolm Rifkind rejecting the idea on the grounds that it would create new divisions in Europe – and, perhaps more importantly for London, could undermine NATO's internal cohesion.[7] The German position on the issue was not unanimous, but it was in Germany that the idea began to be seriously considered and eventually supported by the government. One of the first supporters of the notion was the German Defence Minister Volker Rühe who delivered a clearly pro-enlargement speech at the London based International Institute for Strategic Studies (IISS) in March 1993. The thrust of his argument was that Eastern Europe could not remain a 'conceptual no-man's land': the region was increasingly a zone of instability, threatened by ethnic wars, nationalism and fragmentation, and the means to prevent this was the extension of western institutions eastwards. Rühe also stressed that the enlargement should be quick, as 'Europe did not have time to postpone such actions', and in effect argued in favour of enlarging NATO prior to EU accession, which was at odds with mainstream German thinking on the matter at the time.[8]

However, Rühe's argument was challenged by the Foreign Office – and, more importantly it was not initially underpinned by Kohl who was focusing, at the time on appeasing Russia's concerns.[9] Nevertheless, the Defence Minister succeeded in planting the seeds of the internal German debate. In addition, the enlargement case was soon to receive a decisive boost with the electoral success of ultra-nationalist Vladimir Zhirinovsky, who openly preached Russia's imperialism and territorial expansion. The results of the Russian elections provided a wake-up call for the German establishment, bringing into the public eye vivid images of post-Soviet fascism and the memories of Soviet participation in the 1939 partition of Poland.

Illustrative of the German response to the ultra-nationalists' success in the Duma (the Russian Parliament) was an issue of *Der Spiegel* magazine. The edition put on its front cover a picture of Zhirinovsky dressed in his favourite combat uniform and posed in Hitler's shadow. This was accompanied by a vehement article in favour of Poland's NATO membership written by the magazine's editor Rudolf Augestein and entitled 'Poland in Danger' (*Bedrohtes Polen*).[10] The publication was striking not only for its declaratory and emotional rhetoric 'Poland belongs to Europe, whatever kind of Europe it will be, and this is the way it must be!',[11] but also because until that moment *Der Spiegel* had not been known for being particularly pro-Polish or supportive of NATO enlargement.

The 'Zhirinovsky factor' served to strengthen calls for NATO enlargement within the governing CDU, whose foreign policy spokesperson, Friedbert Pflüger, appealed to the *Bundestag* for a quick completion of the accession process.[12] In the wake of these developments Berlin's official security policy towards Poland evolved into a policy of NATO enlargement. Once the enlargement issue had been broached and accepted as an objective of the alliance at the Madrid summit in 1994, Germany acted as a full and active advocate and shaper of it. This was in line with Warsaw's preferences that, for geopolitical reasons, focused on Berlin in expectation that the latter would be the main advocate of NATO enlargement. With active German support, the first round of NATO enlargement occurred on 13 March 1999, incorporating Poland, the Czech Republic and Hungary into the Alliance.

The case of NATO enlargement demonstrates the massive progress in reconciling Polish and German security perspectives since the end of the Cold War. From belonging to confronting alliances, through the dissolution of the Warsaw Pact, to being partners in NATO, Bonn/Berlin-Warsaw relations had undergone a remarkable evolution. Unsurprisingly, there was widespread opinion amongst Polish elites, that Germany remained Poland's main security partner.[13] The significance of Germany's advocacy of NATO enlargement went beyond the recasting of security relations in East Central Europe. It also had a profound impact on the perception of Germany in Poland. In particular, by promoting Poland's NATO membership and in effect ignoring

Moscow's veto, the Federal Republic departed from the traditional 'Russia first' policy, which had hitherto guided its *Ostpolitik*. Had Bonn–Berlin not done this, the Polish–German reconciliation project would have had little chance of success. This had significant and positive implications for the progress of *Europeanisation*.

The process of bringing German and Polish security policies to converge was clearly a difficult task. However, once a strategic break-through in Bonn's eastern policy had been achieved and NATO enlargement won the day in the Federal Republic, both countries co-operated smoothly to achieve the goal.

The EU enlargement process was different. Although the strategic priorities of German and Polish foreign policies intersected on this issue right from the very early days after 1989, this congruence was only a pre-condition, and hence only the beginning of the actual EU enlargement process.

The politics of EU enlargement

The nature of European integration and its rather under-developed security dimension meant that the idea of fostering EC/EU co-opera-tion with East Central Europe was relatively uncontroversial, so it found early supporters both in Germany and Poland even prior to the end of the Cold War. In Poland, an overwhelming sense of 'belonging to Europe' prevailed among the population throughout the post-war period and, importantly, the idea of co-operating with the EC/EU was always considered in a framework of improving Polish–(West) German relations. As argued earlier, since the 1970s even the Polish Communists had worked towards developing trade relations with the EC, and with West Germany in particular. But the real change of attitude towards West Germany and the EC was to come from the non-communist opposition. In 1976, the dissident group, called the 'Polish Alliance for Independence', broke the unspoken Polish consensus by arguing that the unification of Germany would serve Poland's inter-ests. The Alliance's manifesto put this argument in the following words:

> Unification of Germany in the framework of the European Community would result in Poland having direct contact with the West ... it would create an opportunity for co-operation with the European Communities and finally it would let Poland choose what kind of alliances and organisations it would want to belong to.[14]

The link between German unification and Poland's reintegration with the West made explicitly in this manifesto was to be adopted by major dissident groups in Poland and subsequently strongly influenced the foreign policy of the first non-communist government of Mazowiecki. In West Germany, some ideas in favour of fostering East Central Europe's participation in the common market originated from within the left wing of the SPD, which was looking for ways to revitalise their flagging *Ostpolitik*.[15] While the Cold War prevented these ideas from being seriously considered in the early 1980s, by the end of the decade Bonn was increasingly hinting at the prospects of actual EC membership for Germany's eastern neighbours.[16]

With Mazowiecki's government coming to power in 1989 Bonn was immediately identified by Warsaw as its main advocate in the process of Poland's 'return to Europe'. Bonn also welcomed the principle of Poland's integration with the West which, as argued by Kohl, dramatically enhanced the chances for the unification of Germany.[17] Although, as argued in Chapter 4, Polish–German relations suffered subsequently from the re-opening of the border question in 1989–90, the issue of Poland's membership in the EC/EU was kept alive and acquired further impetus in the wake of the border treaty in November 1990. Bonn's preference for Poland's integration with the EC/EU was not weakened as a result of German unification and the initial rationale (unification) was replaced by an emphasis on stabilising the Federal Republic's regional milieu. These strategic considerations were reflected in Germany's consistent advocacy of the enlargement process, and of Poland's EU membership in particular.

Between the 'Europe agreements' and accession negotiations

In December 1991 Poland, Czechoslovakia and Hungary concluded the so-called 'Europe Agreement', which liberalised trade between the EC and these countries. While the agreements lacked any real meaningful political dimension and did not commit the EC/EU to the principle of enlargement, Germany, together with Britain, managed to push through a clause that recognised these countries' desire to join the EC/EU in the future.[18] Subsequently, Berlin continued to promote the principle of enlargement, by supporting, for example, the report by EU Commissioner Hans Andriessen, which recommended that a set of criteria be established that would be pre-conditions for starting actual membership negotiations with the former Soviet Bloc countries.[19] With

active German support, these criteria were agreed upon at the Copenhagen summit in 1993, leading to the prospect of eastern enlargement
becoming official EU policy. The 'Copenhagen criteria', as they became
known, were both political and economic, referring to the rule of law,
functioning democracy, human rights and an ability to compete in the
common market. As such, the criteria reflected some key preferences
of the German government which, deeply concerned with developments in the former Yugoslavia, was determined that the conditions
set out by the EU should aim to foster stability in its eastern neighbourhood. A certain peculiarity of the Copenhagen criteria was the
inclusion of human and minority rights. This was questionable from
the moral point of view as the EU did not have any such standards
for itself and had therefore to refer to the Council of Europe's Charter
of Human Rights, but the inclusion of this condition was strongly pursued by Germany. Berlin believed that setting a clear normative
standard for the applicant countries would discourage them from
pursuing nationalistic policies which, as the case of Yugoslavia demonstrated, could have resulted in the uncontrollable migration of refugees
to Germany. An additional 'benefit' of the criterion was that it would
effectively exclude Turkey from the enlargement, which was consonant
with Berlin's preference at the time.

Once agreed upon, the Copenhagen criteria spelt out a clear perspective for joining the EU for Poland and other hopefuls, who
responded by putting forward their membership applications between
1993 and 1994. However, while politically the principle of enlargement
seemed accepted, it was clear that the accession countries would struggle to meet all the legal and technical requirements that needed to be
adopted prior to the opening of actual negotiations. Responding to this
predicament the German EU presidency in 1994 established a 'structural
relationship' for East Central Europeans that permitted the candidate
countries to participate in some of the EU's internal affairs,[20] and subsequently Berlin promoted a so-called 'pre-accession strategy' which
gave candidate countries access to some EU programmes, including
legal and technical assistance.[21]

In its advocacy of the enlargement process, Germany initially exhib-
ited a preference for a quick (preferably by 2000) but territorially
limited expansion of the EU, including only Poland, the Czech Republic and Hungary.[22] Berlin initially maintained this position during the
EU's Luxembourg summit in December 1997, when the issue of which
countries should be invited to start negotiations was debated. However,

Berlin eventually bent under pressure from other member states, particularly the Nordic countries, and agreed that the EU should start negotiations with the group of six applicants (Poland, the Czech Republic, Hungary, Estonia, Slovenia, Cyprus), while continuing the so-called 'screening' of other candidates with a view that they should join the negotiations as soon as they could meet the Copenhagen criteria.[23] Consequently, it was agreed at the summit in Berlin in 1999 that six other countries – Lithuania, Latvia, Slovakia, Bulgaria, Romania and Malta – would join the negotiations.

From the moment the actual decision to launch membership negotiations with Poland was reached, the Federal Republic's lobbying in favour of 'speeding-up' the process showed signs of weakening. This happened essentially for two reasons. The first resulted from an ever-greater number of domestic actors becoming involved in the process and influencing the government's policy on the matter. This process, referred to here as 'domestication', will be addressed in Chapter 6. The second difficulty was strategic and had to do with an increasingly poor fit between the two key objectives of German European policy – 'widening' and 'deepening' – which up to this point had been seen in Berlin as perfectly reconcilable. In fact, enlargement was often perceived as a useful argument in favour of the reform of EU institutions and its decision-making procedures.

However, this logic was not universally accepted by the proponents of establishing a genuine political union in the EU, including members of the governing CDU, who tended to see enlargement as potentially contradicting the goal of an 'ever-closer union'. Consequently, a number of proposals emerged from these circles, the most famous of these being the Schäuble–Lamers paper that argued in favour of 'differentiated integration' as a way of preserving the EU's internal cohesion after enlargement.[24] These arguments were not unsympathetically received by Kohl, himself a dedicated 'European'. However, whether Kohl lost his enthusiasm for the notion or encountered too stiff resistance from other members of the EU, it is clear that the principle of 'differentiated integration' – or 'flexibility', as it became known – found only a small mention in the Intergovernmental Conference (IGC) in Amsterdam in 1997.

The Amsterdam treaty, which was supposed to prepare the EU for its enlargement, did not satisfy its domestic critics. It also did not address the growing tensions in Franco-German relations over the eastern enlargement of the EU. France, increasingly uneasy about the idea and its impact upon the balance of power in the EU, was supportive of the principle of 'differentiated integration' with an inner circle being built around France and Germany, and hoping that this would enable Paris to retain its privileged position in the EU.[25]

The EU therefore began the enlargement negotiations in 1998 as a body insufficiently reformed in the view of many members of the German government and opposition. The internal German debate on the matter did not result in any substantially new policies and, with the exception of France, the proposals, which suggested a setting up of a mechanism of differentiated integration did not meet with much enthusiasm abroad. The German government, faced with increasing economic difficulties at home, chose to take on board a more 'pragmatic' stance towards enlargement. This was characterised by retaining political support for the notion but coupling it with an ever-growing emphasis on the need to protect domestic interests as the EU opened up to the East. As mentioned earlier, this post-1997 change in Germany's EU enlargement policy will be addressed in Chapter 6.

Despite these issues and reservations that started to emerge in Germany after 1997 it should be noted that German and Polish enlargement policies were predominantly reconcilable, if not complementary. Most importantly, these policies were based on the strategic perspectives of the two countries that had come to see Poland's integration with the West as beneficial for their security and economic interests. The following section addresses the material and cultural basis of this strategic congruence which, as argued earlier, constitutes a necessary step towards the 'Europeanisation' of interstate relations.

Explaining strategic congruence

While it is apparent that some vital interests of Poland and Germany converged closely through the processes of NATO and EU enlargements, it may remain unclear just 'how' and 'why' it exactly happened. This section seeks to explore two essential sources of these policies and poses two broad types of explanation; 'power maximisation' and 'historical legacies'.

The 'power maximisation' idea stresses material notions of economic and security interests whereas the 'historical legacies' argument emphasises historical experiences and political culture as shaping German and Polish perspectives on enlargement and European integration more broadly. The point made here is that Germany's 'inbred' attachment to multilateralism gelled with Poland's post-1989 desire to 'return to Europe', which resulted in a common position on enlargement. These arguments are addressed, beginning with the material explanation.

Power maximisation and power protection

Power maximisation

It is often argued that the reason why Berlin's and Warsaw's interests came to be reconcilable in the context of Poland's integration with the West was related to the fact that enlargement served to increase the relative powers of both states.[26] As far as Poland is concerned, there are two lines of argument according to which Warsaw would maximise its power through joining western institutions. The first argument is geopolitical in nature, and is based on the assumption that only through joining western institutions would Poland be able to protect its sovereignty against external threats.[27] Furthermore, it is argued that western integration would increase Poland's significance in the East, particularly in Ukraine and Lithuania, where it has traditionally located its interests. The second argument is related to modernisation and the economic expectations derived from EU membership. As stated in the Polish 'National Strategy of Integration', joining the EU would enable Poland to accelerate the process of economic modernisation and 'catching-up' with the West.[28] This argument is normally seen against the background of past enlargements to include less-developed states such as Spain, Ireland and Portugal which, it was believed in Poland, had led to an improvement of economic conditions in these countries. Both of these arguments have been contested, especially by the opponents of EU membership who emerged *en masse* after 1998 in Poland and argued that national sovereignty could not be enhanced through integration. Further criticism was directed at the economic implications of joining the EU on the grounds that integration would affect national industries, resulting in the growth of unemployment and the decline of heavy industry and agriculture.

In Germany's case it was often expected that East Central Europe's integration with the West would further increase Germany's weight in the global economy. This was based on an observation of the expansion of German industry in the region that followed the end of the Cold War. From the early 1990s Poland's trade with Germany accounted for roughly half of all its imports and exports with the EU and about a third of its overall trade. Germany also became a major foreign investor in Poland and in the other countries of the region, with German firms controlling a considerable share of the Polish banking sector.[29] This situation led to the growing dependence of East Central Europe on economic trends in the Federal Republic. At the same time, for Germany, trade with Poland, its largest partner in the region, barely reached two-thirds per cent of its overall exchange.[30]

Modell Deutschland *and Germany's economic domination?*
Evidence of the sort outlined above might lead to the conclusion that Germany's policy in East Central Europe was driven by an attempt to *maximise its power* in Europe, even to the point of domination. The best-known argument of the kind was presented by Andrei Markovits and Simon Reich in a paper published in 1991, entitled 'Should Europe Fear the Germans?', which maintained that Germany was poised to dominate East Central Europe both economically and culturally. The paper based its assumption on evidence of West Germany's success in 'exporting' its preferred model of international economic relations, based on free trade and undervalued currency, throughout the EC in the 1970s and 1980s. The export of *Modell Deutschland* to the rest of the EC brought about considerable advantages for West Germany, whose exports grew while other members of the Community recorded stagnation or decline in their trade exchange with West Germany. Importantly here, Markovits and Reich argued that a similar expansion of the German economy was bound to happen in East Central Europe after 1989, only to an even greater degree due to the region's structural weakness and its cultural attachment to Germany. Should this development occur, the authors maintained, it would lead to a situation in which, while enjoying its unrivalled position in the East, Germany would 'cement its hegemony in Western Europe'. Markovits and Reich clearly saw East Central Europe's integration with the West in terms of a 'zero-sum' game in which Germany was the winner.[31]

The article was written over a decade ago, it is therefore possible to assess its predictions with the benefit of hindsight. Developments in the 1990s demonstrate that few of the article's hypotheses were correct. As noted above, East Central Europe undoubtedly became an area of Germany's economic expansion. It is also true that the countries of the region willingly copied some elements of *Modell Deutschland* – in economics in the form of establishing independent Central Banks, and in politics as seen in the adoption of some elements of the German electoral constitution by Poland, Hungary and the Czech Republic. It would however, be far-fetched if not outright erroneous, to assume that the post-1989 export of *Modell Deutschland* was deliberately harmful to the economic and political interests of the countries of the region. Leaving aside the question of how significant *Modell Deutschland* actually was for post-1989 Poland, the overall balance of Poland's trade with Germany and the actual results of imitating Germany's political institutions speak against the Markovits–Reich hypothesis. True, as a result of liberalising its trade with the EU, Poland recorded an outstanding deficit in its current account in the 1990s (over 10 billion USD in 1998 and over 11 billion USD in 1999), which altogether amounted to over 80 per cent of Poland's entire trade deficit. However, against the Markovits–Reich prediction, the fact that Poland's account was so unbalanced had little to do with German economic expansionism. In fact, Poland's trade relations with Germany remained far more equal than its trade with other members of the EU; throughout most of the 1990s Poland had a relatively small deficit in its trade with Germany, with its imports being on average just 5–10 per cent higher than its exports to its western neighbour. This deficit appears insignificant when compared with the respective figures for Poland's trade with Italy, which show that in 1998–99 Poland bought from Italy twice as much as it sold.[32] In addition, the ratio of Poland's deficit with Germany declined in 2000 and since 2001 Poland's exports to Germany have exceeded its imports.[33] The changing configuration of Polish products sold in Germany – consistently fewer raw materials and more sophisticated products and machinery – is also generally seen as favourable for the Polish economy (Figure 5.1).[34] It would, therefore, be difficult to prove on strictly economic grounds that the Markovits–Reich thesis was validated by developments in the 1990s. In reality, the picture of post-1989 economic relations in East Central Europe has been far more complex. As argued above, the introduction of freer trade in Poland's relations with the EU proved to be more beneficial for EU member states than for Poland. While in 1998 Poland was exporting twice as much as in 1990 (28.2 billion USD and 14.3 billion USD, respectively) its imports grew by more than four times (from 9.5 billion USD in 1990 to 47 billion USD in 1998).[35] Leaving aside the question as to whether the 1990s trade deficit was really avoidable or harmful for Poland (it is argued that a high proportion of it was a result of foreign investment), it is abundantly clear from the data

Figure 5.1 Poland's trade with Italy and Germany, 1998–99

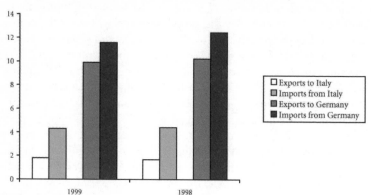

outlined above that Germany was not the prime cause of it. In actual fact, whatever deficit existed in Poland's relations with Germany in the 1990s, it is safe to assume that it was largely compensated by the unrecorded purchases made by Germans shopping in Polish border towns.

As far as cultural emulation is concerned, the expectations of Markovits and Reich that the German language would be widely spoken in East Central Europe has also not come about. In spite of the legacy of a German presence in the region, more people can speak English than German in today's Poland with Russian remaining the best-known foreign language.[36] However, although less prominent in the linguistic sphere, *Modell Deutschland* has had some impact upon the shape of democratic institutions that emerged after 1989. For example, the German model certainly inspired the draftees of the Polish electoral law, which was intended, with mixed success, to produce a German-style party system. The German federal system was also studied when Warsaw embarked in 1998 on devolving its powers to the regions. By no means, however, do these instances show that Germany has been set on dominating Poland culturally. There are two fundamental reasons why this has not been the case. Firstly, with regards to the electoral law, there was not a conscious German 'export' of an idea, but rather the German model acted as a point of inspiration for the Polish draftees who wanted to tackle political instability in the early 1990s. Secondly, it seems that Polish law-makers preferred to 'pick and choose' individual elements of more than one foreign model and then adjust them to their own setting rather than to copy an entire solution from abroad. Therefore, *Modell Deutschland* was almost never taken in its entirety and, in fact, it rarely served as a major foreign solution. For example, although *Modell Deutschland* was predominant in the setting up of a second tier of local government in Poland, the so-called *powiat*, a French unitary model prevailed in establishing the rules governing the third regional tier.[37]

In sum, there is little evidence suggesting that Germany's post-1989 policy towards Poland was predominantly driven by a desire to *maximise* its power in the region and in Europe as a whole and certainly not in the zero-sum model suggested by Markovits and Reich. Part of the reason why this was the case is to do with the changing perception of German security interests in East Central Europe.

Security and stability

With the end of the Cold War, the Federal Republic's position of a *Frontstaat* was transformed – it no longer feared Russian tanks on its streets; instead, it started to fear regional instability in Eastern and South Eastern Europe. As the upheavals in the former Yugoslavia and the Soviet Union were unfolding, the human and economic costs of these developments were especially felt in Germany, where the bulk of refugees chose to relocate. Reacting to these developments, the Federal Republic sought to promote *stability*, which became the leitmotif of its foreign policy towards the countries of the former Soviet Bloc. This, it was believed in Berlin, would best be achieved through the extension of western institutions to the region and first and foremost to Germany's immediate neighbours to the East. By completing the integration of East Central Europe into the West, Germany's sensitive status as a western frontier state would disappear, thereby considerably enhancing its security.[38] Moreover, with Poland's membership in western organisations, the socio-economic transformation of the region would be consolidated, with obvious benefits for the Federal Republic. Finally, Berlin also expected that the future accession of East Central Europe to common immigration rules as defined by the Schengen agreement, would help diminish the level of migration into the Federal Republic.[39]

In principle, this view converged with Polish aspirations, which were also focused on western institutions. However, until the mid-1990s some important differences persisted, regarding which institutions were best suited to address the region's post-Cold War security needs. It is true that from the very early days after the watershed of 1989, Bonn and Warsaw agreed that Poland should join the EC/EU. However, as argued earlier, while from 1992 Poland started to press for member-ship in NATO, Germany was initially divided on the issue, with the Defence Ministry in favour and the Foreign Office against the idea. The major reason why Berlin did not at first unequivocally support War-saw's plea to join NATO was related to diverging assessments of the security situation in the region which, as seen by many in Berlin, was more threatened by *instability* than the prospect of military aggression. As argued by Egon Bahr, one of the key architects of the 1960s and 1970s *Ostpolitik*, NATO was ill-suited to address the security threats that existed in East Central Europe at the time. Moreover, from a secu-rity point of view, Bahr and many others in Berlin argued, the expansion of the Alliance eastwards might prove only to be counter-productive, as it could lead to a growing sense of isolation and defeat in Russia, which in turn could lead to further instability in the region.[40] But Poland was not convinced by these arguments as it remained anx-ious about its 'new-yet-dangerously-familiar' position of a state squeezed between Germany and Russia. This was understandable, given that, until the end of the Cold War (with a twenty-year break during the interwar period) Poland had been without interruption dependent on or directly occupied by either Germany or Russia, or by both of them together. Therefore, it is probably unsurprising that rather than being concerned about instability in the former Soviet Union, Warsaw craved *territorial security*, and saw NATO as the best available instru-ment for such protection. However, these divergences of perspective between Berlin and Warsaw remained only partial, with many in Berlin (e.g. Defence Minister Rühe) sharing the Polish point of view, and in any case, following the rise of the far-right movement in Russia, the German government came around to the idea of NATO enlargement, which it started to support from 1994 onwards.

Despite this convergence of policies, it remained clear that while Poland cherished the goal of NATO membership, Germany preferred other than traditional military and defensive means for promoting sta-bility in the region. Germany's strategy towards Poland therefore remained focused on fostering Polish domestic reforms, first of all on furthering democracy and the social market economy. This was pur-sued through two main means: Germany's promotion of Poland's EU membership and through bilateral devices, most importantly the pro-visions of the 'Good Neighbourliness and Friendly Co-operation' treaty. As argued above, Germany has always promoted the objective of EU enlargement and pressed for Poland's inclusion in the first group of East Central European countries to enter the Community.

While on the whole Germany's enthusiasm for a quick expansion of the EU waned after 1997, Bonn continued to stress that enlargement without Poland's inclusion would be ridiculous.[41]

As well as facilitating Poland finding a harbour within western institutions, Germany also promoted the transformation of the Polish economy through bilateral means. It is in this light that one has to look at the provisions of the Polish–German treaty of 1991, in which Germany promised an extensive transfer of 'know-how' and financial assistance. Most importantly, as envisaged in the treaty, Berlin wrote off a considerable part of the Polish debt and supported Warsaw during its negotiations with foreign creditors. As a result, the burden of foreign loans (seen in the 1980s and 1990s as a major problem for the Polish economy) was considerably eased, with substantial benefits for the reform process.

Defensive power and power constrained

As shown above, both *power maximisation* and the promotion of *security and stability*, were to a greater or lesser extent present in Germany's as well as in Poland's EU and NATO enlargement policies. It could be argued, therefore, that regardless of their particular circumstances both countries' policies were driven by a similar set of considerations. However, although this might be in principle correct, it misses important differences that existed in Germany's and Poland's interest perceptions. For example, while the *power-maximisation* argument seems to be more pronounced in Warsaw's approach towards EU and NATO enlargement, Berlin remained more focused on tackling *instability*. These differences are first and foremost related to the contrasting positions of Poland, as a candidate state which had just regained its sovereignty, and that of the Federal Republic, as a crucial member of both the EU and NATO and a state whose sovereignty before 1989 had been far greater than Poland's.

For Poland, the end of bipolarity meant first of all a great opportunity for re-asserting its nationhood and self-determination. For the first time since the Second World War Poland was able to pursue an independent foreign policy and embark on 'returning to Europe'. Clearly, the fear of Russia and an unhappy experience of being part of the Soviet Bloc played an important role here. Unsurprisingly, therefore, national self-determination and the notion of 'returning to

Europe' were often seen as intertwined in the Polish perspective. It was therefore quite natural for Warsaw to see its membership in western organisations in terms of *power maximisation*. However, in doing so Warsaw's position remained defensive in the sense that, rather than willing to project its power externally it wanted to *protect* its sovereignty and security. Provided that this objective was achieved, Warsaw would feel that its security had increased considerably. The Federal Republic, on the other hand, although not completely sovereign, had already enjoyed a far greater degree of self-determination than Poland before unification. During and after unification many were afraid that Germany's power would now be difficult to contain. As the Markovits–Reich paper illustrates, the possibility of a new form of German domination, in both western and eastern Europe, was seriously debated. However, Germany's policy towards Poland and other countries in the region was not motivated by a power maximisation imperative but rather by the need to protect its domestic status quo against the spread of instability.

To be sure, however, whether intentionally or not, Germany's policy towards East Central Europe served to strengthen its international position and consequently its relative power. Most importantly, through supporting Poland and other East Central European countries in their aspirations to join NATO and the EU, Germany's prestige was boosted in both the candidate countries and among existing member states. While in East Central Europe Berlin was credited with the progress of the EU enlargement process, in the West it came to be perceived as the prime mover in the EU's eastern policy. One of the most tangible outcomes of this development was Poland's pledge, which was also shared by other East Central European states, to support Germany's plea for a permanent seat in the United Nations Security Council.[42] By doing so, Poland and other countries of the region accepted that Germany's status of a great power should be recognised. This was an absolute novelty for Poland, whose foreign policy in the past was focused on preventing the international promotion of Germany.

Correspondingly, Warsaw began to expect that its membership in the EU and NATO would boost its international position in the region vis-à-vis its Eastern neighbours.[43] This followed a number of ideas emerging since the late 1990s suggesting that Poland should become a regional power and turn its position as a linchpin between West and East to its own advantage.[44] However, despite the growing evidence that EU and NATO enlargements might be used by both Poland and

Germany to maximise their power, this does not seem to have been a predominant trend in either country, at least not in a traditional sense. As suggested earlier, Germany's main objective in East Central Europe remained ensuring the continued success of the post-1989 reforms, which paradoxically, led Berlin to *constrain* rather than advance its economic potential in the region. Poland, which indeed appeared to be attracted by the prospects of enhancing its influence in the East, still lacked an equivalent potential to fulfil this aspiration.

To sum up, it is apparent that the process of integrating Poland with the West has served the fundamental interests of both Germany and Poland. This convergence and mutual reinforcement of Polish and German interests has furthered the prospect of the relationship's 'Europeanisation'. Through the eastern extension of European structures both Germany and Poland enhanced their internal and external security. Economic benefits were also mutual, although proportionally more substantial for Poland. By promoting EU enlargement Germany also did not compromise its reputation of being a 'constructive European', while it successfully tackled fears of 'German dominance'. German and Polish foreign policies have therefore become reconcilable. In this respect, it could be argued that the nexus that emerged in Polish–German relations in the context of western integration is reminiscent of Franco-German relations. While Berlin has been consciously constraining its own power Warsaw, like Paris, has been able to re-gain its self-confidence and 'punch above its weight'.

These points notwithstanding, Germany's and Poland's concerns with maximising their powers and promoting stability do not provide a complete explanation of their EU and NATO enlargement policies. In particular, historically and culturally defined interests were also important in determining the positions of both Warsaw and Berlin. Essentially, it is important to see the enlargement policies against the background of both countries' historical experiences. It is to these issues that the chapter now turns.

Historical legacies and Western integration

In the past, both Poland and Germany had stormy and predominately unsuccessful experiences with nation-state-building. Not only were they both latecomers to this process (with the German state emerging in 1871 and the Polish in 1918) but also, once they became states, they were quite soon engulfed in conflicts leading either to dissolution or a

major crisis affecting their statehood and sovereignty. Unsurprisingly
then, historical legacies of German and Polish states figure as one of
the important factors explaining these countries' support for western
integration, which in both capitals has been perceived as mitigating
international conflicts and enhancing their security and stability.

In spite of these similarities, which contributed to the congruence of
Polish and German policies after 1989, there are significant differences in both countries' past experiences with nation-state-building.
Most importantly, Germany itself brought about most previous incur-
sions into its statehood. In contrast, the Polish state was subjected to
various episodes of external aggression, with Germany being an invader
on more than one occasion. These innate differences in the Polish
and German experience are, it is argued here, of great consequence
for their current foreign policies. As demonstrated in the next section, these differences have led to some discrepancies between Polish
and German policies towards EU enlargement, and towards the notion
of supranational integration more generally.

Germany's 'excessive' multilateralism

The Federal Republic has been renowned for its strong preference for
multilateralism and attachment to international institutions as a means
of conducting its foreign policy. As argued by Helga Hafterndorn,
Bonn–Berlin's relationship with international organisations has been
intimate and reciprocal.[45] To explain why this has been the case it is
important to consider Germany's past. In particular two issues are at
the forefront of all arguments about the peculiar nature of
Bonn–Berlin's international behaviour: its unsuccessful experience with
the nation-state and, as a consequence of this, externally imposed constraints upon its sovereignty.[46] With its sovereignty considerably limited
in the wake of the Second World War, Bonn viewed its membership in
international organisations as 'an opportunity to change external
restrictions into voluntary commitments'.[47] Paradoxically, then, the
internationalisation of its surroundings and integration with the West
served to enhance West Germany's autonomy. The decision to join the
ECSC and NATO facilitated West Germany's international rehabilitation, gave it a platform for the conduct of diplomacy and opened possibilities for its economic expansion in Europe and beyond.
Consequently, then, western integration served Bonn's interests well,
and at the same time it kept its allies assured that, enmeshed within
international institutions, the Federal Republic would be prevented

from acting belligerently. This perception was not seriously challenged until 1989.

The end of the Cold War revived the discussion about Germany's role in the international community. Other countries, notably America, called upon Germany to return to normality and act in the international arena in a way that would reflect its economic power. 'Partners in leadership', the term coined by President Bush in 1989, came to symbolise the new international expectations placed upon Germany. These new perceptions were mobilised by some writers in the discipline of International Relations, most spectacularly by John Mearsheimer whose famous article 'Back to the Future' suggested Germany's return to superpower status with all its necessary assets, including the acquisition of nuclear weapons.[48] This line of thinking became known as the 'normalisation debate', and also implied that the post-Cold War Federal Republic would be more assertive in its international behaviour and less inclined to support supranational integration.[49] As regards East Central Europe, the predictable implication of this thesis was that Germany would pursue a unilateral policy towards the region and would refrain from promoting Poland's and others integration with western institutions.

Over a decade after German unification it appears that the prophecies of the 'normalisers' remain unfulfilled. The Federal Republic not only strove to secure the united Germany's membership in NATO, but through the adoption of the Maastricht treaty, it bound itself more strongly than ever to the EC/EU. Most importantly here, as demonstrated in Germany's promotion of NATO and EU enlargements, Bonn–Berlin did not display unilateralism in its policies towards East Central Europe. Consistent with its sustained multilateral approach, Germany's EU enlargement policy remained based on the pursuit of a dual and preferably simultaneous development of the EU: its deeper internal integration coupled with expansion to Poland and other East Central European states. The first feature is directly connected with Germany's policy of strengthening its anchor to the West and the latter serves to 'Europeanise' its relations with East Central Europe.[50]

However, it still remains unclear whether the widening of the EU is really fully compatible with its deepening. Part of the reason why this is questionable has to do with the deep attachment towards national sovereignty held by the new member states, and Poland in particular.

Poland's return to Europe

Two main factors shaped the formation of Poland's European identity. Poland's geographical location, at the crossroads of western and eastern cultures, is the first. The second is the accidental decision of the first Polish ruler, Prince Mieszko, to choose Rome rather than Constantinople as the place of his conversion to Christianity. Following Mieszko's, decision Poland became the easternmost periphery of western Christendom, which led to the emergence of a national myth projecting Poland as the protector of Christendom, of western culture and ultimately of Europe.[51] Polish military victories over the Turks, Tatars and Russians were interpreted in this way and came to form a core part of national mythology. For example, when King Jan Sobieski led the Polish army to rescue Vienna from the Turks at the end of the seventeenth century, this was presented as an act of defending European Christendom rather than simply Poland's interests.[52] After Poland lost its sovereignty and was partitioned throughout the nineteenth century, the country's elites maintained the view that, at least spiritually, Poland remained a part of the West European tradition and although it was unable to be Europe's shield, it became Europe's martyr and its future saviour. This view was maintained by leading poets and writers of the nineteenth century, Adam Mickiewicz and Stanisław Wyspiański, who constructed a Messiah-like vision of Poland's role in Europe, as the state which died to redeem other nations. The modern nationalism that emerged in the nineteenth century therefore included a large element of mythologised history that portrayed the national and European identities of the Poles as inseparable.[53] The images of Poland as Europe's shield re-emerged after the First World War as a reaction to the Polish–Soviet war of 1920, an event which was interpreted in terms of protecting Europe against the 'non-European' Bolsheviks. It was argued that, by defeating the Bolsheviks, Poland prevented the spread of communism to western Europe that would have inevitably lead to the destruction of European culture and identity.[54] Western Europe's inaction during the German and Soviet invasion of Poland in 1939, and the subsequent acceptance of the Soviet dictate in Yalta, thus led to the widespread disappointment and feeling of being betrayed by Europe and the West.

However, after the war, the non-communist intelligentsia and the Catholic Church sustained an image of Poland that was 'artificially and temporally separated from Europe by the Iron Curtain' and 'kidnapped' from the West by the 'Asiatic, and Bolshevik East'. The issue of belonging to Europe thus continued as a vital component of Polish national identity, though the perceptions of what exactly 'Europe' stood for evolved from predominantly cultural and religious to socio-political and largely secular. This was also reflected in the evolving perception of Polish history and its relation to Europe that, on the one hand, was manifested in the toning down of the 'bulwark of Christendom' argument while, on the other, led to an emphasis upon those historical events that could prove Poland's progressive credentials. For example, the fact that Poland had the first written constitution in Europe (1791) was often recalled as proof of Poland's 'Europeaness'. The subsequent partition of Poland that led to the abolition of the constitution was portrayed as an assault, not only on Poland but also on the forces of progress in Europe.

The achievements of Polish and Polish-born scientists, like Copernicus and Marie Curie, or artists like Chopin, were proudly displayed to the world to show that Poles were as European as the Italians or French; the economic accomplishments of the interwar period were exaggerated in order that Poland be seen as a truly European state, capable of organising itself if only given a chance. In sum, before 1989 non-communists elites in Poland held an idealistic image of Europe, of which they wanted to be a part. According to a Polish intellectual Jacek Woźniakowski, for Poles, Europe has always had a positive value, and to be described, as 'a real European' was one of the greatest complements one could receive.[55]

It was thus almost a natural development that when the Iron Curtain disintegrated in 1989, the non-communist government of Poland proclaimed a 'return to Europe' as its main foreign policy objective. In this context, two particular moves of the first non-communist Prime Minister, Mazowiecki, deserve attention, as they came to symbolise how the new Poland saw its European identity. Firstly, making his first official visit abroad, Mazowiecki chose to travel to Rome, which was widely read as being an affirmation of Poland's belonging to Europe's Christian heritage. This element was additionally strengthened by the role played by the Pope John Paul II, himself a Pole, in the emergence of the anti-communist 'Solidarity' movement.[56] Secondly, during his speech in the Council of Europe in Strasbourg in January 1990, Mazowiecki stressed that 'as a nation Poland has always been in the Council of Europe', thus suggesting that modern European values, first of all democracy and human rights, though abused by the state, have always been cherished by the bulk of society.[57] These gestures had the broad backing of public opinion which, as seen in opinion polls from the early 1990s, associated 'Europe' with human rights, economic freedoms, democracy and tolerance – principles that the Poles wanted to see implemented at home.

On the whole, then, while as shown above a strong sense of belonging to Europe has been one of the most crucial factors in determining the general direction of Poland's foreign policy, it is by no means certain what of kind of Europe Poland wanted to be a part. Since 1989 it became apparent that Poland's Europeaness was torn between two tendencies which, for the purpose of this account, are labelled 'traditional' and 'modern'. While the 'traditionalists' see Europe as a club of independent states and predominantly a Christian project, the 'modernists' perceive European integration as intertwined with liberal-democratic values. Attitudes towards Germany roughly converge with these general trends, with the 'traditionalists' being wary about the possibility of German domination and the 'modernists' being more relaxed about their western neighbour. However, whichever of these two tendencies becomes more prevalent, Poland's national identity will always be a potent force. It was consequently unlikely that Warsaw's policy towards the EU would be driven by pro-integrationist and pro-federal objectives similar to those of Germanys. The major reasons for these differences are related to the divergent experiences of nationalism and national identity. Unlike in Germany, nationalism has positive historical connotations in Poland, which results in a situation where Warsaw is less willing to give up on its sovereignty. In the situation where for the last 200 years Polish statehood has been constantly threatened (often by Germany), the notion of national identity grew to symbolise cultural defence against foreign aggression. The Poles have therefore been proud of their national identity and hold a positive image of the nation-state. In fact, the very notion of a 'return to Europe' bolstered Polish nationalism further, as it became apparent that Poland could never have embarked on joining the European project had she not regained its sovereignty in 1989. Thus, neither the 'traditionalists' nor the 'modernists' questioned the idea of the nation-state, which remained a sacrosanct element of Polish politics.[58] While these divergent attitudes towards European integration and the 'modern' state were of only peripheral consequence during the political phase of enlargement, with the beginning of EU membership negotiations in 1998 they started to act as an increasingly divisive factor in Polish–German relations.

From reconcilable interests to a convergence of interests?

On the eve of the *Bundestag's* ratification of the 'Good Neighbourliness and Friendly Co-operation' treaty, Helmut Kohl likened Germany's reconciliation with France to its relations with Poland. The Chancellor declared that while the former was essential to begin the process of uniting Europe, the latter would be equally crucial to its completion. This view fitted well with post-1990 Polish foreign policy, which in a significant part was guided by the principle of a 'return to Europe through Germany'. This congruence of the two countries' strategic perspectives laid the foundations for the new relationship that came to be closer and more intimate than ever before. The role of international organisations, particularly the EU and NATO, was absolutely essential in bringing about this new closeness. In this respect, the patterns of congruence in Polish–German relations was again not dissimilar to the post-war Franco-(West) German process. As argued in this chapter, Germany emerged in the 1990s as the main supporter of eastern enlargement, and it was clear that Poland's EU membership was the main focus of this policy. This was apparent in 1995, when Kohl argued for a swift enlargement to Poland, Hungary and the Czech Republic, in 1997, when Germany opted for starting negotiations with a selected group of countries, including Poland and in mid-2000, when Germany successfully argued against widespread opinion that Poland should be left out of the first group of countries to join the EU. As a result, elements of trust which were missing from the relationship during the Cold War, began to emerge. The process of constructing new neighbourly relations (*gute Nachbarschaft/dobre sąsiedzctwo*) initiated in 1989 was successful in advancing the relationship.

However, as mentioned earlier, Germany's enthusiasm for EU enlargement decreased after 1998, so did Poland's. This situation transpired partly because of historically rooted differences which lay at the base of attitudes towards European integration. Owing to its historical experience Germany regards international institutions not only as useful instruments, but also as a good in themselves. This attachment to multilateralism has clearly posed a challenge for Berlin of how to reconcile its primary European policy objective for an 'ever-closer union' with enlargement which, in the view of some in Berlin, may threaten to undermine the EU's cohesion. Poland's experience with nationhood remains very different to that of Germany's and so are its contemporary implications. Most importantly, the general position of the main

Polish political forces, irrespective of their particular ideological out-look, is less European and more national-minded than is the case with their German counterparts. It is again useful to invoke the Franco-German example to illustrate what this could mean for the relationship's 'Europeanisation'.

The Franco-German process demonstrated that strategic congruence was a vital step towards 'Europeanisation', but that this was just the beginning of the process. In order to build a sound basis for an endur-ing consensus states had to be prepared not only to *reconcile* their strategic perspectives but also to compromise, and in this process *re-define* their national interests. In the 1950s and 1960s, France and West Germany supported European integration for different reasons. While France's approach towards the EC was largely instrumental and moti-vated primarily by a desire to regain its former great power status, West Germany was more genuinely disposed towards further progress of European integration, which enhanced its sovereignty, its access to western markets and promoted its international rehabilitation. These divergent motivations of Paris and Bonn were nevertheless reconcil-able, which proved crucial for the progress of European integration. However, it soon became clear that in order to sustain and advance the rapprochement, France and West Germany needed to compromise and redefine their national perspectives. De Gaulle's inability to do this led to a major crisis in European integration, known as the 'empty chair' crisis – with France pulling out its representative from the Coun-cil of Ministers – and subsequently to a period of stalemate in the relationship.[59]

It was not until President Valéry Giscard d'Estaing and Chancellor Helmut Schmidt agreed to work towards establishing a European Mon-etary System (EMS) that the relationship became again dynamic in the mid-1970s. Essentially here, the Franco-German agreement on the EMS and the prospect of a future European monetary union (EMU) required compromises from the two parties. While the French had to agree that the D-Mark would be the dominant currency in the system – a clear testimony to German economic superiority – Bonn had to convince its public that joining a system composed of many weaker currencies would not lead to economic difficulties at home.[60] In subsequent years, many such compromises were struck, including over the common cur-rency (the Euro) and more recently over the European constitution.

Polish–German rapprochement remained based on a *reconcilability* of strategic interests, which had proved crucial in bringing about EU and, to a lesser extent, NATO enlargements. Since 1998 these processes were politically irreversible, which was a great success for Berlin and Warsaw but opened up the question as to the future of the relationship in an enlarged EU. The divergent attitudes towards European integration in Germany and Poland were not essentially important prior the start of the negotiations, not least because these differences were largely not apparent up to this point. Throughout the 1990s public opinion in Poland continued to support the principle of EU membership without being engaged in the debate about the implications of European integration for national sovereignty. At the same time, the government chose not to express its views on the issue, fearing that this could undermine its position in the run-up to the negotiations. However, as discussed in Chapter 6, the parliamentary elections in 1997 already demonstrated that the nation-state remained sacrosanct in Polish politics, with many parties taking sceptical positions on European integration often inspired by de Gaulle's notion of a Europe of independent states. This tendency only intensified after the start of the negotiations. This essentially meant that the evolution from *reconciling* strategic interests to actually *re-defining* them, as had been the case in Franco-West German relations since the mid-1970s, was by no means certain in Polish–German relations after 1998.

The other essential aspect of 'Europeanisation' is to deepen the reconcilability of interests beyond strategic concerns to areas of economic interest. Here again the Franco-German case proves instructive. While the setting up of the ECSC is seen as a product of Franco-West German rapprochement and a great triumph of the European idea, it is clear that in economic terms the community's success was at best mixed and riddled by conflicts between French steel and West German coal-mining industries. In subsequent years the economic interests of the two countries were often in conflict, not least because the French *dirigisme* was more state-interventionist than the West German social-market economy. However, as European integration progressed, the economic interests of the two countries and individual industrial groups started to be more reconcilable and even mutually supportive. To illustrate this, it suffices to mention the cases of EMS and EMU – or, more specifically, the joint defence of the Common Agricultural Policy (CAP) by the farming lobbies in Germany and France.

The issue of divergent economic interests in the Polish–German case was not apparent as long as Poland remained outside the EU; however, with the start of accession negotiations these differences came to the forefront of the enlargement process and had a negative impact on the relationship. This was particularly apparent with regard to the question of the EU budget – Germany being a net payer and Poland the potential main beneficiary – the issue of Polish migrant workers and the question of CAP reform. All of these and many smaller issues meant that while Germany's political support for Poland's EU membership remained unchanged, the start of actual negotiations in 1998 marked the beginning of an evolution in the German debate on aspects of implementation. A similar process occurred in Poland where, while in principle all major political forces have continued to support the goal of EU membership, they have also demanded that the government defend Poland's interests in the negotiations.[61] In other words, as a result of the start of negotiations in 1998, EU enlargement lost its 'special status' – an exclusive position at the level of 'high politics'. Instead, debating enlargement became exposed to all levels of both German and Polish national systems – the process referred to here as *domestication.* Consequently, the analysis of the process of EU enlargement after 1998 presented in Chapter 6 will look at national-specific domestic factors in both countries, and assess their impact upon the process of 'Europeanisation' after 1998.

Notes

1   Quoted in *Time Magazine*, 22 March 1999, p. 15.
2   See 'Atlantic News', 23 March 1990.
3   See 'Atlantic News', 12 May 1990.
4   See Karl-Heinz Kamp, 'Germany and NATO: The Opening of the Alliance and its Future', Institute for German Studies, University of Birmingham, Discussion Paper, 14/1998.
5   On the initiative, see Stuart Croft *et al.*, *The Enlargement of Europe* (Manchester: Manchester University Press, 1999), pp. 27–32.
6   See 'Atlantic News', 9 October 1991.
7   Andrzej Krzeczunowicz, *Krok po kroku. Polska droga do NATO 1989–1999* (Cracow: Znak, 1999), pp. 94–5, 112
8   See Volker Rühe, 'Shaping Euro-Atlantic Policies: Grand Strategy for a New Era', *Survival*, Vol. 35, No. 2, 1993, pp. 129–37. For Rühe' s role in promoting enlargement, see Henning Tewes, *Germany, Civilian Power and New Europe* (Basingstoke: Palgrave, 2001).
9   See *Der Spiegel*, No. 52, 1993.
10 Rudolf Augestein, 'Bedrohtes Polen', *Der Spiegel*, No. 2, 1994.

11 'Polen gehört zu uns, wird künftig zu einem wie auch immer gestalteten Europa gehören, und damit basta'.

12 Interview with Friedbert Pflüger, Bonn, 2 April 1998.

13 Interview with Poland's former Defence Minister Janusz Onyszkiewicz, 16 February 2001.

14 'Niemcy a Polska', *Kultura*, July–August 1978, p. 127.

15 Interview with Peter Glotz, chairman of the SPD in the 1980s, Erfurt, 12 May 1998. Interestingly, after the end of the Cold War Glotz went on to oppose the eastern enlargement of both the EU and NATO.

16 See Michael Mertes and Norbert J. Prill 'Der verhängnisvolle Irrtum eines Entweder-Oder', *FAZ*, 19 July 1989.

17 See Helmut Kohl (interviewed by Kai Diekmann and Ralf Georg Reuth), *Pragnąłem Jedności Niemiec* (Warsaw: Politeja, 1999), pp. 67–9.

18 See José Ignacio Torreblanca Payá, *The European Community and Central Eastern Europe (1989–1993): Foreign Policy and Decision-Making* (Madrid: Centro de Estudios Avanzados en Ciencias Sociales, 1997), pp. 192–3.

19 On the implications of Andriessen report, see Andrzej Harasimowicz, 'Po podpisaniu układu europejskiego', in *Rocznik Polskiej Polityki Zagranicznej 1992* (Warsaw: PISM, 1994), pp. 62–3

20 See *Presidency Conclusions*, 'Annex IV' Essen, 10 December 1994.

21 See 'Falsche Hoffnungen', *Der Spiegel*, No. 12 December 1994.

22 See 'European Union. Single-Currency-Minded', *The Economist*, 23 December 1995.

23 This decision of the European Council was based on the recommendation of the Commission (see Agenda 2000 (1/1), in Bulletin EU 7/8–1997). For the decision of the European Council, see Agenda 2000 (1/5), in Bulletin EU 12–1997.

24 Wolfgang Schäuble and Karl Lamers, Überlegungen zur europäischen Politik. Positionspapier der CDU/CSU- Bundestagsfraktion vom 1.9.1994, *Blätter für deutsche und internationale Politik*, No. 10, 1994, pp. 1271–80.

25 I. Kolboom, 'Frankreich und Deutschland: Die neuen Akzente', in K. Kaiser and J. Krause (eds), *Deutschlands neue Außenpolitik, Band 3: Interessen und Strategien*, Forschungsinstitut der Deutschen Gesellschaft für Auswärtige Politik, Munich: Oldenbourg Verlag, 1996, pp. 123–4.

26 For example, see Roland Freudenstein, 'Germany, Poland and the EU', *International Affairs*, Vol. 74, No. 1, 1998, pp. 41–55.

27 See Jacek Saryusz-Wolski, *Polska w Europie*, 17/1995; Andrzej Wielowieyski, *Polska w Europie*, 17/1995.

28 See 'National Strategy for Integration' (Warsaw: Committee for European Integration, January 1997), p. 5.

29 See 'Deutsche Bank zdobył przewage', *Rzeczpospolita*, 14 February 2000.

30 'Außenhandel der Bundesrepublik Deutschland nach Ländergruppen und Ländern', Bundesministerium für Wirtschaft – ID 5 – 2 April 99/1.

31   Andrei S. Markovits and Simon Reich, 'Should Europe Fear the Germans?', *German Politics and Society*, Vol. 23, 1991, pp. 1–20.

32   See the data of the Ministry of Economics, Analysis and Forecast Department, 'Poland's Trade in 1999 Per Country Groupings', www.mg.gov.pl /struktur/DaiP.

33   'Obroty handlu zagranicznego ogółem i według krajów w okresie I-VII 2000', www. stat. gov. pl/miesieczne/obr-handlu-zagr/index. htm.

34   See 'Polska wymiana handlowa z Niemcami ma wzrosnąć w 2000 r. o 13 procent', *Gazeta Wyborcza*, 20 October 2000.

35   See 'Dane Ministerstwa Gospodarki, Departament Analiz i Prognoz', www.mg.gov.pl/struktur/DaiP/wsk_gos/tab24pl. htm.

36   The polls conducted in 1998 showed the following hierarchy of foreign languages spoken in Poland: 24 per cent Russian, 9 per cent English, 9 per cent German, 4 per cent French. See 'Czy Polacy znają Świat', CBOS, *Komunikat z Badań*), www.cbos.pl/SPISKOM.POL/1998/ZK001.HTM.

37   On the Polish devolutionary reforms, see 'Poland's Devolutionary Battleground', *Economist*, 7 February 1998; 'Erste Wahl zu den Regionalparlamenten', *FAZ*, 10 October 1998.

38   Interviews with Friedbert Pflüger (CDU) and Marcus Meckel (SPD), Bonn, April 1998.

39   See 'Kampfansage an Flüchtlinge. Schengen-Staaten beschließen Aktionsplan', *Frankfurter Rundschau*, 16 September 1998.

40   See Egon Bahr, *Deutsche Interessen* (Munich: Karl Blessing Verlag, 1998).

41   For example, see Fischer's interview for *Süddeutsche Zeitung*; 'Vorbote einer "großen Krise"', 4 September 2000.

42   See 'Poparcie dla większej Rady, przemówienie Rosattiego w ONZ', *Rzeczpospolita*, 27 July 1997.

43   See 'Polish Policy vis-a-vis Ukraine and How it is Perceived in EU Member States', *Reports & Analyses 2/00* (Warsaw: Centre for International Relations, 2000).

44   Interviews with Zdzisław Najder (a former advisor to Prime Minister), Janusz Onyszkiwicz (former Defence Minister) and Jarosław Guzy (chairman of the Polish Atlantic Club), Warsaw, 14–16 February 2001.

45   Helga Haftendorn, 'Gulliver in the Centre of Europe: International Involvement and National Capabilities for Action', in Bertel Heurlin (ed.), *Germany in the Nineties* (Basingstoke, 1996), p. 92

46   The category of 'penetrated sovereignty', originally invented by Wolfram Hanrieder, is quoted here from Bertel Heurlin, 'The International Position and the National Interest of Germany in the Nineties', in Heurlin (ed.), *Germany in the Nineties*, p. 47.

47   See Haftendorn, 'Gulliver in the Centre of Europe', p. 96.

48   See John Mearsheimer, 'Back to the Future: Instability in Europe After the Cold War', *International Security*, Vol. 15, No. 1, 1990.

49 For the 'normalisation' debate, see Hanns W. Maull and Philip H. Gordon, *German Foreign Policy and German 'National Interest': German and American Perspectives*, American Institute for Contemporary German Studies, Johns Hopkins University, Discussion Paper, No. 5, January 1993.

50 See Friedbert Pflüger, 'Polen – unser Frankreich im Osten'/'Poland and the European Union', *Außenpolitik*, III/95, pp. 225–31.

51 See Zdzisław Mach, 'Heritage, Dream, and Anxiety: The European Identity of Poles', in Zdzisław Mach and Dariusz Niedźwiecki (eds), *European Enlargement and Identity* (Cracow: Universitas, 1997), pp. 35–51.

52 See Norman Davies, *God's Playground: A History of Poland*, Vol. I (Oxford: Oxford University Press, 1981), pp. 480–6.

53 See Davies *God's Playground: A History of Poland*, Vol. II (Oxford: Oxford University Press, 1981), pp. 2–80.

54 Mach, 'Heritage, Dream, and Anxiety', pp. 35–51.

55 Quoted in Mach, 'Heritage, Dream, and Anxiety', pp. 35–51

56 See *ibid.*

57 See the collection of documents edited by Adam Daniel Rotfeld and Walther Stützle, *Germany and Europe in Transition* (Oxford: Sipri and Oxford University Press, 1998), pp. 131–4.

58 See Saryusz-Wolski, *Polska w Europie*, 17/1995.

59 Stephen George and Ian Bache, *Politics in the European Union*, (Oxford: Oxford University Press, 2001), p. 92–3.

60 Loukas Tsoukalis, 'European Monetary Union', in Helen Wallace and William Wallace, *Policy-making in the EU* 4th edn (Oxford: Oxford University Press, 2000), pp. 149–79

61 See Aleks Szczerbiak, 'Explaining Declining Support for EU Membership in Poland', Sussex European Institute Working Paper, No. 34.

6

EU enlargement and Polish–German relations between 1998 and 2001

The age of the 'big leaps', historic gestures and symbols is coming to an end. It will be replaced by hard work on details, interrupted by the 'ups and downs' of political normality. (Friedbert Pflüger, Chairman of the German–Polish Society)[1]

Introduction

After the end of the Cold War, Polish foreign policy was focused on convincing the United States and western Europeans of the merits of expanding NATO and the EU eastwards. By the end of 1997 it was clear that this strategy had been successful – NATO invited Poland, the Czech Republic and Hungary to join the Alliance in 1999 and the EU agreed to begin membership negotiations with these and a handful of other countries in 1998. However, while NATO's decision practically meant that the enlargement was a done deal, in the case of the EU the start of negotiations meant first and foremost an evolution of the process that thereafter would be less political, less strategic, but more technocratic. Most of the candidates, particularly the smaller ones, welcomed this change which, they believed, would mean greater equality and transparency of the process. However, Poland – the largest and strategically the most important of the accession states, did not adjust very well to this new reality and continued to behave as if it deserved special treatment. Consequently, Poland proved to be the most difficult of the accession countries dragging its feet in the negotiations and causing irritation amongst the other candidates.

The development of NATO and EU enlargements was certainly helped by the rapprochement that had taken place in Polish–German relations. However, the start of the negotiations in 1998 considerably challenged the post-Cold War Polish–German consensus. The technical logic of the negotiations was such that it de-emphasised strategic considerations, which had united Poland and Germany, while it brought into fore many particular issues which were often problematic for the two states sharing one of the longest borders in Europe. Germany remained the strongest supporter of Poland's EU membership, but it was also more worried than any other member state about the economic implications of EU enlargement. In the course of the negotiations many such issues – most prominently the question of migrant workers and agricultural subsidies came to dog the relationship and undermine the hard-earned consensus.

The particular nature of the negotiations required a more detailed and technical definition of the member states' and accession countries' positions in the process. Until 1998, the enlargement policies of Poland and Germany were pursued almost exclusively within the realms of their foreign policies. The start of the negotiation process led to all major ministries becoming involved in the process. The same was true for political parties, and in Germany's case also for the *Länder*, which started to perceive EU enlargement as a process that would affect their domestic constituencies. Overall, negotiations led to a greater engagement of more domestic actors attempting to influence national positions and defend their particular interests in the process – a development referred to here as 'domestication'.

The natural consequence of these post-1998 changes was that both Germany and Poland began to construct their policies in such a way as to reflect to a greater degree their specific national conditions. In order to address the relationship during this period it is essential to focus analysis on the domestic mechanisms underpinning the processes of constructing enlargement policies in Germany and Poland. It is also important to consider the perspectives of key domestic actors that were able to influence the process. The chapter considers these issues by looking first at Germany and then Poland. This focus upon domestic actors is followed by a consideration of the impact of Bonn–Berlin's and Warsaw's EU enlargement policies on the general condition of bilateral relations.

Germany's EU enlargement policy after 1998: domestic factors

For Germany, the beginning of EU accession negotiations meant that the process of constructing policies on the issue became part of its 'regular' European diplomacy, which in itself is a complex bureaucratic process involving broad participation from the government, the *Länder* and political parties. It is therefore essential to begin this section by outlining the mechanisms and basic characteristics of Germany's European diplomacy before an analysis of the EU enlargement policies of the key actors involved in the process can be outlined.

The frameworks of Germany's European diplomacy

Germany's European policy is renowned for its ambivalence. On the one hand, consensus has often prevailed in Bonn–Berlin when 'strategic' issues of European integration are under consideration. For example, the key constitutional policies of the EC/EU, such as the EMS, Single Market or EMU, were supported by all major political parties in government and opposition. At the same time, however, Germany's policy in the EU has been criticised for being poorly co-ordinated owing to a de-concentration of its decision-making processes. Thus, unsurprisingly, Germany's European diplomacy is 'famous' for being good on pursuing 'strategic' objectives but poor on 'tactics'.[2]

This ambivalence, it is argued, is a consequence of Germany's specific domestic conditions – or, in other words, its national opportunity structures. The German system of governance is considered highly decentralised first and foremost because of its federal nature but also because of the considerable autonomy enjoyed by individual ministries and non-state actors (e.g. the trade unions), all of which aspire to influence Berlin's European policy. On the one hand, the extensive and constitutionally guaranteed position of the Federal Chancellor (article 65 of the Basic Law) enables a clear articulation of the strategic aims of Germany's European policy. This system – known as Guiding Competence or *Richtlinienkompetenz* – proved effective even when the government adopted unpopular policies – for example, EMU and the abolition of the D-Mark, the symbol of (West) German prosperity. On the other hand, the relative autonomy of individual ministries (*Ressortprinzip*) allows ministries to run their autonomous policies, which are often determined by particular sectoral interests. This phenomenon, known as 'sectorisation', led to the emergence of 'in-house' European policies of individual federal ministries that are sometimes incongruent with the government's main position.[3] Further decentralisation of the government's competencies is a consequence of the participation of the *Länder* in the governing process. In addition, the decision-making process is exposed to differences of opinion within political parties in both government and opposition.

The decision-making process

The process of co-ordinating this multiplicity of positions in Germany's European diplomacy has been conducted via formal and informal devices, with the first being largely insignificant and the second far more important. Falling in the first category is the cross-governmental steering committee (*Europa-Staatssekretäre*), which was set up in the 1980s with a view to bring more cohesion into West Germany's policy vis-à-vis Brussels. However, the new body was quickly paralysed as its decisions were binding only if agreed unanimously by the representatives of all participating ministries, which in practice proved difficult to achieve. Consequently the *Europa-Staatssekretäre* remained largely ineffective and insignificant.[4] Informal devices proved far more consequential for the conduct of Bonn's European policy. For example, under Kohl's Chancellorship an informal practice emerged with regular discussions on EU matters in a triangular relationship established between *Abteilung 2* in the Chancellor's Office (*Bundeskanzleramt*), the *Europaabteilung* in the Foreign Office and *Abteilung E* in the Economics Ministry. This triangle became subsequently known for dealing with 'strategic'- level policy issues (Figure 6.1).

In theory, there was a clear-cut division of labour in the triangle outlined above. Actual European policy was meant to be constructed in the Foreign Office, with the Economics Ministry acting as a post-box between the *Auswärtiges Amt* and other ministries. The Chancellor's Office had no formal powers in this area, except for overall guidance. Significantly, there was no special European division within *Abteilung 2* of the Chancellor's Office. However, in practice the competencies of the *Bundeskanzleramt* were far more substantial than they seemed on paper. For example, it was no secret that the last head of the *Abteilung 2* under Kohl, Joachim Bitterlich, dedicated the bulk of his attention to European issues. The position of the *Bundeskanzleramt* was also strengthened by default as the strength of the Foreign Office suffered under Klaus Kinkel's leadership. The same was true for the Economics Ministry. As a result, many of the 'strategic' ideas and decisions

Figure 6.1   Strategic-level European policy-making in Germany under Kohl

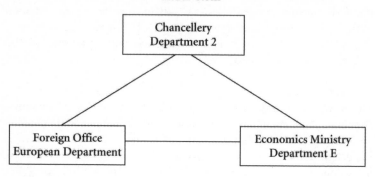

concerning policies towards the EU originated from the Chancellor's Office and were, or were not, co-ordinated with the Foreign Office and Economics Ministry.

The other ministries' European policies continued, however, to enjoy a substantial degree of independence, which led occasionally to the pursuit of a line quite different from that at the strategic level of governance. The most spectacular examples of such incongruity were the positions of the Finance and Agricultural ministries on the Commission's paper *Agenda 2000*, published in early 1998. While the Finance Ministry criticised the paper for overlooking the problem of Germany's disproportionately high net contributions to the EU (the so called *Nettozahlerdebatte*), the Agricultural Ministry considered proposals in *Agenda 2000* too radical in cutting subsidies for farmers. These sectoral interests were in fact often capable of changing the policy of the government, as was the case with *Agenda 2000*. Although *Agenda 2000* was generally considered compatible with the government's strategic objectives (deepening European integration and making the EU ready for enlargement) it was criticised by Bonn on the conflicting grounds put forward by the Finance and Agricultural Ministries.[5]

As regards the involvement of the *Länder* in European policy making, their rights are guaranteed by article 23 of the Basic Law, as amended after the ratification debate on the Maastricht treaty. According to article 23, the *Bundesrat* – the upper house of Parliament that represents the *Länder* – has to be consulted on most matters relating to European policy. In those areas where European legislation may affect the traditional competencies of the *Länder*, the *Bundesrat's* powers are significant. Consequently, the system described by Charlie Jeffery as 'co-operative federalism' (power-sharing between the federation and its regions) entered the field of European diplomacy.[6] As far as EU enlargement is concerned, the entrenched competencies of the *Länder* meant that they were very much involved in the process. Crucially, the *Länder* have been directly involved in the accession negotiations, with Brandenburg acting as representative for the Federal States. In addition, when completed, the enlargement treaties were submitted for the ratification to the *Bundesrat.*[7]

While it can be said that during Kohl's term in office Bonn was remarkably effective in pursuing the Chancellor's 'strategic' vision of Europe, characterised by a consistent push towards greater integration as well as opening the EU to new members, the institutional diffusion described above clearly impaired the co-ordination of 'routine' policies. This latter process was exacerbated by the system of coalition government, which contributed to the sectorisation of Germany's European diplomacy. In addition, at the end of Kohl's chancellorship the governing parties became increasingly split over EU integration. While the liberal FDP remained traditionally pro-European, the conservative CSU developed a penchant for Euroscepticism, including an increasingly reserved attitude towards enlargement.[8]

The change of government and the arrival to power of the red–green coalition following the *Bundestag* elections in September 1998 marked some considerable reorganisation in the decision-making structure of Bonn–Berlin's European policy. The European department of the Economics Ministry was moved to the Finance Ministry and a new European Affairs unit was created in the Chancellor's Office. However, in the period discussed here (1998–2001) the latter development did not bring about much change, since the new Chancellor, Gerhard Schröder, did not display as much interest in European policy as his predecessor. In the absence of the *Bundeskanzleramt*'s leadership in European affairs, it could be assumed that the Foreign Office would perform a stronger role in creating European policy. This view was also supported by the fact that the new Foreign Minister, Joschka Fischer, carried more weight in Europe than his predecessor. However, since a considerable share of the enlargement negotiations was dealt with by the powerful Finance Ministry, the position of the Foreign Office was not initially as formidable as it might have been (Figure 6.2).

Figure 6.2 Key decision-making departments in Germany's
European policy under Schröder

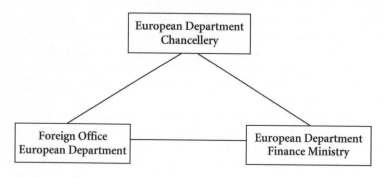

The government and EU enlargement

At the end of Kohl's term in office, Bonn's system of constructing EU enlargement policy became subject to the same dynamics as other issues in Germany's European diplomacy. After the EU agreed to start accession negotiations with the selected group of six countries in 1998, the German administration underwent some changes to cope with this more technical phase. As argued earlier, this resulted in EU enlargement losing its 'special' status, as the process began to be dealt with by European technocrats rather than 'area' specialists.

At the beginning of 1998, the Foreign Office reorganised its system of dealing with enlargement issues, which were moved away from the Political Department, the *Politische Abteilung*, to the Department of European Affairs, the *Europaabteilung*. Before 1998 the main person responsible for EU enlargement in the Ministry was a Mr Vogel, a traditional career diplomat who previously had spent many years working in the West German Embassy in Poland, spoke perfect Polish and had developed a genuine interest in the area. Essentially, Vogel perceived Poland's future EU membership in terms of political rapprochement and reconciliation.[9] His successor, Reinhard Silberberg, was known as a skilful technocrat who had been formerly responsible for preparing the Ministry's position for the 1996–97 IGC, but his interest in East Central Europe was mild at best. It was also made clear to Silberberg that his job would be deal with the technical aspects of enlargement.[10]

This 'technocratisation' of Bonn's EU enlargement policy increased further with the change of government in September 1998. The task-force for enlargement in the Ministry of Economics was moved to the Finance Ministry and its competencies were extended to include those issues previously dealt with by the Foreign Office. Crucially, the Finance Ministry took over all responsibilities for the chapters of the accession negotiations that were considered significant for the economy.[11] Needless to say, these have been the most difficult and the most important aspects of the negotiations. Silberberg left the Foreign Office to head a newly created European division in the Chancellor's office. His deputy, a Mr Klekner, when interviewed in November 1998 (two months after the change of government), spoke firmly about Germany's need to defend its national interests during the enlargement negotiations.[12]

As was the case with broader issues of European diplomacy, the structure of decision-making mechanisms had a strong impact upon individual ministries' perspectives on EU enlargement. Under Kohl's Chancellorship, a largely positive perception of EU enlargement prevailed within the 'strategic triangle' between *Abteilung 2* in the Chancellor's Office, the *Europaabteilung* in the Foreign Office and *Abteilung E* in the Ministry of Economics, as outlined above. The view generally held in this triangle was that EU enlargement would enhance Germany's security and that it would create opportunities for its economic position in East Central Europe.[13]

The expectations of Germany's security being enhanced through enlargement were almost always at the front of arguments posed in support of the notion. These tended to concern 'soft' security issues such as tackling illegal migration, international crime and environmental concerns. It was expected that with the future extension of the Schengen agreement to the candidate countries, and especially to Poland, many of these problems would simply migrate further eastwards.[14] The economic arguments in favour of EU enlargement were usually very broad and based on the expectations of intensified trade exchange and acquisition of competitive advantages through joint production involving low-cost labour from future member states.[15]

However, as far as the 'non-strategic' divisions of the government were concerned, it was clear that the perception of EU enlargement was different than at the 'top level', and more focused on short-term costs rather than prospective benefits of enlargement. Importantly, as was the case in other issues of European diplomacy, the perspectives of individual ministers were often capable of changing the government's collective position.[16] This was largely a consequence of the 'sectorisation' of the government's policy discussed above, which became a particularly prominent phenomenon after the launch of the negotiations.

These sectoral interests had, however, been infringing on Bonn's EU enlargement policy even before the accession talks began. For example, they were apparent in the German position during the negotiations of the Polish and other East Central European Association Agreements with the EU in 1990–91. Although Bonn's policy was to support the prospect of full membership for these countries, it took a number of protectionist positions in the economic sphere. Thus, Bonn objected to trade liberalisation in agricultural goods and disapproved of the Polish proposal to remove barriers on the export of coal and steel from East Central Europe.[17] Germany also rejected any kind of opening (even partial) of the EU's labour market. Furthermore, Bonn initiated a number of anti-dumping procedures often used against competitive exports from East Central Europe.[18]

The most striking example of the 'harmful' impact of short-term economic interests upon the cohesion of Bonn's EU enlargement policy under Kohl was the failure of the government to support the reform of CAP. The critical position of the Ministry of Agriculture was backed by the Chancellor's Office, which remained sympathetic to the concerns expressed by largely pro-CDU farmers.[19] Therefore, although both the Foreign Office and the Ministry of Economics thought that the Commission's proposal, as outlined in *Agenda 2000*, was perfectly reasonable, they were incapable of changing the view of the Chancellor.[20]

Ironically however, according to some German experts, contrary to its established opinion the agricultural lobby was in fact in favour of enlargement, expecting that potential export opportunities in East Central Europe would help solve their over-production problems. In addition, notwithstanding the apparent employment problem in Germany in the 1990s, there was a constant shortage of labour in the agricultural sector and farmers had come to rely on cheap and well-motivated workers from East Central Europe. German farmers, it was reported, would welcome therefore the migration of Polish, Czech and other seasonal workers to the Federal Republic.[21]

On the other hand, the prospect of migrant workers from East Central Europe coming to Germany was strongly opposed by the Ministry of Labour, which demanded long transition periods before a full implementation of the free movement of people could be extended to the new members.[22] The case of enlargement was complicated further by the policy of the Finance Ministry to minimise Germany's net contributions to the EU by making the system of payments proportionate to *per capita* gross domestic product (GDP).[23] In sum, internal contradictions and discrepancies between the government's broader objectives, sectoral interests and its EU enlargement policy became apparent even at the end of Kohl's chancellorship.

As argued above, this tendency increased further with the change of government in September 1998. The new, more domestically focused government argued more assertively for what it called a 'fairer' allocation of EU resources and for lowering Germany's payments to the EU.[24] Under a left-wing Finance Minister, Oskar Lafontaine, who resigned in a spectacular manner in March 1999, Bonn also pursued a policy of tax harmonisation and synchronisation of employment policies, both of which served further to undermine EU enlargement.[25] Although, as noted above, calls for budgetary reforms were initiated by the former coalition, the new government pursued its policy in a way that antagonised poorer member states and disinclined them to support enlargement. More importantly, for the first time, Bonn directly linked budgetary reform with the eastern expansion of the EU, declaring a 'no enlargement without financial reform' *(Keine EU Erweiterung ohne Finanzreform)* policy.[26] Lafontaine's EU employment policy could not be easily reconciled with extending the free movement of workers to those countries where the costs of labour units were considerably cheaper than in Germany. Finally, the tax harmonisation proposal caused a lot of antagonism in the EU, chiefly in Britain,[27] and pushed the enlargement question further down the EU's agenda.

In sum, it is clear that the start of EU membership negotiations led to the de-centralisation of the federal government's EU enlargement policy and the emergence of a division between the 'strategic' and 'technical' levels of policy-making. This broadening of participation in enlargement policy also stretched outside the government to include the *Länder*, whose voice became increasingly important in the process of constructing Germany's policy towards enlargement.

The Länder

According to Charlie Jeffery and Stephen Collins, EU enlargement represents for the *Länder* the same qualities as 'apple pie' has for Americans, no-one can really refuse it and everyone considers it a 'good thing'.[28] Indeed, the *Länder* have never opposed enlargement and have often declared it to be a desirable development. In 1993 the European Ministers' Conference of the *Länder* had issued a declaration of support for Poland's, the Czech Republic's, Slovakia's and Hungary's EU membership. They also welcomed the outcome of the 1996–97 IGC 'as preparing the way for enlarging the EU to the East'. However, as was the case with the national government, after late 1997 the attitude of the *Länder* towards enlargement was transformed from an unreserved positive to what Jeffery calls 'a range of "yes, but ..." qualifications'.[29] The *Länder* not only began to raise various reservations about individual aspects of enlargement but (again like individual ministries at the governmental level) they started to perceive the notion through the prism of their particular and often conflicting interests.

Inevitably, once enlargement entered its technical stage the focus began to shift onto its immediate costs rather than its long-term political ramifications. This was especially true for those *Länder* that shared borders with prospective new member states, which were concerned that while investment might migrate further East, the cheaper Polish and Czech labour force would move West. In addition *Agenda 2000* proposed a number of solutions that involved cuts in the resources so far received by the poorer East German *Länder*. Thus, unsurprisingly, the *Länder* reacted with mixed feelings to this proposal. The *Bundesrat* published a resolution in which the *Länder* reaffirmed their support for enlargement and welcomed the decision of the European Council (Luxembourg, December 1997) to start negotiations with the selected group of six countries. It was also noted in this document that EU enlargement was in the *Länder's* own interest. But the resolution also stressed that the special concerns of the regions bordering with prospective members needed to be taken into consideration. The *Bundesrat* also called the proposed reform of the structural and cohesion funds 'too drastic', especially with regards to the eastern *Länder*.[30]

The reaction of the *Länder* to the publication of *Agenda 2000* thus saw the emergence of the 'yes, but ...' attitude in their EU enlargement policies. The '*but ...*' element of this qualification was to become more prominent in due course. For example, it was significant how the European Ministers' Conference of the *Länder* welcomed the start of the membership negotiations in March 1998. The declaration issued at the meeting in April 1998 in Bremen once again expressed the *Länder's* support for the process but it also put forward a number of reservations that needed to be tackled prior to the actual implementation of enlargement. In particular, European ministers stressed that transition periods for new members were imperative in some fields, such as the free movement of people. The negative impact of enlargement upon the border regions was also repeatedly stressed.[31]

In this context, it is interesting to see that the policies of those *Länder* bordering East Central Europe were in fact far from unanimous. The two most striking examples of divergent attitudes and interests were Brandenburg and Bavaria. Both Brandenburg and Bavaria were prominent in the process, the former because Potsdam represented all of the *Länder* during the negotiations and the latter due to its informal leadership of a sceptical line towards enlargement and what Jeffery calls 'issue linkage' with other areas of European policy. Formerly a part of the GDR, Brandenburg remained one of the poorest areas of today's Germany. However, in spite of its structural weakness, arguably partially caused by increasing economic integration with the western regions of Poland, Brandenburg took a positive stance towards EU enlargement and worked towards deepening cross-border integration. Bavaria, one of the wealthiest *Länder*, had in the past supported EU enlargement; however, since 1998 it had argued in favour of delaying the process.[32]

Both Brandenburg and Bavaria not only had differing attitudes but also divergent interests in EU enlargement. This was due to their unequal standards of wealth and hence opposing positions on the EU's Structural Funds policy. Brandenburg pursued a line in favour of channelling additional resources within the framework of the EU's structural policy to the most sensitive and disadvantaged areas. Therefore, as long as enlargement was not endangering Brandenburg's benefits from the funds, Potsdam did not have an incentive to object to it. In fact, because much of Brandenburg's European philosophy was based on the theory of solidarity and the expectation that wealthy western European regions should subsidise poorer ones, Potsdam often saw new members states as potential allies in the 'struggle against the richer regions'.[33]

Bavaria, which contributed more than it benefited from EU funds, 'linked' its support for enlargement with the reform of the Structural Funds which, according to Munich, should be deregulated. In particular, Bavaria argued that 'it would rather subsidise its poorer areas itself and stop paying for others'.[34] This, in turn, was opposed by Brandenburg on the grounds that the proposal was damaging to the EU's principle of solidarity. In addition, although neither *Land* supported the reform of the CAP, as proposed in *Agenda 2000*, they did so for different reasons and thus proposed conflicting ideas. Bavaria was in fact willing to keep CAP unreformed, or alternatively to accept that agricultural funding should be re-nationalised. As expressed by Bavarian Prime Minister, Edmund Stoiber: 'We in Bavaria know best how to reward our farmers.'[35] In other words, Bavaria would not mind subsidising its own farmers as long as other regions got no aid from the EU. This again was opposed by Brandenburg, which clearly could not afford to 'reward' its farmers. Potsdam argued that if Munich's proposal went through, the heavily subsidised Bavarian farmers would gain a competitive advantage.[36]

Fighting in the name of 'de-regulation', and indeed using the enlargement argument in this context, did not stop Bavaria from demanding that the EU should introduce a number of extra regulations because of enlargement. In particular, Bavaria lobbied strongly for long transition periods on the movement of workers from East Central Europe and for the rigid implementation of border controls by future members. In addition, in spite of its relative wealth, Bavaria demanded that it and other border regions be given extra resources from the EU to compensate for their 'vulnerability' to the effects of enlargement. In support of these demands, Munich was successful in organising a lobby group of EU regions bordering East Central Europe. This group met for the first time in Graz in Austria in January 1998 and issued a typical 'yes, but ...' declaration about enlargement that included most of the Bavarian demands.[37]

However, the Bavarian position was subsequently undermined by Brandenburg which, although signed up to the Graz declaration, threatened to boycott the next meeting of the group if East Central European regions were not invited to participate.[38] Finally, Brandenburg's position found the support of other members of the group and East Central Europeans were invited. In effect, although the declaration agreed in July 1998 sustained the 'yes, but ...' spirit of the former meeting, it focused more on the benefits rather than the costs of enlargement.[39] The cases of Brandenburg and Bavaria demonstrate that the states bordering with the prospective EU members showed a strong interest in enlargement, which they also *linked* with their domestic policies and preferences. However, the fact that the policies of Potsdam and Munich were so divergent in this instance demonstrated the lack of agreement amongst the *Länder* with regard to this important area of European diplomacy.

Political parties

Until the mid-1990s the cross-party consensus on the conduct of an EU-friendly policy allowed consecutive German governments to proceed with a policy of embedding Germany's interests in a supranational context to achieve its foreign policy goals. However, this consensus also became weakened. The increasingly Eurosceptic CSU began to dispute Kohl's policy of parallel 'deepening' and 'enlarging' as early as the mid-1990s.[40] The SPD, while in opposition, also expressed concerns about the costs of expanding the EU eastwards as well as criticising the government's policy on CAP and EU Structural Funds.[41] In addition, the previous positive attitude of the German public towards the process of European integration continuously weakened throughout the 1990s. The financial burden of unification considerably limited Federal resources, which led to the emergence of public reluctance against subsidising other than domestic policy priorities. Perhaps the most clear reaction of the Kohl government to these internal social pressures was its 'new assertiveness', displayed during the EU budgetary debate. While reaffirming that national contributions to the EU's treasury should not exceed the level of 1.27 per cent of GDP, the government's policy did not diverge from the SPD's view. The CSU and Bavarian government went even further, and suggested a lowering of the German share below the threshold advocated by Bonn.[42]

Although the economic benefits of expanding the EU beyond the Federal Republic's eastern border had been appreciated by German elites, the majority of the general public identified mainly with the negative aspects in this process (such as migration, cheap labour, crime, environmental degradation), and consequently objected to eastern enlargement.[43] These public fears were clearly reflected in the positions of individual political parties. The CSU initially argued in favour of a quick completion of EU eastern expansion; however, even before the September 1998 elections, it changed its position and started to dispute the notion, arguing from a conservative position of 'law and order' with concerns over influxes of cheap labour from East Central Europe. Ironically, the same argument – the threat of cheap labour – was raised by the SPD, although the Social Democrats did not appeal to 'law and order' arguments, but expressed their concerns about the domestic employment market.[44]

The run-up to the general election in the autumn of 1998 resulted in EU enlargement being instrumentalised for domestic purposes by

the parties of the governing coalition. The CSU, aided by some politicians on the right of the CDU, attacked the allegedly hasty timetable
for enlargement, they also demanded conditions for the Czech Republic's and Poland's membership in the EU – for example, that these
countries show a readiness to return former German properties con-
fiscated by the Czechoslovak and Polish authorities after 1945. On
29 May 1998, the CDU, CSU and FDP voted in the *Bundestag* in
favour of the *Heimatvertrieben* resolution, in which these parties
demanded that in the context of EU enlargement Poland and the
Czech Republic should respect the rights of those Germans who had
lost their properties at the end of the war and let them return to
their *Heimat*.[45]

The SPD and the Greens voted against the resolution and the future
Chancellor, Gerhard Schröder, rejected linking the issue with EU
enlargement.[46] On the other hand, some members of the SPD attacked
enlargement on 'pragmatic' grounds, stressing that neither the EU nor
the applicant countries were ready for it and warned that, should
enlargement happen, Germany would be the main sponsor.[47]

With the change of government in autumn 1998, the parties of the
new governing coalition, the SPD, and the Greens, initially advocated a
more cautious approach towards EU enlargement. For the SPD it was
imperative that the EU's financial system be reformed so that Germany
would not have to shoulder the bulk of enlargement-related costs. The
Greens were less concerned with the economic burden of enlargement,
but were anxious that the widening of an unreformed EU might endan-
ger its internal cohesion and hinder further integration. However, after
it became apparent that change in Germany's EU enlargement policy
would have led to a difficult predicament in relations with Poland and
that it would not be well received in the West either, the SPD and the
Greens altered their cautious rhetoric. In the meantime the CDU
attacked the parties of the new government for irresponsible behaviour
on the issue.[48]

Interestingly, however, the *Frankfurter Allgemeine Zeitung* reported
in July 2000 that the two biggest parties of the *Bundestag*, the CDU
and the SPD, had secretly agreed to delay enlargement, preferably until
2005.[49] Although this news was denied by Günter Verheugen, a prominent member of the SPD and the EU Commissioner responsible for
enlargement,[50] the two main parties were subsequently unanimous in
their opposition to the Polish demand to name the accession date. In
sum, although no German party questioned the principle of EU

enlargement, it was nonetheless clear that after 1998 they were in no rush to see it implemented.

Assessment

The German government's efforts to put the question of enlargement firmly on to the EU's agenda were remarkably successful. As a result, the accession preparations entered a more 'technical' stage when membership negotiations started in 1998. Structural and personnel changes within the German civil service showed that the business of dealing with enlargement was to be de-politicised and relegated to the field of normal European affairs. The theme of EU enlargement was also mobilised by German political parties for electoral purposes.

After 1998, EU enlargement came to impact more directly on the German domestic scene, and consequently the Federal Republic's policy became increasingly vulnerable to the influences of interest groups, which often rendered Bonn–Berlin's position contradictory. At the end of Kohl's chancellorship a striking example of such a discrepancy was Bonn's policies of supporting enlargement while arguing in favour of lowering Germany's contributions to the EU budget, and objecting to the reform of the CAP. The subsequent red–green administration chose to concentrate on other than enlargement policies, most notably the issue of Germany's net contribution and deepening European integration prior to its opening to the East. Whereas the first of these policies was pursued by Schröder himself, the second was taken forward by Fischer, as seen in his pro-federal proposal for Europe delivered at the Humboldt University in May 2000.[51] It is clear that these priorities signified a waning of the government's support for a quick enlargement, as demonstrated in Germany's opposition to naming a date.

Diversities of policies and interests were also apparent in the enlargement policies of the German *Länder*, as demonstrated in the cases of Bavaria and Brandenburg. Considering the *Länder* involvement in the negotiations and the *Bundesrat's* right to reject the enlargement treaties, their policies should not be overlooked. The differences occurring at the Federal as well as the *Länder* level were further exacerbated by the political parties, which increasingly came to look at enlargement through the prism of their domestic considerations. A similar 'domestication' of EU enlargement policies occurred in Poland.

Domestic politics in Poland and EU enlargement

Convergence and divergence of national structures

The national context in which Warsaw formulated its European policy bore some structural similarities to that of the Federal Republic, which was a consequence of Poland borrowing some solutions from Germany in its post-1989 transformation. Of these 'borrowed solutions', probably the most significant was the introduction in Poland of a 'German-style' electoral system based on proportional representation (PR) with a 5 per cent threshold. The system effectively narrowed the number of Polish parliamentary parties from over thirty in 1990 to between five and six by 1998. This system fostered the practice of coalition governments. Beyond national politics, Poland also used some elements of the German example while embarking on regional decentralisation. This was particularly apparent in the second tier of local administration, established in 1998 and called the '*powiat*', which was modelled on the German *Kreise* (district).

However, in spite of these similarities, the domestic circumstances in which German and Polish European policies emerged were structurally quite different. Germany was an established democracy and Poland still a young, unconsolidated democracy. Notwithstanding some constitutional similarities in organising political representation as mentioned above, the differences between the two party systems and political parties remained vast. True, the two countries had a comparable number of parliamentary parties (five–seven), but the similarities ended here. While the mainstream German parties (CDU, SPD, FPD) developed and survived over the course of at least fifty years (the SPD since the late nineteenth century) Polish parties emerged and sometimes won elections (such as AWS, Electoral Action Solidarity) only to disappear over the parliament's four-year period. It was also clear that those Polish parties that had survived since 1989 (SLD, Alliance of Democratic Left; PSL, Polish Popular Alliance) were still in the process of constructing their identities and writing or re-writing their programmes. This relative immaturity of Polish parties produced a political system that was far less stable than that in Germany. For example, between 1989 and 2001 Poland had ten Prime Ministers while Germany had had only seven Chancellors since the inception of the Federal Republic in 1949.

Further differences concerned the structures of national and local governments. Although the constitutional position of the Polish Prime

Minister was formally strong, it was by no means comparable with that of the Federal Chancellor and his special *Richtlinienkompetenz*. In addition, the prestige of the Prime Minister's office was overshadowed by the position of the President who, unlike in Germany, was directly elected. Another major difference appeared in territorial structures and the degree of regional decentralisation. While Germany operated a federal system Poland, despite the 1998 de-centralisation law, was a unitary state. Consequently, unlike in Germany, Polish regions were not involved in European policy in a meaningful way. This mixture of deliberate constitutional convergence, coupled with continuing divergences between the two states is of consequence here. For example, as in the Federal Republic, the Polish system of coalition government effectively safeguarded against European policy being dominated by a one-party approach. Yet, it also resulted in comparably poor co-ordination within the government. However, the latter did not occur on the same level of government in the two countries; the prominent phenomenon of ministerial 'sectorisation' in Germany did not materialise in Poland to a comparable degree. However, there were difficulties in Poland with co-ordinating positions at the top 'strategic' level of government, which, as noted above, had been successfully tackled in Germany. Arguably, this latter feature was a consequence of the relatively weak position of the Polish Prime Minister and the unstable political environment in which he/she operates.

The government

The decision-making structure of Poland's European diplomacy is considerably decentralised, highly politicised and personality-driven (Figure 6.3). There are a whole range of actors involved in the process but during the period after 1998 the four principal individuals were the Prime Minister, the Foreign Minister, the head of the Office of the Committee of European Integration (UKIE) and the Chief Negotiator of Poland's accession to the EU. This plurality of institutions involved in Poland's European diplomacy originates from the period of unsuccessful political 'cohabitation' between the anti-communist President Lech Wałęsa and the government made up of two communist successor parties, the SLD and the PSL. While Wałęsa remained in office (1990–95), he controlled the so-called 'presidential Ministries', which, along with Defence and the Interior also included the Foreign Office. As a result of the 1993 parliamentary elections, won by the ex-communists and their

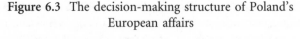

Figure 6.3   The decision-making structure of Poland's
European affairs

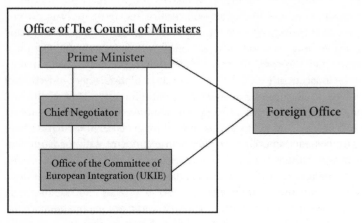

allies, Wałęsa had to share power with his political opponents. Little co-operation emerged, and in effect the ex-communists looked for ways to constrain Wałęsa's influence in foreign and European affairs. This led to the establishment of UKIE, which, attached to the Prime Minister's Office and controlled by the ex-communist SLD, emerged as a competitor to the Department of European Affairs in the Foreign Office.

Once established, this dual governance of Warsaw's European policy became a permanent feature, surviving Wałęsa's departure from office, the change of constitution that considerably limited presidential powers and the departure of the ex-communists from government in September 1997. The new centre-right government was formed by the pro-European Freedom Union (UW) and the Electoral Action Solidarity (AWS), that contained a substantial Eurosceptic element. In order to reconcile the conflicting positions of these parties, the new Prime Minister, Jerzy Buzek, from the AWS, chose to apply a system of 'checks and balances' in the government's conduct of European policy. Consequently, the Foreign Office went to the pro-European Bronisław Geremek from the UW and UKIE was taken by a Eurosceptic member of the AWS, Ryszard Czarnecki.

At the beginning of 1998 the new centre-right government had to appoint a Chief Negotiator for Poland's accession to the EU, which emerged as a new and important post in Warsaw's EU affairs. The issue quickly became a contentious one as it put a spotlight on the government's internal squabbles over the division of competencies in the area of EU enlargement. An obvious front-runner for the post was Jacek Saryusz-Wolski, who had formerly negotiated the terms of the EC/EU Association Agreements. However, being famously ambitious, Saryusz-Wolski did not want to be answerable to anyone but the Prime Minister. He also demanded that his new office would be independent from both the Foreign Office and the UKIE.[52] This infuriated the head of UKIE, Czarnecki, who threatened to resign if Buzek agreed to Saryusz-Wolski's conditions.[53] Up against a wall, Buzek rejected Saryusz-Wolski and eventually appointed Jan Kułakowski, Poland's former Ambassador to the EU, a European technocrat with no particular political affiliations. Kułakowski's competencies were subsequently split in a truly ingenious manner between the Prime Minister's Office (where he was appointed as State Secretary), the UKIE (where Kułakowski had his second office) and the Foreign Office (with which he promised to co-operate).[54] In practice, however, while the Chief Negotiator worked closely with the Prime Minister his links with both the UKIE and the Foreign Office became loose. In theory, the division of labour between the Chief Negotiator, the Foreign Office and the UKIE was clear. The Foreign Office's task was to prepare policy guidelines and to look at bilateral relations with member states, and its policy guidelines were subsequently supposed to be turned into policy directives by the UKIE, which was also responsible for the task of co-ordinating the work of other ministries.[55] Finally, the Chief Negotiator's team prepared Poland's position for the negotiations on the basis of instructions from both the Foreign Office and the UKIE.

However, in practice, there was a lot of policy overlap between and within these departments and a fair amount of political as well as personal competition. These tensions were only further exacerbated in the wake of the EU's refusal to finance 34 million ECU worth of projects, which were prepared by Warsaw within the framework of the PHARE programme.[56] Minister Czarnecki, whose UKIE was responsible for preparing the projects, accused Brussels of playing politics and Czarnecki's Eurosceptic friends from the AWS recalled various conspiracy theories.[57] In the meantime, the Foreign Office, run by Geremek from the UW, confirmed that Czarnecki's team had not allowed itself enough time to prepare the projects. In addition, Czarnecki's deputy, Piotr Nowina-Konopka, also from the UW, publicly confirmed that Brussels was right to accuse his boss of incompetence. The scandal over the loss of PHARE funds brought the coalition to the brink of collapse and it also fuelled Eurosceptic sentiments in the AWS. Finally, both Czarnecki and his deputy were sacked and the running of the UKIE was taken over by a non-political Under-Secretary of State, Maria Karasińska-Fendler, who was to be directly answerable to the Prime Minister. However, the downgrading of the position of the head of UKIE did not solve the emerging competence problem between the UKIE and the Chief Negotiator's office. In addition, following the PHARE funds' scandal, the UKIE lost its influence over the management of the EU's funds, which were taken over by the powerful Finance Ministry. As a result, the already quite decentralised structure of European policy-making in Poland was further dispersed (Figure 6.4).

As a result of these changes the UKIE's influence was substantially reduced. The Office lost its ability to influence the management of financial aid and, while the position of the Chief Negotiator was boosted, the UKIE's say in the negotiating process diminished. This led the new head of the office, Maria Karasińska-Fendler, to complain about the unnecessary overlap of competencies. Determined to prove her point, Karasińska-Fendler resigned in December 1998, but her resignation was not accepted for a further four months. In the subsequent period between April 1999 and April 2000 the UKIE was effectively without a leader while the squabbles between the AWS and UW made it impossible to find a compromise candidate to head the Office. Finally, in April 2000, Jacek Saryusz-Wolski accepted the position of State Secretary in the Committee of European Integration and became the UKIE's new boss. Saryusz-Wolski's appointment eased, without solving completely, the problem of overlapping competencies with the Negotiator's Office since the Chief Negotiator was now made answerable to the head of UKIE.

It was also clear that Saryusz-Wolski, a person of much greater stature than any of his predecessors, was more than just a civil servant and that he had strong views on European integration, including his sceptical approach towards the notion of supranational integration.[58] He also had a reputation in the EU for being a tough negotiator, whose ability to compromise had often been doubted in the past. Saryusz-Wolski's appointment thus effectively meant the re-politicisation of the UKIE.

One might have expected that with a strong personality in charge of the UKIE Warsaw's internal squabbles over competencies in European affairs would have been resolved and its policy taken a more unanimous shape. Clearly, the decision-making structure within the Prime

Figure 6.4   Changes in the decision-making structures of Poland's European affairs

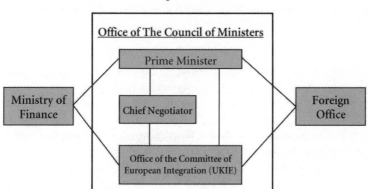

Minister's Office became more straightforward; in addition, in the wake of the UW's withdrawal from government in June 2000 an element of political competition was eliminated from Warsaw's European diplomacy. The Foreign Office was now taken over by Władysław Bartoszewski, a non-political intellectual, loosely affiliated with the centre-right in the same manner as Saryusz-Wolski.

Still, a structural dualism in Warsaw's EU policy persisted, with Saryusz-Wolski on the one hand and Bartoszewski on the other. Only a month after Bartoszewski's appointment, it became clear that his policies were not always congruent with those of the head of the UKIE. For example, while Saryusz-Wolski criticised Joschka Fischer's pro-federal speech given at the Humboldt University in May 2000, Bartoszewski welcomed it and praised it in one of his own first speeches after becoming Foreign Minister.[59]

It is obvious, therefore, that Warsaw still had a long way to go before its European policy became coherent. Some of the discrepancies were caused by the immaturity of the political system and will probably become less acute with the greater consolidation of political parties over time. However, if Poland follows the German example its European diplomacy will probably never be fully centralised. There are some strong indications that this might be the case; as argued above, Poland's electoral law favours coalition governments, which in turn lead to a de-centralised management of European affairs. In addition, the Polish foreign policy system involves the strong participation of the President. One may thus expect that in the foreseeable future Warsaw will continue to speak with more than one voice vis-à-vis Brussels.

Political parties and European integration

During the transition period following 1989 the Polish party system remained in a state of flux. Despite this, at least until 2001, Polish politics was divided by a clear-cut cleavage between the communist successor parties (SLD and PSL) and the forces originating from the pre-1989 dissident movement. The well-organised communist successor parties quickly adjusted to new competitive politics and after 'westernising' their programmes continued as major political forces, returning to power in 1993 and again in 2001. However, the ex-dissident scene remained highly unstable and composed of many smaller parties divided by almost everything and united only by their common past. During the period discussed here (1998–2001) the communist successor parties were in opposition and ex-dissidents were in government initially forming a coalition between the AWS and the UW. This coalition collapsed in 2000 and the AWS formed a minority government that survived until the September 2001 elections.

Overall there were five major parties in the Polish Parliament, the *Sejm*, during the period discussed in this chapter:

- The *AWS*, the senior party in government, was really an umbrella organisation consisting of many smaller parties representing three major types of associations: the trade union 'Solidarity', the Catholic and Christian-Democratic parties and the liberal-conservative parties. The AWS was a typical transitional party marked by weak leadership and internal incoherence. It had been hastily put together shortly before the 1997 elections by various fractions determined to oust the 'reds'; it split while in government and disintegrated altogether after the elections in 2001.

- The *SLD*, the major party of opposition, was a reformed former communist party that aspired to become a western-style Social-Democratic party. It was a major party of government between 1993 and 1997 and again after the 2001 landslide electoral victory.

- The *UW* was a party of former liberal dissidents. It co-governed in coalition with the AWS until June 2000, when it withdraw its ministers.[60] In the 2001 elections the UW failed to pass the 5 per cent threshold and subsequently found itself outside Parliament.

• The rural *PSL*, before 1989 a communist satellite party, represented one particular interest group – the farmers. It co-governed with the SLD during 1993–97 and after the 2001 elections, but it left the coalition in 2003 over a disagreement concerning the terms of agricultural subsidies in the context of the CAP.

• The far-right *Movement for the Reconstruction of Poland (ROP)* remained in opposition before and after 1997. It disintegrated after the 2001 elections and was replaced by a more pious and ostensibly anti-EU party called the League of Polish Families.

As in the German case, before 1997–98, EU enlargement did not serve as a reference point for Polish parties to demonstrate their divisions. All the major parties had agreed that Poland should join the EU; in fact, the issue was one of the few areas of political consensus in Poland. With the prospect of actual membership negotiations looming, this consensus was not broken (in as much as none of the larger parties opposed Poland's EU membership) but differences emerged with regard to the negotiation strategy and the future of European integration. As a result, the political scene divided between the supporters of a quick EU membership, who did not attach any special conditions to this principle, and the proponents of the 'yes, but …' qualification, who maintained that Poland should enter the EU only as long as its specific national demands were met.

The first occurrences of a serious European debate took place in the run-up to the Parliamentary elections in September 1997. During its campaign the newly formed AWS referred to the Gaullist idea of a 'Europe of the States' *(Europa Narodów)* and stressed that, once in the EU, Poland would retain its own distinctive identity. It was argued that the AWS use of the Gaullist notion was produced for internal party purposes, to help reconcile the divisions between its pro-European and Eurosceptic factions.[61]

In opposition to the AWS 'Europe of the States' the ex-communist SLD promoted the concept of 'Europe as the Fatherland of the Nations' *(Europa jako Ojczyzna Narodów)*, denoting a more pro-federal approach. Since the 1997 elections the SLD had started to portray itself as a Euro-friendly socialist party. On the other hand, the SLD did not match its pro-European rhetoric with support for the economic and political reforms recommended by the EU Commission. The liberal

UW, as expected, appeared the most pro-European and pro-reformist, while the rural PSL embarked on a typical 'yes, but ...' position as well as asserting its dislike for any further reforms that pre-conditioned enlargement.[62]

The 1997 elections also saw the emergence of a link between Euroscepticism and anti-Germanism. This was also often connected with a pro-Atlantic bias, as some Eurosceptic politicians expected that NATO would counter-balance the EU – which they alleged was dominated by Germans. As argued by one of the most influential members of the Catholic-national wing of the AWS, Henryk Goryszewski, 'Europe after Maastricht is dominated by Germany, whereas in NATO there is a strong presence of Americans – the only ones who are able to balance the German influence'.[63] Another leader of the Eurosceptic wing of the AWS, Marian Piłka, expressed a similar opinion: 'Poland should oppose the supranational development of the EU that would lead to the rise in dominance of the strongest Member State – Germany, and subsequently the loss of our sovereignty, ... the Europeanisation of NATO leads an increase in German power, a development that would result in turning East Central Europe into a sphere of German influence.'[64] At the other end of the Polish discourse was the UW, which was clearly quite comfortable about Germany and chose to attract voters by displaying images of Kohl and Mazowiecki, one of the UW's founders and its first leader, embracing in the famous gesture of reconciliation from 1989.[65]

In the wake of the elections, won by the AWS and UW, and the launch of the accession negotiations in November 1998, some significant reshaping of the European debate occurred. Most significantly, the political consensus on Poland's EU membership was broken as a group of ultra-Eurosceptic dissidents left the AWS and formed their own parliamentary faction called 'Our Circle' (Nasze Koło) which explicitly opposed EU membership.[66] The AWS did not become free of its Eurosceptics, however, who were still prominent in the party and exerted their influence. As a result, the AWS continued to struggle with reconciling its internal differences while also trying to satisfy its coalition partner, the pro-European UW. In order to keep everyone on board, the AWS started to exploit its Christian-Democratic heritage and argue that Europe was essentially a Christian project. Like a 'Europe of the States' idea, this argument aimed to reconcile the AWS Eurosceptic wing with the notion of European integration. It also had the merit of being acceptable to the UW and pro-Europeans in the AWS.

In embarking on a more Euro-friendly course, the AWS received support from a most unlikely partner – the Catholic Church. This was particularly surprising considering that in the immediate wake of the end of the Cold War Polish bishops had viewed integration with the EU with deep suspicion. However, when prompted by Pope John Paul II, who encouraged the bishops to promote European integration, the Church slowly began to support Poland's EU membership. In 1999, the Polish episcopate went to Brussels to meet the EU Commission; since then the bishops have been unreservedly in favour of EU integration.[67] However, although the 'Christian EU' argument helped to ease tensions within the centre-right, it antagonised the centre-left and led to a weakening of the cross-party consensus on European matters. The SLD's perception of EU integration was clearly very different from that of the AWS. The Social Democrats remained convinced that the EU was a predominantly secular entity and as such could even be a useful instrument against the 'clerical' centre-right. For example, the SLD's leader, Leszek Miller, stressed that the EU promoted a secular state, and a clear separation of religion from politics and as such it deserved the support of the Social Democrats.

The tensions between the coalition partners, UW and AWS, climaxed after the row over the mishandled application for PHARE funds. In effect, European integration stopped being a unifying factor in Polish politics and became a point of division between the government and opposition, as well as within the government itself. As a result, no significant cross-party co-operation was established on European issues, which led to the slowing down of the pace of adopting the *acquis communitaire*. To make matters worse, the opposition began to undermine the government's position presented for negotiations with the EU. During their trip to Brussels, SLD politicians reportedly criticised the government's position on the acquisition of land and second homes (where the government requested an eighteen-year transition period) and on the farming sector's access to EU funds (the government wanted full access; and the SLD thought this was unrealistic).[68]

With slow progress in the negotiations and in the adoption of European legislation, the EU threatened Warsaw that Poland might be relegated to the second group of applicant countries and therefore would not be able to join the EU in the first wave of enlargement. This warning clearly had a mobilising effect, as all major parties of the Parliament agreed to set up an extraordinary Committee of European Law. The Committee has been subsequently armed with special competencies that allowed the Parliament a 'short-cut' adoption to the *acquis communitaire*.[69] Although a consensus on European integration finally transpired in Parliament, some political divisions continued to affect Poland's preparation for EU membership. This point notwithstanding, aside from the views of the relatively minor group of ultra-Eurosceptics from 'Our Circle', the principle of EU membership was not challenged during the 1997–2001 Parliament's life.

Assessment

In the second half of the 1990s Poland's EU enlargement policy evolved from being a straightforward political objective and a central component of the notion of 'returning to Europe' into a more problematic and contested issue. Much of this change was perhaps a natural consequence of the 'domestication' of the EU enlargement agenda, following the start of negotiations. While it could be expected that European integration would start to divide party politics it was rather surprising that (unlike in Germany) it also divided the top branches of the government. Naturally, with the negotiations commencing, it was inevitable that the role of individual ministries would grow and differences of opinion would appear. Nonetheless, it was not equally predictable that the centre of the government's decision-making process would be so difficult to define. Unlike most member states and accession countries, Warsaw decided against concentrating its European diplomacy in the Foreign Office, but rather to split competencies between the Prime Minister's Office and the Foreign Office. In addition, the Office of the Negotiator temporarily emerged as an additional decision-making centre. Clearly, much of this de-centralisation was rooted in the specificity of the political system in Poland – characterised by coalition government and the President's role in foreign affairs. In addition, the unconsolidated nature of the party system produced a split government, with a weak Prime Minister unable to provide clear leadership in European affairs. The AWS and UW remained divided between themselves as well as internally over European integration. These divisions resulted in turn in the poor co-ordination of European policy between the Prime Minister's Office and the Foreign Office as well as within the Prime Minister's Office itself.

Overall, Poland's European diplomacy during the 1997–2001 period demonstrated that a combination of unconsolidated democracy coupled the 'domestication' of the European agenda produced a policy that was both 'poor on strategy and poor on tactics'.

'EU-isation', domestication and Polish–German relations

Germany can rightly claim credit for the fact that the first phase of enlargement began and that Poland found itself firmly on track to join the EU. Bonn–Berlin's support for enlargement was the main reason for the dramatic improvement in the relationship, which was manifest in the favourable changes in public perceptions of Germany in Poland. When in 1990 *Der Spiegel* published a survey on the attitudes of Poles towards the Germans, the outcome was still rather pessimistic, with more than 50 per cent of Poles declaring that they did not like their western neighbours, 41 per cent indifferent and only 9 per cent actually liking the Germans.[70] In the same survey, 59 per cent confessed that they still viewed Germany as a threat. Subsequent research into public opinion in Poland showed that in the period between 1993 and 1996 positive attitudes towards the Germans were consistently rising. Whereas in 1993, 23 per cent were positively disposed towards the Germans, 22 per cent indifferent and 53 per cent were of a negative view, in 1996 these figures were almost reversed. 43 per cent declared a liking for the Germans, 23 per cent remained indifferent and only 31 per cent held a negative view (Figure 6.5).[71]

The changing nature of the relationship was also reflected in Warsaw's foreign policy. Since the mid-1990s the Federal Republic figured in many official declarations and foreign policy statements as a 'special friend' and Poland's most important partner in Europe. Particular popularity and respect in Poland was earned by the German Christian-Democratic party and its former leader Helmut Kohl. Even Kohl's dubious policy towards the Oder-Neisse dispute in 1989–90 was forgiven and forgotten when he declared in 1995 that Poland should join the EU before the year 2000.[72]

On the other hand, soon after the launch of membership negotiations it became apparent that the interrelationship which had been established between EU enlargement and Polish–German rapprochement could also become problematic for the relationship. As argued earlier, the start of the negotiations in 1998 coincided not only with Bonn adopting a far more cautious position on enlargement, but also with Warsaw becoming more demanding vis-à-vis the EU. This was perhaps a natural response to the development of the enlargement

Figure 6.5 Changing Polish attitudes towards the Germans, 1993–96

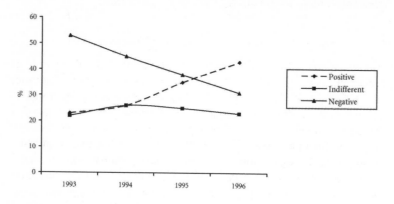

process, which, in the late 1990s, was increasingly impacting upon the domestic affairs of both Poland and Germany, the process referred to as 'EU-isation' in Chapter 1. It is clear that both in Germany and Poland the 'EU-isation' of the enlargement agenda, that intensified after the start of the negotiations, resulted in its *domestication* – a multiplication of actors involved in the shaping of enlargement policies. This development meant that both Poland and Germany arrived at the negotiating table with much more constrained and convoluted postures than they had had in the former strategic stage of the enlargement process. Despite this, neither Bonn nor Warsaw questioned the basic principle of EU enlargement, which they both continued to see as the bedrock of their rapprochement. However, in some policy areas, such as land acquisition or the free movement of workers, discord emerged which was subsequently instrumentalised for domestic purposes in both countries. This development undoubtedly affected the pace of the relationship and led to a number of much-publicised disagreements between Bonn–Berlin and Warsaw.

The first serious blow to Warsaw's confidence in the Federal Republic's role as its advocate emerged in the wake of the CDU–CSU–FDP coalition's vote in May 1998 in support of the *Heimatvertrieben* resolution. The arrival of the SPD–Green (red–green) government in 1998, with its 'new realism' in EU enlargement, was a further setback for the relationship. While Kohl could be forgiven for playing a nationalistic tune for domestic purposes, he somehow managed to establish himself in Poland as the chief promoter of EU enlargement. The SPD was different. It had a record of ignoring the pre-1989 dissidents and of co-operating with Polish communists. Many in the SPD opposed NATO enlargement and remained ambivalent about expanding the EU. This was coupled with a perception of the Greens as a leftist, anti-American force, both of which were viewed with suspicion by the AWS–UW coalition and the majority of the new foreign policy elite in Poland.

Thus when, during his visit to Poland in October 1998, Joschka Fischer declined to set a target date for enlargement and Gerhard Schröder warned at the EU Summit in Pörtschach in December 1998 against too quick an opening of the EU to the East, Warsaw felt that it had lost its advocate. Following this, the Polish Foreign Minister expressed his scepticism about the red–green coalition by saying: 'The CDU and Helmut Kohl, we knew that they were our friends but the new government we are not sure.'[73] The Polish press was full of articles accusing the SPD–Green coalition of pursuing a nationalistic 'new *Realpolitik*' that would lead to the isolation of Poland and renewal of the German–Russian bond. At the same time it was hardly noticed in Warsaw that the new government had inherited from Kohl a European policy which was already contradictory, unsustainable – and, most importantly, increasingly reserved about enlargement. It was, however, widely noted that while setting an agenda for its EU Presidency (in the first half of 1999), the red–green government prioritised issues other than enlargement.[74]

Warsaw's EU enlargement policy was also criticised in Germany. Poland was accused by the German press of slowing down the process and of making other, allegedly better-prepared, countries wait while Poland lagged behind in the negotiations.[75] The affair over Warsaw losing PHARE funds and the subsequent power struggle between different departments over the management of European policy were widely and critically commented upon in Germany. The disagreements within the governing coalition about Europe were observed with similar concern in Bonn–Berlin. The German press became prone to portray the AWS as a Eurosceptic force dominated by its traditional 'catholic-national' wing. It was also indicated that a major influence was being exerted on the AWS by industrial lobbies and trade unions that allegedly intended to block the passage of legislation required for the compliance with EU's *acquis*.

This rather unfavourable climate began to improve after 1999. In spite of Warsaw's early criticism of Berlin's EU Presidency, the enlargement negotiations accelerated during this period. Berlin strongly opposed any plans that would not include Poland in the first wave of enlargement and Joschka Fischer repeatedly stated that without Poland the notion was not conceivable. Finally, during the Nice summit in December 2000, Berlin and Warsaw fought together against the French proposal to discriminate new members by granting them proportionally lesser voting powers than they were entitled to by virtue of their demography.[76]

To conclude, the case of post-1998 Polish–German relations in the context of EU enlargement shows two fundamental points. The growing impact of European integration on the domestic scene provoked responses from multiple domestic agents, which inevitably put pressures on national governments. The findings of this chapter have shown that Polish and German European policies, were at times, dominated by domestic considerations. This seemed to have been the case in the latter stages of the Kohl government, as seen in its *Heimatsvertriebene* resolution, and in the early phase of Schröder's chancellorship. A second point is that the intensification of 'EU-isation', and the growth of domestic actors involved in the process, does not necessarily mean that governments will always let domestic interests lead their policies. It is clear that the post-1989 rapprochement acted in the Polish–German case as the constraining factor against enlargement policies being determined solely by short-term considerations.

Conclusion

In the 1990s NATO and EU enlargements became the engines of Polish–German reconciliation, rapprochement and co-operation. As frameworks for the relationship, the enlargement processes illustrated points of co-operation but, as demonstrated by the events after 1998, they also prompted divisions and discord, when the aspirations of domestic actors diverged. Since 1998, the Federal Republic has not had a single, comprehensive EU enlargement policy. Instead there have been the policies of the Foreign Office, the Finance Ministry and the Chancellor's Office, as well as those of other ministries. There have also been the policies of Bavaria and Brandenburg, as well as of other *Länder*. Party politics have additionally contributed to aggravating the complexity of the German system. It is true that some common grounds remain: most importantly, neither a single Ministry nor state questioned the underlying principle of enlargement. Nonetheless, as argued in the chapter, the differences were often substantial. Secondly, because of the complexity of the issue and growing criticism of it at home, the 'yes, but …' attitude came to dominate Bonn–Berlin's EU enlargement policy. Thirdly, from being a key advocate for a quick enlargement, Germany came to prefer a slower pace, as demonstrated in the objection to naming a date for enlargement.

In Poland, as in the Federal Republic, a diversification of EU enlargement policy also took place, albeit within different domestic conditions and having different outcomes. Most importantly, European affairs fell prey to the unfinished process of Poland's transition to democracy, characterised by changing and unclear divisions of bureaucratic competencies and an unstable party system. The ever-increasing number of centres of European policy-making led to poor co-ordination and, as in Germany, the emergence of several, instead of one, EU enlargement policy. The de-centralisation of Warsaw's European policy was further increased by the weakness of political parties, particularly of the AWS, which remained divided into a number of factions. In Germany, the diversification of European policy mainly concerned the lower levels of government and did not impair the government's ability to pursue strategic aims and objectives. In Poland, however, the diversity of policies occurred at the very centre of government, seriously affected Warsaw's capacity to come up with a coherent vision of European integration.

The issue of EU enlargement became central to the 'Europeanisation' of German–Polish relations. As long as the Federal Republic was perceived in Poland as an advocate of the enlargement, the relationship continued to improve dramatically. This was reflected in both Polish foreign policy and also in public opinion in Poland. However, when enthusiasm for enlargement diminished in Germany, the link existing between EU enlargement and Berlin–Warsaw relations came to have a rather ambivalent impact upon the relationship. This ambivalence only became more apparent after 2001, when Poland and Germany started to voice increasingly divergent views towards the future shape of the EU. In this context, some commentators raised the question whether Polish–German rapprochement would be sustainable after enlargement. On one hand Poland's EU membership in 2004 represents a joint success for the two countries that had consistently pursued this policy since 1989. On the other hand, the actual realisation of enlargement opens up the question as to whether the 'Europeanisation' of the relationship is sufficiently advanced to encourage Berlin and Warsaw to put their differences aside and work together in an EU of twenty-five members. Developments between 2001 and 2004 do not give grounds for much optimism when considering this question.

Notes

1 Friedbert Pflüger, 'Polen – unser Frankreich im Osten'/'Poland and the European Union', *Aussenpolitik*, III/95, pp. 225–310.

2 See Simon Bulmer, Charlie Jeffery and William E. Paterson, *Germany's European Diplomacy: Shaping the Regional Milieu* (Manchester and New York: Manchester University Press, 2000), p. 9.

3 Bulmer, Jeffery and Paterson, *Germany's European Diplomacy*, pp. 22–52.

4 See Dietrich Rometsch and Wolfgang Wessels, *The European Union and Member States* (Manchester: Manchester University Press, 1996), p. 73

5 See 'Erklärung der Bundesregierung zur Agenda 2000', Bonn, 18 March 1998.

6 Charlie Jeffery, 'Niemieckie landy a "normalizacja" dyskusji o rozszerzeniu UE', in William E. Paterson, Barbara Lippert, Marcin Zaborowski *et al.*, *Wspólnota Sprzecznych Interesów* (Warsaw: CSM, 1999), pp. 47–50.

7 Interview with Peter Sonnehol, a Foreign Office official responsible for liasing with the *Länder*, Auswärtiges Amt, Referat E II, Bonn, 11 May 1998.

8 See press interview with Klaus Kinkel, 'Das ist Verrat an der Geschichte', *Focus*, 18 May 1998.

9 Interview with Mr Vogel, Auswärtiges Amt, Arbeitstab Ostmitteleuropa, Bonn, 23 April 1998.

10 Interview with Reinhard Silberberg, Auswärtiges Amt, Arbeitstab EU/Mittel- und Osteuropa, Bonn, 21 April 1998.

11 Confidential interview in the Finance Ministry, Bonn, 10 December 1998.

12 Interview with Mr Klekner, Auswärtiges Amt, Arbeitstab Osterweiterung, 13 November 1998.

13 Interviews in the Abteilung 2 (Chancellor's Office), the Europaabteilung (Foreign Office), and the Abteilung E (Economics Ministry), 1 April–15 May 1998.

14 Interviews in the Federal Ministries between March and December 1998.

15 Interview with Reinhard Silberberg, Auswärtiges Amt, Arbeitstab EU/Mittel- und Osteuropa, Bonn, 21 April 1998.

16 For example, see 'Erklärung der Bundesregierung zur Agenda 2000', Bonn, 18 March 1998.

17 See José Ignacio Torreblanca Payá, *The European Community and Central Eastern Europe (1989–1993): Foreign Policy and Decision-Making* (Madrid: Centro de Estudios Avanzados en Ciencias Socialeas, 1997), pp. 199, 200–1.

18 Barbara Lippert, 'Shaping and Evaluating the Europe Agreements – The

Community Side', in Barbara Lippert and Heinrisch Schneider, *Monitoring Association and Beyond: The European Union and the Visegrad States* (Bonn: Europe Union Verlag, 1995), p. 320.

19 Interview in the Abteilung 2 (Chancellor's Office), 23 April 1998.

20 Interviews in the Ministry of Economics and Foreign Office, March–April 1998.

21 Interview with Dr Stefan Comes, Deutsche Gesellschaft für Auswärtige Politik (DGAP), 16 April 1998.

22 Interview in the Ministry of Labour and Social Affairs, Bonn, April 1998. See also 'Warschau will von Anfang an ein vollwertiges EU Mitglied sein', *FAZ*, 26 February 1998.

23 See 'Northern States Pay the Union Piper but Santer Calls the Tune', *European Voice*, 23–29 July 1998.

24 See 'Schröder fordert niedrigere deutsche Zahlungen an die EU', *FAZ*, 9 December 1998.

25 'Germany to Push Ahead with EU Tax Harmonising Plans', *Financial Times*, 24 November 1998.

26 See 'Bundesregierung: Keine EU-Erweiterung ohne Finanzreform', *FAZ*, 3 December 1998.

27 See 'Britain Out of Harmony Again', *The Economist*, 28 November 1998.

28 See Charlie Jeffery and Stephen Collins, 'The German Länder and EU Enlargement: Between Apple Pie and Issue Linkage', in V. Handl, J. Hon, O. Pick *et al.*, *Germany and East Central Europe Since 1990* (Prague: Ustav mezinarodnich vztahu, 1998), pp. 89–98.

29 See Bulmer, Jeffery and Paterson, *Germany's European Diplomacy*, p. 112.

30 'Entschließung des Bundesrates zur Mitteilung der Europäischen Kommission "Agenda 2000" – eine stärkere und erweiterte Union', Beschluss des Bundesrates, 28 November 1997.

31 See 'Erweiterung der Europäischen Union', Beschluss-Top3, 19 Europaministerkonferenz in Bremen, 22–23 April 1998.

32 'CSU warnt erneut vor überstürzten Beitritten', *Süddeutsche Zeitung*, 12 May 1998.

33 Interview with Brandenburg State Secretary Irmgard von Rottenburg, Vertretung des Landes Brandenburg beim Bund, Bonn, 7 May 1998.

34 Interview in Vertretung des Freistaates Bayern beim Bund, 28 April 1998. See also: *Anmerkungen zur Reform der EU-Strukturpolitik und zur Zukunft der Beihilfenkontrolle.*

35 Quoted in Jeffery, 'Niemieckie landy a "normalizacja" dyskusji o rozszerzeniu UE', p. 54.

36 Interview with Petra Erheler, Vertretung des Landes Brandenburg beim Bund, Bonn, 8 May 1998.

37 See 'Grazer Konferenz Resolution der an die mittel- und osteuropäischen Länder angrenzenden Regionen der EU-Mitgliedstaaten betreffend die

Herausforderungen der EU-Osterweiterung', Amt der Steiermärkischen Landesregierung, Graz, 29 January 1998.

38 Conversations with Petra Erheler, Brundenburg government official, January 1999.

39 See 'Hofer 20-Punkte-Katalog zur EU-Erweiterung, Entschließung der 2. Konferenz der EU-Grenzregionen am 24/25 Juli in Hof', Bayerische Staatskanzlei, Munich.

40 See Theo Waigel, 'Wer soll das bezahlen?', *Focus*, 3 July 1995.

41 'Finanzierung der EU-Osterweiterung', *Das Parlament*, 20 December 1996.

42 'In Sachen Europa hat Bayern ein Forderungspaket geschnürt', *Mainpost*, 3 December 1998.

43 In 1997 only about 30 per cent of Germans supported Poland's membership in the EU and 52 per cent were against it: See *Eurobarometer*, 47, Annex B. 20, Spring 1997.

44 See 'Gerhard Schröder w Warszawie. Nie stawiajmy warunków', *Rzeczpospolita*, 18 June 1998.

45 'Rechte für die Heimatvertriebenen', *FAZ*, 30 May 1998.

46 'Niefortunna Rezolucja. Verheugen: Po zwycięstwie SPD będzie inaczej', *Rzeczpospolita*, 7 July 1998.

47 See 'SPD Warns on EU Enlargement', *Financial Times*, 2 June 1998.

48 See 'Kritik der Union an der Europa-Politik der Regierung/Bundesdebatte vor dem Wiener Gipfel', *FAZ*, 11 December 1998.

49 See 'Keine EU-Beitritte vor 2005 oder 2006. Ein stilles Einvernehmen der großen deutschen Parteien', *FAZ*, 8 July 2000.

50 See 'Lista zaniedbań w rękach Millera. Kto spowalnia negocjacje?', *Rzeczpospolita*, 12 July 2000.

51 See 'From Confederacy to Federation – Thoughts on the Finality of European Integration', speech by Joschka Fischer at the Humboldt University, 12 May 2000.

52 See 'Jacek Saryusz-Wolski będzie głównym negocjatorem', *Rzeczpospolita*, 18 December 1997.

53 See 'Najlepszy kandydat w czwartek', *Prawo i Życie*, 3 February 1998.

54 See interview with Kułakowski 'Misja specjalna', *Wprost*, 22 February 1998.

55 See 'Zespół negocjacyjny w sprawie negocjacji o członkostwo Rzeczypospolitej Polskiej w Unii Europejskiej – Schemat stanowiska negocjacyjnego', Warsaw 15 July 1998.

56 See 'Polska traci 34 miliony ECU', *Rzeczpospolita*, 26 May 1998.

57 See 'SLD czeka, ZChN broni', *Rzeczpospolita*, 28 May 1998.

58 See interview with Sarysz-Wolski, 'Polska przeciwna Europie o dwóch prędkościach', Euro.pap.com.pl, 17 July 2000.

59 For Bartoszewski's speech, see 'Speech by the Minister for Foreign Affairs of Poland, Władysław Bartoszewski, at the Centre for European Policy Studies Brussels, 25 July 2000'; for Sarysz-Wolski's views on European

Federation and 'two-speed Europe', see Sarysz-Wolski, 'Polska przeciwna Europie o dwóch prędkościach', Euro.pap.com.pl, 17 July 2000.

60 See 'Coalition Adrift', *The Economist*, 3 June 2001.

61 See Jacek Kucharczyk, 'Porwanie Europy: Integracja europejska w polskim dyskursie politycznym 1997–1998', in Lena Kolarska-Bobińska *et al.* (ed.) *Polska Eurodebata* (Warsaw: Instytut Spraw Publicznych, 1999).

62 Kucharczyk, '"Za, a nawet przeciw": partie politiczne wobec perspecktywy integracij europejskiej w wyborach' 97', in Lena Kolarska-Bobińska *et al.* (ed.), *Polska Eurodebata* (Warsaw: Instytut Spraw Publicznych, 1999). pp. 231–44.

63 Klaus Bachmann, *Polska Kaczka i Europejski Staw* (Warsaw: CSM, 1999), p. 36

64 Marian Piłka, 'Europa, Tak Ale ...', *Życie*, 18 February 1997.

65 Kucharczyk, '"Za, a nawet przeciw"', p. 224.

66 Kucharczyk, 'Porwanie Europy', p. 298.

67 See 'Wizyta długo oczekiwana', *Rzeczpospolita*, 5 November 1997.

68 See '"SLD" krytykuje rząd w Warszawie', *Rzeczpospolita*, 11 July 2000.

69 See 'Szybka ścieżka z wybojami', *Rzeczpospolita*, 11 July 2000.

70 See Andrzej Sakson, 'Niemcy w świadomości Polaków', in Anna Wolf-Poweska (ed.), *Polacy Wobec Niemców: Z Dziejów Kultury Politycznej Polski 1945–1989* (Poznannnn: Instytut Zachodni, 1993), p. 428.

71 See 'Stosunek Polaków do Innych Narodowści, Komunikat z Badań' (Warsaw: CBOS, November 1998).

72 On Kohl's declaration in Warsaw, see 'Razem jest nam po drodze', *Rzeczpospolita*, 10 July 1995.

73 See 'Geremek: nie wiemy czego oczekiwać', *Gazeta Wyborcza*, 29 October 1998.

74 See Janusz A. Majcherek, 'Widmo Nowej Realpolitik', *Rzeczpospolita*, 3 November 1998; Aleksander Smolar, 'Unia na Horyzoncie', *Rzeczpospolita*, 19–20 December 1998.

75 See 'Die EU erweitert: Tür zu', *Die Welt*, 8 June 2000.

76 See Piotr Buras, 'The Most Serious Challenges Facing Poland's European Policy,' *Policy Reports & Analyses No. 4/2000*, (Warsaw: CIR 2000) www.csm.org.pl/en-index.htmlp.

Conclusion

This study has focused on the themes of conflict, co-operation and 'Europeanisation' in Polish–German relations between 1944 and 2001. As demonstrated in the course of the book, the relationship has evolved in a breathtaking manner over the last fifty years. The Nazi crimes during the Second World War and the territorial decisions taken by the allies in Tehran, Yalta and Potsdam resulted in a severe Polish–German conflict rooted in historical memory and sealed by an externally brokered border dispute. The subsequent division of Europe froze the relationship in what seemed a 'permanent conflict', with West Germany and Poland belonging to confronting alliances and deeply divided over disputed territory as well as the status of East Germany. While some elements of 'co-operation' started to emerge in Warsaw-Bonn relations from the 1970s onwards they remained limited to official circles and the prevailing Cold War conditions prevented any real breakthrough in the relationship. With the end of the Cold War the prospect for a military conflict between Poland and Germany was for the first time deemed impossible and by the end of the twentieth century economic, societal and political ties between the two neighbours developed to a degree unprecedented across the former East–West divide.

To illustrate the evolution of Polish–German relations, an analogy can be used with relations between neighbours who had badly fallen out, then, wanted to co-operate but were worried what other 'bigger' neighbours would say and eventually, after the hostile neighbours moved out, started to talk to each other and discovered many common interests in the process. However, it still remains unclear whether the neighbours' offspring, who increasingly like each other, will one day marry. There are three phases in this relationship, all of which were dealt with in the book and are summarised briefly below.

The three phases of the relationship

The neighbours who fell out

Chapter 2 focused on addressing the roots of conflict in the relation-ship which, as argued here, was multilayered in nature. The German–Polish 'interlocking conflict of interests', as it was defined in the chapter, was rooted in hostile perceptions of the two nations vis-à-vis each other in the aftermath of the Second World War and sustained by the realities of the post-war division of Europe. The chap-ter argued that with the end of the Second World War the relationship was at its lowest point ever. After Nazi Germany initiated war, six mil-lion Poles, one-fifth of the entire population, were killed. Under the German occupation most of Polish Jewry was exterminated and many other groups in society, including the intelligentsia, were singled out and subjected to mass executions carried out by the Nazi authorities. The whole of the occupied population lived under a regime that was much harsher than in the occupied nations of western Europe. With the end of the war, Poland was physically and economically devastated. In addition, half of the country remained under Soviet occupation with millions of Poles deported to various parts of the Soviet Union and others resettled to formerly East German areas where Poland was allowed by the allies to expand after the war as compensation. Poland's westward expansion led to the expulsion of millions of Germans from the annexed territories. Although, as prescribed by the allies, these expulsions were supposed to be conducted in a 'humane spirit' this was often not the case.

All of these developments meant that reconciliation between Poland and Germany would be an onerous task, which soon after the war became even more difficult as Europe and Germany split between two rival blocs. Consequently, the historical and territorial conflict was rein-forced by a conflict of ideology and politics. This combination of circumstances produced open hostility in the Polish–West German rela-tionship while Poland's relations with East Germany remained artificially friendly at the governmental level but reluctant between the two societies. This situation continued throughout most of the Cold War period, but in the mid-1950s, and later on in the late 1960s and early 1970s attempts were made to overcome the state of 'permanent freeze' in Warsaw's relations with Bonn.

The neighbours who wanted to co-operate but were afraid of other neighbours

Chapter 3 addressed the periods of 'thaw' in Polish–(West) German relations and discussed the reasons for the failure of these policies to deliver a meaningful breakthrough. The first such period followed de-Stalinisation in Poland in the autumn of 1956. The new nationally minded leader of the Polish communists, Stanisław Gomułka, was elected against the wishes of the Soviets and was therefore looking for ways to establish a more balanced relationship with the West. However, it was clear that any such co-operation would not be achievable without a degree of normality in relations with the Federal Republic, which remained highly irregular by this point, with Bonn refusing to establish diplomatic relations with Warsaw. The relationship subsequently went through a testing period during which economic co-operation intensified but no significant breakthrough came about. By 1957 Gomułka veered back towards the Soviet Union and returned to his anti-Western and anti-German position.

The second attempt followed from the new *Ostpolitik* of the SPD–FDP coalition that came to office in September 1969. The new government of Willy Brandt was determined to overcome the Cold War status quo and establish more regular relations with Eastern Bloc countries. A 'normalisation' of relations with Poland was crucial to the success of this project and Bonn moved quickly to address the issue. In December 1970 a comprehensive Polish–(West) German treaty was signed, resulting in the two countries establishing official relations and the Bonn Republic recognising the post-war Oder-Neisse border in its own name – though not as the successor German state. This agreement proved to be of fundamental significance for improving relations between the two governments and, most importantly, it 'liberated' Poland from relying on Soviet security guarantees. On the other hand, the new *Ostpolitik* failed to extend the benefits of '*détente*' beyond the level of governments; moreover, it was marked by the reluctant attitude of West German authorities towards the democratic opposition in Poland.

The chapter argued that the reason why the pre-1989 co-operation between Bonn and Warsaw remained limited was predominantly structural. As long as the two states belonged to confronting alliances, no considerable breakthrough in their relations was obtainable. This situation changed with the demise of bipolarity in 1989–90.

The neighbours who became reconciled

The end of the Cold War and the unification of Germany removed the structural constraints from the relationship, creating for the first time since the end of the Second World War a conducive climate for a genuine 'rapprochement' between Poland and Germany. While structural conditions were favourable, the two nations continued to distrust each other and the immediate period after 1989 saw an ambivalent relationship which was marked by the old conflict (the re-opened border dispute) but at the same time ever-more dynamic co-operation in other areas. In the early 1990s Warsaw and Bonn began to co-operate over the issue of Poland's integration with western institutions and found out in the process that their strategic interests were closely aligned. This process led to the debate about the 'Europeanisation' of the relationship and it was noted that the foreign policy perspectives of the two nations were reconcilable and mutually supportive.[1] However, as seen in Chapter 5, for Europeanisation to develop it is necessary to move beyond a simple reconcilability of interests towards an actual convergence of interests. Chapters 5 and 6 dealt with EU enlargement and argued that such an evolution remains a distant prospect for the relationship. Despite this rather sombre view of the further prospects for the 'Europeanisation' process, it is clear that enormous progress has been achieved in the relationship. The reconciliation process is well advanced and dialogue between the two nations is relatively broad, including business communities, youth exchange programmes and numerous cross-border initiatives. In other words, relations between the neighbours are good but it is not clear how much better they may become, and whether they can ever be as intimate as Franco-German relations.

Franco-German relations as a model for Polish–German relations

The book has frequently referred to the case of Franco-(West) German relations as a likely model for emulation in Polish–German relations. There are many points of comparison between these two relationships including geographical proximity, a difficult history and concerted efforts to overcome the past and develop close ties in a European context. As noted by an influential member of the CDU, Friedbert Pflüger, Poland is Germany's France to the East, in terms of both its geostrategic importance and the relationship's past.[2] Arguably Poland's position at the critical juncture between Western and Eastern Europe is just as strategically significant as France's contiguity with the Mediterranean and the Iberian Peninsula. With its 38 million inhabitants, Poland is less populous than France, but it is still by far the largest state in East Central Europe.

In the past, France and Germany (or the Germanic states) threatened each other with armed conflict; Napoleonic France invaded and controlled most of the German states. The unification of Germany in 1871 followed from the military defeat of France and the subsequent world wars solidified the hostile perceptions of the two nations vis-à-vis each other. The Polish–German past experience was equally, if not more, traumatic. Prussia, together with Russia and Austria, successfully plotted to divide among themselves the Polish–Lithuanian commonwealth that ceased to exist in the late eighteenth century, with western Poland being occupied by the Prussian state. After Poland was resurrected in 1918 it was threatened by the Weimar Republic and then Nazi Germany leading eventually to the outbreak of the Second World War.

It is true that the past experience of Franco-German relations may appear more balanced, with both nations threatening each other at some point, while relations between Germany and Poland are often portrayed as fitting more closely into the aggressor (Germany) and victim (Poland) paradigm. However, this latter view is disputed in Germany, particularly by the expellees and their descendants who tend to see themselves as victims and the Polish state as the aggressor. More importantly, however, there is no doubt that both Franco-German and Polish–German relations experienced a very difficult past, which needed to be addressed while building new relationships.

There are also clear similarities in these rapprochement processes. Although, for the reasons discussed in the book, the Franco–(West) German rapprochement began almost forty years before the Polish–German process could take place, it is clear that there are many common points to note. Most significantly, there is a clear preference in both cases to reconcile 'through Europe' rather than on a strictly bilateral basis. Consequently, there is a strong European and multilateral dimension in these two processes that is based on finding a 'common project'. In the Franco–(West) German case the first, and perhaps the most important, such project was the setting up of the ECSC in the early 1950s. This was followed by many other similar initiatives in the context of the EC and subsequently the EU. In the

Polish–German case the issue of EU Eastern enlargement acted as a unifying factor for the two nations.

The other major similarities include a preference for institutionalising these relationships through creating bilateral governmental and non-governmental fora. These include regular consultations between the executives (including most ministers and some heads of departments), youth exchange and other joint educational programmes (e.g. a joint Polish–German university in Frankfurt am Oder/Słubice) and many agreements between the regional and local governments. All of these and many other institutions have their origins in bilateral treaties, in the Franco–(West) German case in the Elysée treaty of 1961 and in the Polish–German case in the 'Good Neighbourly Relations and Friendly Co-operation' treaty of 1991.

There are therefore many points of comparison between these two cases and there is no doubt that the Franco–(West) German process was looked at and consciously emulated when Warsaw and Bonn embarked on their rapprochement after the end of the Cold War. On the other hand, there are some fundamental differences between these relationships, two of which need to be mentioned here. First, is the length of the two processes. As mentioned earlier Franco–(West) German reconciliation is forty years older, and hence considerably richer in experience than the Polish–German process. While Franco–(West) German relations appear strong when looked at from a contemporary perspective, it is often forgotten that this has not always been the case since the beginning of their rapprochement. For example, while Bonn and Paris agreed to set up the ECSC in 1951 they fell out over the failed project for establishing a European Defence Community and subsequently over the 'empty chair' crisis created by de Gaulle in the mid-1960s. In fact, the relationship remained very 'un-special' between Adenaeur's departure in 1963 and the late 1970s when Bonn and Paris agreed to set up the EMS. Later on, France's behaviour during the run-up to the unification of Germany was often perceived from Bonn as highly un-co-operative. It is therefore on decades of good but also less good experiences that the current strength of the Franco–German relationship is built. Polish–German rapprochement is just over a decade old, during which time no comparable experience and capital of trust could be gathered. It is therefore clear that in the Polish–German case both sides are still in the process of 'learning' about each other.

The second difference has to do with the relatively asymmetric nature of these relationships. While, arguably, the Franco–German relationship became asymmetric after unification this was not the case prior to it. Before 1990 France and Germany each had their relative strengths and weaknesses that often complemented each other and led to a balanced relationship. The West German economy was more powerful than the French, but France retained much greater political prestige and, with its nuclear capability, it was also militarily superior to its Eastern neighbour. Perhaps more importantly here, France and West Germany were equal partners in the setting up of the ECSC, EC and other European initiatives. Each side had its own benefits from these projects but they needed each other and other member states needed them to co-operate. With the end of the Cold War French assets lost some of their value, Germany was no longer a pariah state and French nuclear weapons looked obsolete in the new international reality. However, as demonstrated by their joint work on the European constitution, it is clear that France and Germany continue to co-operate in the EU, and still see themselves as the driving forces of European integration.

No comparable equilibrium ever existed in Polish–German relations. Economically Poland is not only weaker but in fact dependent on the German economy and politically on Berlin's support to join western institutions and to get a good deal in this process. Almost in every other field, including military strength, Germany is superior to Poland. What Germany says it needs in return from Poland is that the latter remain stable and that its borders, particularly in the East, be secure and tight enough to stop illegal migration. This hardly constitutes the basis for a partner-like relationship; instead, it is clear that Germany has acted as Poland's advocate and Poland, though increasingly resenting this role, is Germany's protégé.

Where this relationship may appear more balanced is again in the context of European integration. As a relatively large state, Poland could become a meaningful actor in the EU. As Poland's positions on the EU constitution and European security and defence demonstrate, Warsaw certainly has an appetite to punch above its weight.[3] What is, however, striking is that Warsaw's 'independent' behaviour in the EU is received with thinly disguised annoyance in Berlin. After all, protégés are supposed to follow and not oppose their advocates. The relationship therefore remains unbalanced and asymmetric, and will continue to be so for the time being. This fact, combined with the relatively short experience of the rapprochement process, means that in practice the 'Europeanisation' of Polish–German relations is nowhere near as advanced as the equivalent Franco–German process.

'Europeanisation'

The question of 'Europeanisation' formed the conceptual thread running through this book. The concept was used to address the Polish-German consensus-building process in a broader European framework. As such, 'Europeanisation' was defined as a normative process with multilateral and institutional dimensions. The book set out to develop the understanding of this concept and to assess its broader applicability. Chapter 1 identified two types of 'Europeanisation' present in the existing International Relations literature. The first type belongs to the discipline of political science and EU studies and is used to describe the ways and means through which EU integration affects the domestic interests, norms and arrangements of member states and candidate countries. This debate was re-named in the book and referred to as 'EU-isation'. The second idea of 'Europeanisation' is normative in nature and remains particularly relevant for states with a 'troubled' past, which tend to perceive the European idea as evoking liberal democracy, progress and the rejection of chauvinism. As such, 'Europeanisation' is understood as being closely connected with the processes of liberal transformation in European states that used to be run by dictatorial regimes, such as Germany and Poland. In this interpretation, the notion of 'Europeanisation' has political, economic and international dimensions. This book was concerned with the latter.

But where do these norms concerned originate? The book pointed to three sources: philosophical, historical and policy-related. Philosophically, 'Europeanisation' is based in Kant's theory of 'stable peace', which emphasises the importance of domestic freedoms (democracies do not fight each other) and multilateral arrangements (a voluntary federation of states). Clearly, prior to 1939, these principles were not universally accepted and certainly not practised in Europe. However, the traumatic experience of the Second World War led to a normative revolution in West European international relations, which re-defined the norms of 'appropriate behaviour' very much in line with Kantian principles. After the end of the Cold War it became clear that much of East Central Europe subscribed to this philosophy too. Finally, there is a policy-related point of reference. The relationship where Kantian principles have been practised and which was deeply embedded in the past is the relationship between France and (West) Germany. The relationship therefore constitutes a practical point of emulation for other states in Europe who once might have conflicted but now wish to co-operate.

Chapter 1 identified four conditions that need to be place in order for the 'Europeanisation' agenda to start having a political impact:

- *Conducive international structure.* This condition was identified as essential to 'permit' the process of consensus-building among states. While with the end of the Second World War the international structure was favourable for initiating a rapprochement in Franco–(West) German relations, the reverse was true for West Germany's relations with Poland. On the other hand, the importance of international structure remains passive: it can accommodate or obstruct the process, but it does not actively facilitate it. For example, Franco–(West) German co-operation became intensive only since the early 1960s although the structural conditions had been conducive since the late 1940s. As demonstrated in Chapters 2 and 3, bipolarity prevented any meaningful rapprochement in Polish–(West) German relations. However, as seen in Chapter 4, the end of the Cold War was not in itself sufficient to establish more co-operative relations between these nations.

- *Democratic government.* This is an essential component of Kantian theory: states that are freer are less likely to act belligerently towards other states, particularly when these are also democratic. This argument was validated throughout the book. It was clear, for example, that Bonn's *Ostpolitik* would not be possible without the democratisation of the Federal Republic and the subsequent profound transformation of West German society. At the same time the fact that Poland was not a democratic state until 1989 had a critical impact upon its policy towards West Germany that, with some exceptions, remained inflexible. With the end of communism in 1989 Poland and Germany had compatible governments; this proved crucial for setting in motion the rapprochement process.

- *Institutional integration.* This is again an essential component of Kant's argument that stresses the notion of 'voluntary federation' among 'free states'. The importance of western integration for the relationship was extensively discussed in Chapter 5 and 6. The outcome of these discussions was that it was through European integration that Poland and Germany established congruence in their strategic interests, a vital aspect of 'Europeanisation'.

- *Reconciliation.* The process of dealing with the past and overcoming historically rooted differences is essential to the process of broadening rapprochement beyond the governmental level. As shown in Chapter 3, following Bonn's *Ostpolitk,* a degree of co-operation had already emerged in Polish–(West) German relations in the 1970s. However, since this policy remained deliberately narrowed to the government level it failed to address the historical grievances that existed within the two societies. This was clearly illustrated in opinion polls in the 1970s and the 1980s that showed a prevailing mistrust towards the German state and the suspicion of belligerent overtones in Polish views of both East and West Germany.[4] This tendency decidedly altered after the collapse of communism in Poland. New Polish–German treaties and agreements set out a number of institutions promoting reconciliation. A conscious effort was also made to reach out with the message of reconciliation, to broader sectors of these societies.

Chapters 2 and 3 discussed developments in the relationship during the Cold War period. It was clear that 'Europeanisation' was not an option in the conditions of structural conflict that divided communist Poland and capitalist West Germany. With the end of the Cold War the structural constraints were removed and the external conditions were for the first time conducive with a genuine rapprochement in the relationship. However, as discussed in Chapter 4, during the 1989–91 period the relationship remained handicapped by a prevailing suspicion and inexperience in practising genuine co-operation between Bonn and Warsaw. With the main divisive issue (the Oder-Neisse border) resolved in 1990–91, the relationship started to improve dramatically, particularly with the two countries co-operating over the issue of NATO and EU enlargements. It is in the latter context that 'Europeanisation' started to be increasingly mentioned as a normative imperative but also as a genuine prospect for the relationship. However, as demonstrated in the case of Franco–(West) German relations, 'Europeanisation' becomes an enduring process only if the states concerned find that their key strategic interests are reconcilable and congruent, but also when they show an ability to compromise and redefine their interests vis-à-vis each other. In other words, as argued in Chapter 5, 'Europeanisation' requires an evolution from interest 'reconcilability' to interest 'convergence'. So far, the developments in Polish–German relations indicate that such an evolution remains a distant prospect.

Final words

Polish–German relations have always been of great importance for Europe's peace and stability – or rather, more often, for its discord and instability. This book has dealt with developments during the 1944–2001 period, during which time both the relationship and Europe experienced major transformations. At the end of the Second World War Europe was in ruins and the relationship was dominated by extreme hatred. By the end of 2001 the EU was embarking on its constitutional reform and enlargement to the East – two policies that would spell an end to the division of the continent.

History shows that Europe's fortunes have been closely interconnected with developments in Polish–German relations. Nazi Germany's war with Poland in 1939 brought catastrophe to the rest of Europe. During the Cold War, relations between Bonn and Warsaw were often a magnification of broader international developments, especially during phases of East–West détente. Furthermore, despite many of the issues raised in this book, the post-1989 Polish–German rapprochement remains the singular, most successful and important relationship to emerge across the former East–West divide. It is impossible to imagine that Europe will grow stronger, more prosperous and secure without further progress in Polish–German relations.

Notes

1 A. Hajnicz, *Ze Sobą czy Przeciw Sobie* (Warsaw: Presspublika, 1995).
2 F. Pflüger 'Polen- unser Frankreich im Osten'/'Poland and the European Union', *Außenpolitik*, III/95, pp. 183–92.
3 See Marcin Zaborowski and Kerry Longhurst, 'America's Protégé in the East? The Emergence of Poland as a Regional Leader', *International Affairs*, October 2003, pp. 1009–28.
4 See A. Sakson, 'Niemcy w świadomości Polaków', in Anna Wolf-Poweska, (ed.), *Polacy Wobec Niemców: Z dziejów Kultury Politycznej Polski 1945–1989* (Poznan: Instytut Zachodric, 1993), pp. 408–28.

Select bibliography

Secondary sources

Agh, Attila, *Democratization and Europeanization in Hungary* (Budapest: Hungarian Centre for Democracy Studies, 1995).

Andersen, Svein S. and A. Eliassen Kjell, *Making Policy in Europe: The Europeification of National Policy Making* (London and New Delhi: Sage, 1993).

Bachmann, Klaus, *Polska Kaczka i Europejski Staw* (Warsaw: CSM, 1999).

Bahr, Egon, *Deutsche Interessen* (Munich: Karl Blessing Verlag, 1998).

Barcz, Jan, *Udział Polski w Konferencji '2 + 4': aspekty prawne i proceduralne.* (Warsaw: PISM, 1994).

Baring, Arnulf (ed.), *Germany's New Position in Europe* (Oxford and Providence: Berg, 1994).

Bender, Peter, *Die Neue Ostpolitik und ihre Folgen: Vom Mauerbau bis zur Vereinigung* (Munich: Deutscher Taschenbuch Verlag, 1995).

Berger, Thomas, 'Norms, Identity, and National Security in Germany and Japan', in Katzenstein (ed.), *The Culture of National Security*: 317–56.

Bingen, Dieter, *Die Polenpolitik der Bonner Republik von Adenauer bis Kohl, 1949–1990* (Baden-Baden: Nomos, 1998).

Bornemann, John and Nick Fowler, 'Europeanization', *Annual Review of Anthropology*, 26, 1997: 487–514.

Borodziej, Włodzimierz, *Od Poczdamu do Szklarskiej Poręby. Polska w Stosunkach Międzynarodowych 1945–1947* (London: Aneks, 1990).

Börzel, Tanja A. and Thomas Risse, 'When Europe Hits Home: Europeanization and Domestic Change,' *European Integration online Papers* (EIoP), Vol. 4, No. 15, 2000, http://eiop.or.at/eiop/texte/2000–015a.htm.

Brandt, Willy, 'Der Kniefall von Warschau', in Pflüger and Lipscher (eds), *Feinde werden Freunde*: 51–60.

Brandt, Willy, *My Life in Politics* (London: Hamish Hamilton, 1992).

Bullock, Alan, *Ernest Bevin, Foreign Secretary 1945–1951* (New York and London: W. W. Norton, 1983).

Bulmer, Simon J., 'Shaping the Rules? The Constitutive Politics of the European Union and German Power', in Katzenstein (ed.), *Tamed Power* pp. 1–49.

Bulmer, Simon, Charlie Jeffery and William E. Paterson, *Germany's European Diplomacy: Shaping the Regional Milieu* (Manchester and New York: Manchester University Press, 2000).

Bulmer, Simon and William Paterson, 'West Germany's Role in Europe: "Man-Mountain" or "Semi-Guliver?"', *Journal of Common Market Studies*, Vol 28, 1989: 95–117.

Buras, Piotr and Marek A. Cichocki, Olaf Osica and Janusz Reiter, 'The Most Serious Challenges Facing Poland's European Policy', *Policy Reports & Analyses*, No. 4/200 (Warsaw: CIR, 2000), www.csm.org.pl/en_index.htmlp.

Brzeziński, Zbigniew, *The Soviet Block, Unity and Conflict* (Cambridge MA: Harvard University Press, 1960).

Churchill, Winston S., *The Second World War: Closing the Ring*, Vol. V (London: Cassell, 1952).

Churchill, Winston S., *The Second World War: Triumph and Tragedy*, Vol. VI (London: Cassell, 1954).

Conzelmann, Thomas, '"Europeanization" of Regional Development Policies? Linking the Multi-Level Governance Approach with Theories of Policy Learning and Policy Change', *European Integration online Papers* (EIoP), Vol. 2, No. 4, 1998, http://eiop.or.at/eiop/texte/1998–004a.htm.

Cordell, Karl (ed.), *Poland and the European Union* (London and New York: Routledge, 2000).

Croft, Stuart *et al.*, *The Enlargement of Europe* (Manchester and New York: Manchester University Press, 1999).

Davies, Norman, *God's Playground: A History of Poland*, Vols I and II (Oxford: Oxford University Press, 1981).

Davies, Norman, 'Introduction', in *Europe: A History* (Oxford: Oxford University Press, 1996): 1–46.

Davies, Norman, 'One Thousand Years of Polish–German Camaraderie', in Roger Barlett and Karen Schönwälder (eds), *The German Lands and Eastern Europe* (Basingstoke: Macmillan, 1999): 260–76.

De Zayas, Alfred M., *Nemesis at Potsdam: The Anglo-Americans and the Expulsion of the Germans* (London and Boston: Routledge & Kegan Paul, 1979).

Dienstbier, Jiri, *Sneni o Evropie* (Prague: Lidove Noviny, 1990).

Fisher, Louis, *The Road to Yalta* (New York and London: Harper & Row, 1972).

Freudenstein, Roland, 'Germany, Poland and the EU', *International Affairs*, Vol. 74, No. 1: 41–55.

Frowein, Jakob Abr., 'Rechtliche Probleme der Einigung Deutschlands', *Europa Archiv*, No. 7, 1990: 325–6.

Garton Ash, Timothy, 'Germany's Choice', *Foreign Affairs*, July–August 1994: 65–81.

Garton Ash, Timothy, *In Europe's Name: Germany and the Divided Continent* (London: Vintage, 1994).

Garton Ash, Timothy, 'Mitteleuropa?', *Daedalus*, Vol. 119, 1990: 16–17.

Gierek, Edward (interviewed by Janusz Rolicki), *Przerwana Dekada* (Warsaw: Wydawnictwo Fakt, 1990).

Gordon, Philip H., 'Berlin's Difficulties: The Normalisation of German Foreign Policy', *Orbis*, Spring 1994.

Grant, Charles, 'The Return of Franco–German Dominance?', CER Bulletin, 28, 2003, Centre for European Reform, www.cer.org.

Haftendorn, Helga, 'Gulliver in the Centre of Europe: International Involvement and National Capabilities for Action', in Bertel Heurlin (ed.), *Germany in the Nineties* (Basingstoke: Macmillan, 1996): 91–103.

Hajnicz, Artur, *Ze Sobą czy Przeciw Sobie* (Warsaw: Presspublika, 1995).

Hampton, Mary, 'Poland, Germany and NATO Enlargement Policy', *German Comments*, No. 49/1998: 85–94.

Handl, Vladimir, Kerry Longhurst and Marcin Zaborowski, 'Germany's Security Policy towards East Central Europe', *Perspectives – The Central European Review of International Affairs*, 14, 2000.

Harasimowicz, Andrzej, 'Po podpisaniu układu europejskiego', in *Rocznik Polskiej Polityki Zagranicznej 1992* (Warsaw: PISM, 1994).

Herzog, Roman, 'Die osteuropäischen Staaten und die Europäische Union', *Bulletin des Presse- und Informationsamtes der Bundesregierung*, No. 78, 1997.

Hild, Helmut, 'Was hat die Denkschrift der EKD bewirkt?', in Pflüger and Lipscher (eds), *Feinde werden Freunde*: 90–103, 106–10.

Homyer, Josef ', '25 Jahre nach der Versöhnungsbotschaft der polnischen und deutschen Bischöfe', in Pflüger and Lipscher (eds), *Feinde werden Freunde*: 245–59.

Hyde-Price, Adrian, 'Building a Stable Peace in Mitteleuropa: The German–Polish Hinge', www.bham.ac.uk/IGS/DiscussionPapers.htm.

Hyde-Price, Adrian, *Germany and European Order: Enlarging NATO and the EU* (Manchester and New York: Manchester University Press, 2000).

Jeffery, Charlie, 'Niemieckie landy a "normalizacja" dyskusji o rozszerzeniu UE', in William E. Paterson, Barbara Lippert, Marcin Zaborowski *et al.*, *Wspólnota Sprzecznych Interesów* (Warsaw: CSM, 1999).

Jeffery, Charlie and Stephen Collins, 'The German Länder and EU Enlargement: Between Apple Pie and Issue Linkage', in V. Handl, J. Hon, O. Pick *et al.*, *Germany and East Central East Central Europe Since 1990* (Prague: Ustav mezinarodnich vztahu, 1998).

Kamp, Karl-Heinz, 'Germany and NATO: The Opening of the Alliance and its Future', Institute for German Studies, University of Birmingham, Discussion Paper, 14/1998.

Kant, Immanuel, *Perpetual Peace*, ed. Lewis White Beck (Indianapolis and New York: Bobbs-Merrill, 1957).

Katzenstein, Peter J. (ed.), *The Culture of National Security: Norms and Identity in World Politics* (New York: Columbia University Press, 1996).

Katzenstein, Peter J., 'Introduction: Alternative Perspectives on National Security', in Katzenstein (ed.), *The Culture of National Security*: 1–26.

Katzenstein, Peter J. (ed.), *Mitteleuropa – Between Europe and Germany* (Providence and Oxford: Berghahn, 1997).

Katzenstein, Peter J. (ed.), *Tamed Power: Germany in Europe* (Ithaca and London: Cornell University Press, 1997).

Katzenstein, Peter J., 'United Germany in an Integrating Europe', in Katzenstein (ed.), *Tamed Power*: 2–26.

Keohane, Robert O., *International Institutions and State Power* (San Francisco and London: Westview Press, 1989).

Keohane, Robert O. and Joseph S. Nye, *Power and Interdependence*, 2nd edn (Harvard: HarperCollins, 1989).

Kersten, Krystyna, 'Stulecie Przesiedleńców: Przymusowe Przemieszczenie Ludności – Próba Typologii', in Klaus Bachmann and Jerzy Kranz, *Przeprosić za Wypędzenie?* (Cracow: Znak, 1997), pp. 100–12.

Kiwerska, Jadwiga, 'W Atmosferze Wrogości (1945–1970)', in Wolff-Poweska (ed.), *Polacy Wobec Niemców*: 45–94.

Kohl, Helmut, *Pragnąłem Jedności Niemiec* (Warsaw: Politeja, 1999).

Kolarska-Bobińska, Lena *et al.* (eds), *Polska Eurodebata* (Warsaw: Instytut Spraw Publicznych, 1999).

Kolboom, I., 'Frankreich und Deutschland: Die neuen Akzente', in K. Kaiser and J. Krause (eds.), *Deutschlands neue Außenpolitik. Band 3: Interessen und Strategien*, Forschungimstitut der Deutschen Gesellschaft für Answärtige Politik (Munich: Oldenbourg Verlag, 1996): 123–4.

Koszel, Bogdan, 'Między Dogmatyzmem a Pragmatyzmem (1971–1989)', in Wolf-Poweska (ed.), *Polacy Wobec Niemców*: 94–141.

Krzeczunowicz, Andrzej *Krok po kroku. Polska droga do NATO 1989–1999* (Cracow: Znak, 1999).

Kubiak, Jacek, 'Uwagi o stosunku opozycji demokratycznej do zagadnień niemieckich', in Wolf-Poweska (ed.), *Polacy wobec Niemców*: 359–407.

Kucharczyk, Jacek, 'Porwanie Europy: Integracja europejska w polskim dyskursie politycznym 1997–1998', in Kolarska-Bobińska *et al.* (eds), *Polska Eurodebata*: 297–332.

Kucharczyk, Jacek, '"Za, a nawet przeciw"': partie polityczne wobec perspektywy integracji europejskiej w wyborach '97', in Kolarska-Bobińska *et al.* (eds), *Polska Eurodebata*: 219–46.

Kundera, Milan, 'The Tragedy of Central Europe', *New York Review of Books*, 26 April 1984.

Lavdas, Kostas, *The Europeanization of Greece: Interest Politics and Crisis of Integration* (Basingstoke: Macmillan, 1997).

Lehmann, Hans Georg, *Der Oder-Neisse-Konflikt* (Munich: Beck, 1979).

Lippert, Barbara, 'Shaping and Evaluating the Europe Agreements – The Community Side', in Barbara Lippert and Heinrisch Schneider, *Monitoring Association and Beyond: The Europen Union and the Visegrád States* (Bonn: Europe Union Verlag, 1995): 311–25.

Lipski, Jan Józef, 'Polen, Deutsche und Europa', in Józef Lipski, *Wir müssen uns alles sagen/Musimy sobie wszystko powiedzieć* (Warsaw: Deutsch-Polnischer Verlag, 1996).

Longhurst, Kerry and Arthur Hoffmann, 'German Strategic Culture in Action', *Contemporary Security Policy*, Vol. 20, No. 2, 1999: 34–55.

Mach, Zdzisław, 'Heritage, Dream, and Anxiety: The European Identity of Poles', in Zdzisław Mach and Dariusz Niedźwiecki (eds), *European Enlargement and Identity* (Cracow: Universitas, 1997): 35–51.

Malinowski, Krzysztof, 'Asymetria Partnerstwa: Polityka Zjednoczonych Niemiec wobec Polski', in Zbigniew Mazur (ed.), *Rola Nowych Niemiec na Arenie Międzynarodowej* (Poznań: Instytut Zachodni, 1996): 270–302.

Markovits, Andrei S. and Simon Reich, 'Should Europe Fear the Germans?', *German Politics and Society*, Vol. 23, 1991: 1–20.

Maull, Hanns W. and Philip H. Gordon, *German Foreign Policy and German 'National Interest': German and American Perspectives*, American Institute for Contemporary German Studies, Johns Hopkins University, Discussion Paper, No. 5, January 1993.

Mearsheimer, John, 'Back to the Future: Instability in Europe after the Cold War', *International Security*, Vol. 15, No. 1, 1990: 5–56.

Michałowski, Stanisław, 'RFN wobec rozszerzenia Uni Europejkiej', *Sprawy Międzynarodowe*, 2/1998.

Michta, Andrew and Ilya A. Prizel (eds), *Polish Foreign Policy Reconsidered* (New York: St Martin's Press, 1995).

Mikołajczyk, Stanisław, *Polska Zgwałcona* (Chicago: Wici, 1981).

Nadeau, Remi, *Stalin, Churchill and Roosevelt Divide Europe* (New York and London: Praeger, 1990).

Nelson, Daniel, 'Regional Security and Ethnic Minorities', in Aurel Braun and Zoltan Barany, *Dilemmas of Transition – The Hungarian Experience* (Lanham, MD: Rowman & Littlefield, 1999): 301–23.

'Niemcy i Polska', *Kultura*, July/August 1978: 123–9.

Nitschke, Bernadetta, 'Położenie Ludności Niemieckiej na Terenach na Wschód od Odry i Nysy Lużyckiej w 1945 roku', *Przegląd Zachodni*, No. 3 (Poznan: Instytut Zachodni, 1997).

Nowak-Jeziorański, Jan, *Polska Wczoraj, Dziś i Jutro* (Czytelnik: Warsaw, 1999).

Pailer, Wolfgang, *Na Przekór Fatalizmowi Wrogości: Stanisław Stomma i Stosunki Polsko-Niemieckie* (Warsaw: Wydawnictwo Polsko-Niemieckie, 1998).

Pasierb, Bronisław, 'Funkcje Problemu Niemieckiego w Pierwszym Okresie Polski Ludowej', in Bohdan Jałowiecki and Piotr Przewłocki (eds), *Stosunki*

Polsko-Niemieckie. Integracja i Rozwój Ziem Zachodnich i Północnych (eds), (Katowice, 1980): 95–108.

Payá, José Ignacio Torreblanca, *The European Community and Central Eastern Europe (1989–1993): Foreign Policy and Decision-Making* (Madrid: Centro de Estudios Avanzados en Ciencias Socialeas, 1997).

Pflüger, Friedbert, 'Polen – unser Frankreich im Osten', in W. Schäuble and R. Seiters (eds), *Außenpolitik im 21. Jahrhundert. Die Thesen der Jungen Außenpolitiker* (Bonn: Bouvier Verlag, 1996): 183–92.

Pflüger, Friedbert, 'Polen – unser Frankreich im Osten'/'Poland and the European Union', *Außenpolitik*, III/95: 225–31.

Pflüger, Friedbert, *Die Zukunft des Ostens liegt im Westen. Beiträge zur Außenpolitik* (Düsseldorf and Vienna: Econ Taschenbuch Verlag, 1994).

Pflüger, Friedbert and Winfried Lipscher (eds), *Feinde werden Freunde* (Bonn: Bouvier, 1993).

'Polen und Deutschland', *Osteuropa*, February 1979: 101–5.

'Polish Policy vis-a-vis Ukraine and How it is Perceived in EU Member States (Transcript of a Debate)', *Reports & Analyses 2/00*, Centre for International Relations, Warsaw, www.csm.org.pl/en_index.html.

Poznański, Kazimierz, 'Economic Adjustment and Political Forces: Poland since 1970', *International Organization*, Vol. 40, No. 2, 1986: 279–312.

Pridham, Geoffrey, 'Patterns of Europeanisation and Transnational Party Cooperation: Party Development in Central and Eastern Europe', ECPR Paper, Mannheim, March 1999.

Puślecki, Zdzisław, *Polska w Okresie Transformacji a Zjednoczone Niemcy* (Warsaw and Poznan: Wydawnictwo Naukowe PWN, 1996).

Radaelli, Claudio M., 'Whither Europeanization? Concept Stretching and Substantive Change', *European Integration Online Papers* (EioP), Vol. 4 No. 5, 2000, http://eiop.or.at/eiop/texte/2000-oo8a. htm.

Rakowski, Mieczysław F., *Dzienniki Polityczne 1958–1962* (Warsaw: Iskry, 1999).

Rakowski, Mieczysław F., *Dzienniki Polityczne 1967–1968* (Warsaw: Iskry, 1999).

Risse-Kappen, Thomas, 'Collective Identity in a Democratic Community: The Case of NATO', in Katzenstein, *The Culture of National Security*: 357–99.

Rittberger, Volker, 'Die Bundesrepublik Deutschland – Eine Weltmacht?', *Aus Politik und Zeitgeschichte*, B 4–5, 1990: 3–19.

Rometsch, Dietrich and Wolfgang Wessels, *The European Union and Member States* (Manchester: Manchester University Press, 1996).

Rotfeld, Adam Daniel and Walther Stützle (eds), *Germany and Europe in Transition* (Oxford: Sipri and Oxford University Press, 1998).

Rühe, Volker, 'Shaping Euro-Atlantic Policies: Grand Strategy for a New Era', *Survival*, Vol. 35, No. 2, 1993: 129–37.

Sakson, Andrzej, 'Niemcy w świadomości Polaków', in Wolf-Poweska (ed.), *Polacy Wobec Niemców*: 428.

Saryusz-Wolski, Jacek, *Polska w Europie*, 17/1995.

Schmidt, Carlo, 'Politische Reisen: Polen 1958', in Pflüger and Lipscher (eds). *Feinde werden Freunde* (Bonn: Bouvier Verlag), pp. 29–39.

Schmidt, Helmut, *Die Deutschen und ihre Nachbarn* (Berlin: Siedler, 1990).

Schmidt, Helmut, 'Schwieriger Besuch in Warschau 1966', in Pflüger and Lipscher (eds), *Feinde werden Freunde*: 49–50.

Schöpflin, George, *Nations, Identity, Power* (London: Hurst, 2000).

Schwarz, Hans-Peter, *Konrad Adenauer: From the German Empire to the Federal Republic, Vol. 1: 1876–1952* (Oxford and Providence: Berghahn, 1995).

Schwarz, Hans-Peter, *Konrad Adenauer: A German Politician and Statesman in a Period of War Revolution and Reconstruction, Vol. 2: The Statesman: 1952–1967* (Oxford and Providence: Berghahn, 1995).

Skubiszewski, Krzysztof, 'Polityka Zagraniczna Państwa w 1991 roku', in *Rocznik Polskiej Polityki Zagranicznej 1991* (Warsaw: PISM, 1993): 15–25.

Stomma, Stanisław, *Czy Fatalism Wrogości?* (Cracow: Znak, 1980).

Suchocka, Hanna, 'Znaczenie orędzia Biskupów Polskich z 1965 r. dla budowania Tożsamości nowej Europy', *Przegląd Zachodni*, 96/1, February–March 1996: 17–29.

Szczerbiak, Aleks, 'Explaining Declining Support for EU Membership in Poland', Sussex European Institute Working Paper, No. 34.

Teltschik, Horst, *329 Tage: Innenansichten der Einigung* (Berlin: Siedler Verlag, 1991).

Tewes, Henning, 'The Emergence of Civilian Power: Germany and Central Europe', *German Politics*, Vol. 6, No. 2, August 1997: 95–117.

Tewes, Henning, *Germany, Civilian Power and New Europe* (Basingstoke: Palgrave, 2001).

Tomala, Mieczysław, *Patrząc na Niemcy. Od Wrogości do Porozumienia 1945–1991* (Warsaw: Polska Fundacja Spraw Międzynarodowych, 1997).

Vinton, Louisa, 'Domestic Politics and Foreign Policy, 1989–1993', in Ilya Prizel and Andrew A. Michta (eds), *Polish Foreign Policy Reconsidered: Challenges to Independence* (New York: St Martin's Press, 1995): 35–49.

Waltz, Kenneth N., *Man, the State, and War* (New York and London: Columbia University Press, 1959).

Weitz, Richard, 'Pursuing Military Security in Eastern Europe', in Robert O. Keohane, Joseph S. Nye and Stanley Hoffmann, *After the Cold War: International Institutions and State Strategies in Europe, 1989–1991* (Cambridge MA: Harvard University Press, 1993): 354–68.

Wendt, Alexander, 'Anarchy is What States Make of It: The Social Construction of Power Politics', in James Der Derian (ed.), *International Theory: Critical Investigations* (New York: New York University Press, 1995): 129–77.

Wielowieyski, Andrzej, *Polska w Europie*, 17/1995.

Wojciechowski, Zygmunt, 'Polityka Wschodnia Niemiec a Katastrofa Wspłczes-nej Cywilizacji', in *Przegląd Zachodni – Antalogia Przeglądu Zachodniego 1945–1990*, No. 2 (Poznan: Instytut Zachodni, 1995): 123–35.

Wolf-Poweska, Anna, 'Dylematy Nowej Kultury Politycznej', in *Raport o Zjednoczeniu Niemiec: Problemy, Wyzwania, Strategie* (Poznan: Instytut Zachodni, 1992): 78–89.

Wolf-Poweska, Anna (ed.), *Polacy Wobec Niemców: Z Dziejów Kultury Politycznej Polski 1945–1989* (Poznan: Instytut Zachodni, 1993).

Wolf-Poweska, Anna, 'Poszukiwanie Dróg Dialogu', in Wolf-Poweska (ed.), *Polacy Wobec Niemców*: 31.

Zaborowski, Marcin, 'Does Germany Support the Eastern Enlargement of the European Union?', *The Polish Quarterly of International Affairs*, Vol. 4, 1998: 77–92.

Zaborowski, Marcin, 'Polens Westgrenze – Zwischen Rationaler Politik und Historischer Erinnerung', *Welttrends*, No. 23, 1999.

Zaborowski, Marcin and Kerry Longhurst, 'America's Protégé in the East? The Emergence of Poland as a Regional Leader', *International Affairs*, October 2003: 1009–28.

Zakaria, Fareed, 'Realism and Domestic Politics', *International Security*, Vol. 17, No. 1, 1992: 462–85.

Zelikow, Philip and Condoleezza Rice, *Germany Unified and Europe Transformed: A Study in Statecraft* (Cambridge, MA: Harvard University Press, 1995).

Selected press articles

'Apel o Realizm', *Rzeczpospolita*, 30 Oct. 1998.

'Atlantic News', 23 March 1990, 12 May 1990, 9 October 1991.

'"Atomowa wpadka", usłyszeć nasz glos', *Gazeta Wyborcza*, 25 November 1998.

'Auditors Challenge Budget Rebate Call', *European Voice*, 11–17 June 1998.

Augestein, Rudolf, 'Bedrohtes Polen', *Der Spiegel*, No. 2 1994.

Batt, Judy and Katarzyna Wolczuk, 'Keep an Eye on the East', *Financial Times* (international edn) 23 February 2001.

'Berlin Reject Polish offer', *FAZ Weekly*, 3 May 2003.

'Britain Out of Harmony Again', *The Economist*, 28 November 1998.

'Bundesregierung: Keine EU Erweiterung ohne Finanzreform', *FAZ*, 3 December 1998.

'Coalition Adrift', *The Economist*, 3 June 2001.

'CSU warnt erneut vor überstürzten Beitritten', *Süddeutsche Zeitung*, 12 May 1998.

Czarnecki, Ryszard (interview), *Rzeczpospolita*, 5 November 1997.

'Die EU erweitert: Tür zu', *Die Welt*, 8 June 2000.

'Ekolodzy czekają na opine ekspertów', *Rzeczpospolita*, 18 December 2000.

'Erste Wahl zu den Regionalparlamenten', *FAZ*, 10 October 1998.

'EU North and South Split on Spending Freeze', *Financial Times*, 7 December 1998.

'Europe's Spoils Up for Grabs', *Financial Times*, 14 December 1998.

'European Union: Single-Currency-Minded', *Economist*, 23 December 1995.

'Falsche Hoffnungen', *Der Spiegel*, 12 December 1994.

'Finanzierung der EU-Osterweiterung', *Das Parlament*, 20 December 1996.

Fischer, Joschka (interview), 'Boimy się wielkich Niemiec', *Rzeczpospolita*, 13 October 1995.

Fischer, Joschka and Geremek Bronisław, 'Polacy i Niemcy u progu nowego tysiąclecia', *Rzeczpospolita*, 17 February 2000.

Garztecki, Marek, 'Bałkanizacja przed europeizacją', *Rzeczpospolita*, 8 January 1994.

'Geremek: nie wiemy czego oczekiwać', *Gazeta Wyborcza*, 29 Oct. 1998.

Geremek, Bronisław and Joschka Fischer, 'Deutsch-polnische Beziehungen – Schlüssel zum Aufbau einer stabilen Europäischen Union', *Der Tagesspiegel*, 17 February 2000.

'German Minister Rebuffed over NATO Nuclear Strategy', *Financial Times*, 9 December 1998.

'Germany to Push Ahead with EU Tax Harmonising Plans', *Financial Times*, 24 November 1998.

'Germany's Ostpolitik', *The Economist*, 7 December 1996.

'In Sachen Europa hat Bayern ein Forderungspaket geschnürt', *Mainpost*, 3 December 1998.

'Keine EU-Beitritte vor 2005 oder 2006, Ein stilles Einvernehmen der großen deutschen Parteien', *FAZ*, 8 July 2000.

Kinkel, Klaus (interview), 'Das ist Verrat an der Geschichte', *Focus*, 18 May 1998.

Kohl, Helmut (interview), *FAZ*, 8 January 1994.

Kopp, Reinhold, 'Renaissance des Nationalen', *Frankfurter Rundschau*, 12 November 1993.

'Kritik der Union an der Europa-Politik der Regierung/Bundesdebatte vor dem Wiener Gipfel', *FAZ*, 11 December 1998.

'Księża chcą do Unii', *Rzeczpospolita*, 24 March 1998.

Kułakowski, Jan (interview) 'Misja specjalna', *Wprost*, 22 February 1998.

Kühnhardt, Ludger, 'Bonn muss Zeitplan für die Osterweiterung einhalten. Rot-Grün darf EU-Beitrittskandidaten nicht verunsichern', *Focus*, 52/1998.

'Lista zaniedbań w rękach Millera. Kto spowalnia negocjacje?', *Rzeczpospolita*, 12 July 2000.

Majcherek, Janusz A., 'Widmo Nowej Realpolitik', *Rzeczpospolita*, 3 November 1998.

'Mamy mówić jednym głosem', *Rzeczpospolita*, 12 July 2000.

Mertes, Michael and Norbert J. Prill, 'Der verhängnisvolle Irrtum eines Entweder-Oder', *FAZ*, 19 July 1989.

'Northern States Pay the Union Piper but Santer Calls the Tune', *European Voice*, 23–29 July 1998.

'Ostrzeżenia nie było', *Rzeczpospolita*, 4 June 1998.

Piłka, Marian, 'Europa, tak ale …', *Życie*, 18 February 1997.

'Poland's Devolutionary Battleground', *The Economist*, 7 February 1998.

'Polen will auf den Atomschirm der NATO nicht verzichten', *FAZ*, 7 December 1998.

'Polska traci 34 miliony ECU', *Rzeczpospolita*, 26 May 1998.

'Poparcie dla większej Rady, przemówienie Rosattiego w ONZ', *Rzeczpospolita*, 27 July 1997.

'Razem jest nam po drodze', *Rzeczpospolita*, 10 July 1995.

'Rechte für die Heimatvertriebenen', *FAZ*, 30 May 1998.

Reiter, Janusz, *Gazeta Wyborcza*, 14 February 1990.

Rozważni i Romantyczni', *Gazeta Wyborcza*, 30 October 1998.

Rückschlag für Polens EU-Pläne, *Süddeutsche Zeitung*, 8 June 2000.

Sarysz-Wolski (interview) 'Polska przeciwna Europie o dwóch prędkościach', Euro.pap.com.pl, 17 July 2000.

'Saryusz-Wolski będzie głównym negocjatorem', *Rzeczpospolita*, 18 December 1997.

'Sein Oder Nicht Sein', *Der Spiegel*, 18 May 1998.

'Schengen-Staaten Wollen Kontrollen Verschärfen' *Mainpost*, 17 September 1998.

'Schröder fordert niedrigere deutsche Zahlungen an die EU', *FAZ*, 9 December 1998.

'Schröder gibt Polen Vorrang bei EU-Beitritt', *Süddeutsche Zeitung*, 7 December 2000.

'Schröder w Warszawie. Nie stawiajmy warunków', *Rzeczpospolita*, 18 June 1998.

Schröder, Gerhard and Jerzy Buzek, 'Wspólna przyszłość ma na imię Europa', *Rzeczpospolita*, 18 November 2000.

Skubiszewski, Krzysztof, *Polska Zbrojna*, 19–22 June 1992.

'SLD czeka, ZChN broni', *Rzeczpospolita*, 28 May 1998.

'"SLD" krytykuje rząd w Warszawie', *Rzeczpospolita*, 11 July 2000.

Smolar, Aleksander, Unia na Horyzoncie, *Rzeczpospolita*, 19–20 December 1998.

'Spór o elektrownie załagodzony', *Rzeczpospolita*, 14 November 2000.

Stanisław, Stomma and Stefan Kisielewski, 'Dwugłos o idealizmie i realizmie w polityce', *Tygodnik Powszechny*, No. 1/1956.

'Stoiber geht mir auf den Geist', *Süddeutsche Zeitung*, 13 May 1998.

Stanisław Stomma (interview), 'Porządkowanie Europy', *Rzeczpospolita*, 2 May 2000.

'Der Streit über die Reform der Europäischen Union hält an', *FAZ*, 7 December 1998.

Świat 1998 czyli Sprawa Polska', *Życie* , 8 January 1999.

'Szybka ścieżka z wybojami', *Rzeczpospolita*, 11 July 2000.

Tewes, Henning and Roland Freudenstein, 'Die deutsch-polnischen Beziehungen brauchen den Neuanfang', *FT Deutschland*, 27 June 2000.

'Tide Turns Towards Setting a Target Date for Ending Accession Talks', *European Voice*, 27 July–2 August 2000.

'Trzy powody odłożenia integracji', *Rzeczpospolita*, 13 July 2000.

Urban, Thomas, 'Polnische Blockade', *Süddeutsche Zeitung*, 30 May 2000.

Urban, Thomas, *Süddeutsche Zeitung*, 25 October 1989.

'US Rejects German Call on NATO Nuclear Stance', *Financial Times*, 24 November 1998.

'Vertriebene "nicht auf dem Sprung". Steinbach: Polen ist nicht EU-reif ', *TAZ*, No. 5576 vom 08 July 1998 Seite 5 Aktuelles.

Waigel, Theo, 'Wer soll das bezahlen?', *Focus*, 3 July 1995.

'Warschau will von Anfang an ein vollwertiges EU Mitglied Sein', *FAZ*, 26 February 1998.

Selected documents and speeches

Agenda 2000 (1/1), Bulletin EU, 7/8–1997.

Agenda 2000 (1/5), Bulletin EU 12–1997.

'Agenda 2000: Stellungnahme der Ministerpräsidenten der Länder', Stuttgart, 24 October 1997, www.bayern.de/Europa/EuropaAktuell/1997/150–2.html.

'Außenhandel der Bundesrepublik Deutschland nach Ländergruppen und Ländern', Bundesministerium für Wirtschaft – ID 5–2 April 99/1.

Bachmann, Klaus and Jerzy Kranz (eds), *Przeprosić Za Wypędzenie?* (Cracow: Znak, 1997); in German: *Verlorene Heimat: Die Vertreibungsdebatte in Polen* (Bonn: Bouvier, 1998).

Bartoszewski, Władysław, 'Speech by the Minister for Foreign Affairs of Poland, Władyslaw Bartoszewski, at the Centre for European Policy Studies Brussels, 25th July 2000'; www.msz.gov.pl/polzagr/bruksela.html.

Churchill, Winston S., *His Complete Speeches*, Vol. VII 1943–1949 (New York and London: Chelsea House Publishers, 1974).

'Directions of Foreign Policy of the Republic of Poland Presented by his Excellency Professor Bronisław Geremek the Minister of Foreign Affairs at the 78th Session of the Parliament on May 9th 2000', www.msz.gov.pl/english/polzagr/expose2000ang.html.

Documents on Germany (Washington, DC: United States Department of State, 1985).

Documents on Polish–Soviet Relations 1939–45, Volume II 1943–45, Doc. No.

308: 520; Doc. No. 309: 521; Doc. No. 310; 522; Doc. No. 34; 49; Doc. No. 41, 42: 61–8; Doc No. 51: 83–6; Doc. No. 97: 171; Doc. No. 99–100: 173–6; Doc. No. 272–6: 476–85 (London: The Sikorski Institute, 1964).

'Entschließung des Bundesrates zur Mitteilung der Europäischen Kommission "Agenda 2000" – eine stärkere und erweitere Union', Beschluss des Bundesrates, 28 November 1997.

'Erklärung der Bundesregierung zur Agenda 2000', Bonn, 18 March 1998.

'Erweiterung der Europäischen Union', Beschluss-Top3, 19. Europaministerkonferenz in Bremen, 22–23 April 1998'.

Foreign Relations of the United States 1946 (FRUS), Vol. V (Washington, DC: Department of State Publication, 1969): 576–20.

Foreign Relations of the United States 1946 (FRUS), Vol. V (Washington, DC: Department of State Publication, 1969): 712.

Foreign Relations of the United States 1946 (FRUS), Vol. V (Washington, DC: Department of State Publication, 1969): 729.

Foreign Relations of the United States 1946 (FRUS), Vol. VI (Washington, DC: Department of State Publication, 1969): 376–8, 462–4.

Foreign Relations of the United States 1946 (FRUS), Vol. VI (Washington, DC: Department of State Publication, 1969): 387–92.

Foreign Relations of the United States 1946 (FRUS), Vol. VI (Washington, DC: Department of State Publication, 1969): 420–2.

Foreign Relations of the United States 1946 (FRUS), Vol. VI (Washington, DC: Department of State Publication, 1969): 462–4.

Foreign Relations of the United States 1946 (FRUS), Vol. VI (Washington, DC: Department of State Publication, 1969): 485–7.

Foreign Relations of the United States 1946 (FRUS), Vol. VI (Washington, DC: Department of State Publication, 1969): 494–9.

Foreign Relations of the United States 1947 (FRUS), Vol IV (Washington, DC: Department of State Publication, 1969): 411–14.

Foreign Relations of the United States 1947 (FRUS), Vol. IV (Washington, DC: Department of State Publication, 1969): 445.

Foreign Relations of the United States 1947 (FRUS), Vol. IV (Washington, DC: Department of State Publication, 1969): 427–9.

Foreign Relations of the United States 1948 (FRUS), Vol. II (Washington, DC: Department of State Publication, 1972): 341–2.

Foreign Relations of the United States 1948 (FRUS), Vol. II (Washington, DC: Department of State Publication, 1972): 344.

Foreign Relations of the United States 1958–1960 (FRUS), Vol. IX (Washington, DC: Department of State Publication, 1993): 25, 34, 110–11, 220, 259.

'From Confederacy to Federation – Thoughts on the Finality of European Integration', speech by Joschka Fischer at the Humboldt University, 12 May 2000.

Gomułka Władyslaw, *O Problemie Niemieckim. Artykuły i przemówienia* (Warsaw: Książka i Wiedza, 1971).

'Grazer Konferenz Resolution der an die mittel- und osteuropäischen Länder angrenzenden Regionen der EU-Mitgliedstaaten betreffend die Herausforderungen der EU-Osterweiterung', Amt der steiermärkischen Landesregierung, Graz, 29 January 1998.

'Hofers 20-Punkte-Katalog zur EU-Erweiterung, Entschließung der 2. Konferenz der EU-Grenzeregionen am 24/25 Juli in Hof', Munich, Bayerische Staatskanzlei.

Jacobsen, Hans-Adolf und Tomala Mieczysław (eds), *Bonn-Warschau 1945–1991, Die Deutsch-Polnischen Beziehungen, Analyse und Dokumentation* (Cologne: Verlag Wissenschaft und Politik, 1992).

Kohl, Helmut, speech in the Bundestag on 8 March 1990 in 'Bulletin des Presse- und Informationsamtes der Bundesregirung', 1990, No. 32, 1990: 268.

Kohl, Helmut, 'Zehn-Punkte-Plan zur Überwindung der Teilung Deutschlands und Europas, vorgelegt von Bundeskanzler Helmut Kohl in der Haushaltsdebatte des Deutschen Bundestages am 28 November 1989', *Europa Archiv*, No. 24, 1989: D 728–30.

Marshall, Secretary of State, a speech in Moscow on 9 April 1947, in Julian Makowski, *Zbiór Dokumentów*, No. 5(20) (Warsaw: Drukarnia Automa, May 1947): 213–20.

Memorandum from a Conversation between Gomułka and Brezhnev, 4 March 1969, quoted in Tomala, *Patrząc na Niemcy*: 169–72.

Memorandum from the Talks between Gomułka and the GDR's Prime Minister, Willy Stophe, in Lansk (Poland), 25–27 September 1970, quoted in Tomala, *Patrząc na Niemcy*: 269–70.

Ministry of Economy, Analysis and Forecast Department, 'Poland's Trade in 1999 Per Country Groupings', www.mg.gov.pl/struktur/DaiP.

'National Strategy for Integration' (Warsaw: Committee for European Integration, January 1997).

'Obroty handlu zagranicznego ogółem i według krajów w okresie I-XII 2000r.', www.stat.gov.pl/serwis/miesieczne/obr_handlu_zagr/index. htm.

Poland, Germany and European Peace Official Documents 1944–1948 (London: The Polish Embassy Press Office, 1948).

'Prague Conference on Germany', in *Poland, Germany and European Peace. Official Documents 1944–1948* (London: The Polish Embassy Press Office, 1948): 74–7.

'Der Rapacki Plan, Memorandum der Regierung der Volksrepublik Polen zur Frage der Abschaffung einer atomwaffenfreien Zone vom 14. Februar 1958', in Hans Ester, Hans Hecker and Erika Poettgens (eds), *Deutschland, aber wo liegt es? Deutschland und Mitteleuropa. Analysen und historische Dokumente*, Amsterdam Studies on Cultural Identity 3 (Amsterdam and Atlanta GA Rodopi, 1993): 207–11.

Rotfeld, Adam Daniel and Walter Stützle (eds), *Germany and Europe in Transition* (Oxford: Sipri and Oxford University Press, 1998).

Wolfgang Schäuble and Karl Lamers, Überlegungen zur europäischen Politik. Positionspapier der CDU/CSU- Bundestagsfraktion vom 1.9.1994, *Blätter für deutsche und internationale Politik*, No. 10, 1994: 1271–80.

'Secret Additional Protocol to German–Soviet Treaty of Nonagression', 'Soviet Statement to Poland, September 17, 1939', 'Confidential Protocol to German–Soviet Treaty, September 18, 1939', in George F. Kennan, *Soviet Foreign Policy 1917–1941* (Princeton: D. Van Nostrand, 1960): 178–82.

'Zespół negocjacyjny w sprawie negocjacji o członkostwo Rzeczypospolitej Polskiej w Unii Europejskiej – Schemat stanowiska negocjacyjnego', Warsaw, 15 July 1998.

Index